The Iliad *as Politics*

THE PERFORMANCE OF POLITICAL THOUGHT

DEAN HAMMER

UNIVERSITY OF OKLAHOMA PRESS : NORMAN

3 1257 01437 7740

Published with the assistance of the National Endowment for the Humanities, a federal agency which supports the study of such fields as history, philosophy, literature, and language.

Library of Congress Cataloging-in-Publication Data

Hammer, Dean, 1959–

The Iliad as politics : the performance of political thought / Dean Hammer
    p. cm. — (Oklahoma series in classical literature ; v. 28)
    Includes bibliographical references (p.) and index.
    ISBN 0-8061-3366-X (hc : alk. paper)
    1. Homer. Iliad. 2. Politics and literature—Greece—History—To 500. 3. Political poetry, Greek—History and criticism. 4. Political science—Greece—History—To 500. 5. Greece—Politics and government—To 146 B.C. 6. Epic poetry, Greek—History and criticism. 7. Achilles (Greek mythology) in literature. 8. Trojan War—Literature and the war. 9. Homer—Political and social views. I. Title. II. Series.

PA4037 .H36 2002
873'.01—dc21

2001048072

The Iliad as Politics: The Performance of Political Thought is Volume 28 in the Oklahoma Series in Classical Culture.

1 2 3 4 5 6 7 8 9 10

To Carol
With all my love

Contents

Acknowledgments

Over the years, I have received valuable comments and continued encouragement from many people. My earliest conversations about the *Iliad* were with Thomas Banks, who first suggested that I teach it in a class. As he has read my work over the years, he has saved me from many an embarrassing mistake. Walter Donlan provided generous encouragement in my first scholarly foray into Homer, and continued to offer helpful advice as this project progressed. He is a model of scholarly rigor and intellectual generosity. Kurt Raaflaub's encyclopedic grasp of Homeric scholarship, combined with his clarity of argument, is truly humbling. I owe much to his effort to bring together classicists and political theorists. Kerry Whiteside is a colleague and a true friend who has been a willing participant in our daily conversations about all things theoretical. I cannot overstate the value of my students, as well, who have thought with me about the *Iliad*. Class discussions over the years have stimulated my own thinking about the *Iliad*, and my work on this project has, in turn, stimulated my students' thinking. Several students have commented on portions of the manuscript, including

Michael Kicey and Marina Lutova. I want to particularly thank
Stella Reno for carefully and critically reading the entire manuscript and giving me valuable suggestions about how to make
the work accessible to students. And I would like to thank others
who have read and commented on sections of the manuscript
over the years, including Jane Borelli, Mary Douglas, Richard
Ellis, David Konstan, Ted Lendon, William Marty, and Kyle
Pasewark.

I profited immensely from a fellowship at the Center for
Hellenic Studies, which provided me with an extraordinary
library, uninterrupted time to focus on my research, and an
intellectual environment that was truly invigorating. I have also
received continued support from the Franklin and Marshall
College grants committee.

I would like to thank the editors of the following journals for
permission to use portions of previously published articles:
"The Politics of the *Iliad*," *The Classical Journal* 94 (October–
November 1998); "The Cultural Construction of Chance in the
Iliad," *Arethusa* 31 (January 1998); "'Who Shall Readily Obey?':
Authority and Politics in the *Iliad*," *Phoenix* 51 (1997); "Achilles
as Vagabond: The Culture of Autonomy in the *Iliad*," *Classical
World* 90 (July/August 1997); "Homer, Tyranny, and Democracy,"
Greek, Roman and Byzantine Studies 39 (1998; pub. 2000); and
"The *Iliad* as Ethical Thinking: Politics and Pity," *Arethusa* 35
(2002).

THE *ILIAD* AS POLITICS

Introduction

This book emerges from both a scholarly and teaching engagement I have had with the *Iliad* over the last decade. I originally began using the *Iliad* in my classical political theory course as a way of providing a rich context for understanding Plato and Aristotle. As the years passed, though, the *Iliad* assumed increased prominence in the course, not just in the amount of time I spent on the epic, but on how I came to understand the work. Quite without my realizing it fully, the *Iliad* evolved in the course and in my own thinking from a backdrop for understanding the more systematic political theory of Plato and Aristotle to a composition that stood on its own as a work of political thought.

That the *Iliad* is rarely viewed in this light can be explained, in large part, by a philosophical tradition, beginning with Plato's banishment of Homer from his republic. In positing a split between epic and philosophic knowledge, Plato contended that the problem with the Homeric epic was that it was an imitation (*mimesis*) of phenomenal appearance since it depicted the shadowy world of human action and emotion. As Robb has argued in his intriguing work on the origins of literacy in Greek society, Plato was engaged in an ontological, epistemological, and psychological critique of this poetic act of *mimesis*.[1] First, Plato questioned the ontological status of epic poetry, suggesting that epic poetry is a "third remove" from truth since the art of the poet is one of imitating "appearance as it appears" (*Rep.* 597e, 598b, trans. modified). Second, Plato rejected any epistemological claim of the epic poet, arguing that "the art of representation" is "able to reproduce anything" only because it has "little grasp of anything, and that little is of a mere phenomenal appearance" (598b). If Homer had "actual knowledge" of what he "imitates," suggests Plato at one point, then the poet would devote himself to these "truths" rather than to their representations (599b, trans. modified). The problem of poetry is that it is easy to produce without actual knowledge of the truth (599a).

Finally, and Plato saves his strongest words for this element of *mimesis*, the epic poet has the "terrible power to corrupt (*lôbasthai*) even the best characters" (605c). It is a corruption that recalls the outrages against honor and the defilement of corpses recounted by Homer, as when Agamemnon promises to Peisandros that the "mutilation" (*lôbên*) of his corpse shall "punish the shame of your father" (11.142). For Plato, the poet performs a similar mutilation, this time of the soul, as the poet "indulges the instinctive desires of a part of us," including the "hunger for tears and for an uninhibited indulgence in grief" (606a). Poetry, as it enlivens in each of us emotions of pity, laughter, and sorrow, creates a world in which humans are made vulnerable to the loss of friends, the fear of death, and the tragedy of circumstance. These feelings of dependency and vulnerability corrupt the attainment of the "good life" (387e). For, argues Plato, the best life is one that is self-sufficient (*autarkês*) so that there is the least need of others (387e).

Though tempered in recent years by examinations of both the philosophic contributions of literature and the literary basis of philosophy, this distinction between the epistemological status of poetry and philosophy persists in our understanding of the epic. The first task of philosophy, Havelock reminds us, was "escaping from" the "narrative flux" of the Homeric language, a flux revealing of "error of thought."[2] Theory could claim a reflectiveness and rationality that arose from its propositional logic. The epic, on the other hand, could speak to our emotions and imagination, but could make no claim to knowing either philosophic truths or political questions of community organization. What has often emerged is a distinction, made both implicitly and explicitly, between political theories—which are depicted as systematic, reasoned, reflective, and critical accounts of the political world—and the epic—which is often characterized as an uncritical appropriation of myths, legends, stories, and superstitions.[3] As evidence, commentators point to a seemingly irrational cosmology alive with divine forces, to inconsistencies in the stories that make up the epic, and to the oral nature of epic verse in which the aim was to tell a particular story and not to analyze the foundations of thought. Edmunds summarizes the scholarly sentiment when he suggests that "most of us do not think of Homer as a political thinker. Homeric scholarship, when it has been concerned at all with the political in Homer, has attempted to find evidence for the history of political institutions—assemblies, councils, law-courts—that might have been in existence in Homer's own time and to combine that evidence with the archaeological record, with facts from later Greek history, and with comparative evidence."[4]

This book is an attempt to "think of Homer as a political thinker" or, stated slightly differently, to understand the *Iliad* as a work of political thought. In making this argument, I am actually making two claims: that the epic is engaged in critical reflection and that this reflection is political in nature. Both of these claims are controversial, and both require some explanation.[5]

I turn to the first of these claims. Though the epic has long attracted the Western imagination for the beauty of its poetry and the power of its depiction of human tragedy, less often conceded is that the epic is engaged in critical reflection. Certainly, the view that the *Iliad* is not critically reflective dates from at least the time of Plato. But the argument was given a different theoretical basis by Milman Parry's insight, and Lord's continuation of the work, that not only did the *Iliad* arise from oral composition, but the method of "composition *during* oral performance" imposed a structure on Homeric verse that emphasized the functionality, more than the interpretability, of a Homeric language.[6]

Because Parry, and later Lord, were interested overwhelmingly in the "how" of the poet's craft of composition, it is perhaps not surprising that they would look for the poet's tools. And these tools appeared to Parry and Lord as ready-made formulas and themes.[7] Specifically, metrical lines and half lines were built by formulas and epithets ("godlike Achilles," "clever Odysseus," etc.), and songs were constructed by the use of themes. This formulaic system of language is characterized by its efficiency, which consists of two components: "simplicity" and "extension."[8] By "simplicity," Parry means that no formula duplicates another formula that expresses the same idea in the same metrical unit. And by "extension," he means that all formulas with the same form have different meanings. This does not mean that the system is static. But the invention or modification of formulas occurs always within this oral-formulaic system in which an idea is "generated as the formula," subject to the requirements of simplicity and extension.[9] This structural operation is important not only for poetic composition but for understanding the meanings that emerge. Meaning inheres in the formula, a meaning that has been fixed by tradition. The epic poet, operating within the system of oral language, employs a formula "to express a given essential idea."[10] For the poet working within this formulaic system, "composition was a process of memory" in which the composer, in "the stress of the moment," had to "remember the words, the expressions, the sentences he had heard from other bards who had taught him the traditional style of heroic poetry." The poet, furthermore, "had to remember the place or the places which traditional words and expressions occupied in the complex mould of the hexameter."[11] The poet, in effect, had before him a tradition of "preserved words and phrases which, once happily discovered, could be drawn on for the making of poetry."[12] The "apprentice bard," in learning to construct a poem, would draw on this tradition, using "few words or phrases of his own, or none at all."[13] The art of the practiced oral poet, though, was not one of simply repeating these formulas, but lay "in the ability to compose and recompose the phrases for the idea of the moment on the pattern established by the basic formulas."[14]

The rediscovery of the oral nature of epic composition often led to the unfortunate, and not completely justified, conclusion that the language of the epic was univocal, unreflective, and unconceptual.[15] Underlying Parry and Lord's approach to epic composition, suggests Lynn-George, is a "conventional dichotomy between language and thought, which was later to be distributed between the oral and the written."[16] The language of the oral poet, given the need to fit together phrase after phrase in the proper rhythm and meter, appeared as purely instrumental. Phrases in the formulaic language of the poet were used not to convey "meaning" but because they were functionally useful.[17] Ideas, from this perspective, became a function of language, as when Parry defines the formula as "a group of words which is regularly employed under the same metrical conditions to express a given essential idea." The poet, Parry notes, could express "only ideas for which he has a fixed means of expression."[18] The unity of phrase and meaning precluded the possibility of different interpretations emerging from the performance. As Parry writes,

"But in practice, if we keep in mind the directness which is from every point of view the mark of Homeric style, and firmly exclude any interpretation which does not instantly and easily come to mind, we shall find that there is hardly a case where a variety of opinion is possible."[19]

Whereas Parry and Lord focused on how oral composition placed structural demands on the epic, Eric Havelock would examine the conceptual limits placed on the Homeric epic by an oral consciousness.[20] Havelock characterized the Homeric epic as a "compilation of inherited lore," a "tribal encyclopedia" of conventions, practices, and procedures. In his later work, Havelock continued to emphasize this essentially "utilitarian" function of the poems. The Homeric epics were structured, suggests Havelock, to include "a mass of directive information, appropriate to the society to which the poems are addressed and which was guided by them."[21] This is because an oral language requires "mythos," or the telling of "the acts of persons and the happenings of events," and is "unfriendly" to "logos," or "abstracted and conceptual speech."[22]

Havelock sets up a series of juxtapositions between an oral and philosophic language and a corresponding oral and philosophical consciousness, an emergent consciousness that he associates with the pre-Socratics. In an oral culture, there is no "terminology suitable to describe an external world" nor even the realization "that such a 'world' or cosmos existed to be described." In a literate culture, however, a conceptual vocabulary emerges, particularly the creation of the "timeless present" that can posit permanent relationships. In an oral culture, the environment is viewed as activated by "personal agents" rather than "impersonal forces." An oral culture conceives of events as a "discontinuous multiplicity" of particular beginnings and endings rather than providing a "single comprehensive statement which would somehow include them all by reducing them to aspects of the single whole." But more than articulating differences, Havelock's broader conclusion is that "error of thought has its parallel in error of language."[23] The conscious task of the pre-Socratics, suggests Havelock, was to critique not just the content of Homer and Hesiod, but the error of thought that arises out of orality.[24] The claim of the pre-Socratics, argues Havelock, was that "the resources of poetry as commonly exploited in performances are unsuitable for the expression of philosophy" because of "the idiom of common speech and thought, which narrativizes our experiences, recounting it as a series of events, of becoming and perishing."[25]

We should not be surprised, then, when Havelock views political relationships in the epic, including debate and council, as "composed summarily and formulaically" and offered "only as the story prompts their intrusion."[26] There is a "moral dimension" to the epic. But that, too, is not guided by any conceptual apparatus but is a "pragmatic response to the general rules which impose 'responsibilities' and confer 'rewards' for performance."[27] Havelock seems to equate the situational nature of narrative, in which concepts are not specified in advance but emerge through human action and interaction, with the moral orientation of pragmatism and utility. This is, presumably, the same conclusion Havelock would draw from any fictional rendering, contemporary or otherwise, in which situation and response define plot and character. The result, for Havelock, is a Homeric (and fictional) world devoid of any conceptual substance. For this reason Havelock, in an image that recalls the epistemological distinction made by Plato between poetry and philosophy, describes how the notion of justice from Homer to Plato has "passed from shadow to substance."[28] It is striking, and illustrative of the epistemological bias of contemporary political theory, that abstract, philosophic concepts are substantive whereas the concrete particulars of human action appear as shadows.

I do not mean to suggest that Havelock encompasses the entirety of post-Parry scholarship, though he is important for us here because of his focus on political aspects of the *Iliad.* Many classicists have either rejected the distinction Parry draws between oral and written texts for interpretation[29] or have used Parry as a point of departure to explore Homer's artistic creativity.[30] To the extent that other scholars reclaim Homer's artistry, they often do so by discussing the Homeric epics in terms of almost purely aesthetic forms that appear divorced from any sociopolitical context. Thus, Ford, in combining the "negative poetics of Lord, Havelock, and Walter Ong," sets out what the epic, given its oral nature, is not: "poetry is not a rhetorical effect"; poetry is not history; poetry is "not an art of storytelling"; it is an effort neither to create "monumental makings" nor to leave something behind but is meant to exist in the moment of performance.[31] Homer presents an epic that invites "no reading, no interpretation" because of its denial of any enduring "physical form."[32] The performative dimension of the epic should lead us to understand its aim not as "an art of storytelling" but as "always and only pleasure" that pretends "not even to need a human audience."[33]

There is an irony to Ford's analysis, as he unflinchingly provides a reading—indeed, an interpretation—that employs a contemporary vocabulary that would have been incomprehensible in the Homeric world. My interest is less in pointing to these ironic implications, and more in clarifying where I part company with this particular oral-cultural approach. Though I agree with Ong that "orality situates knowledge within a context of struggle" by "keeping knowledge embedded in the human lifeworld,"[34] I disagree with the epistemological status given to this rendering of experience. Though oral poems serve as an important means of cultural transmission (and, thus, appear primarily instrumental for Havelock and Ong), my suggestion is that situating or embedding knowledge in human struggle gives rise to a reflective aspect in which the poem raises questions about the organization of human experience. The epic, as it was composed in performance, appears as public poetry that was engaged in a reflection on the activity of organizing community life. Let me lay out briefly how epic composition introduces a critical dimension to epic poetry.

First, the *public activity of performance* ties the epic to a broader set of cultural issues contemporaneous with its telling. Redfield, for example, has argued quite persuasively that though the epic draws on traditional stories, the poet tells "not those stories, but the story of a plot he had himself invented." In the development of plot and characters, the poet "employs and persuades us to certain assumptions about the sources and conditions of action."[35] The composition of the poem, as it conveys both coherence and meaning to its audience, rests, then, on a comprehension of culture: on the attitudes and assumptions that make the plot believable.[36] Even though the poet draws on an epic tradition, the interaction of the poet and audience results in the poet re-creating "the past to fit the needs of the present or else rejecting outmoded formulae and elements of plot."[37] The "interaction between singer and audience was essential," Raaflaub notes, as "fantasy and archaisms were balanced by the listeners' need to identify with the human drama and ethical dilemmas described by the singer." The heroic deeds of exceptional individuals were combined with "material reflecting social, economic and political conditions, values and relationships that were familiar to the audience."[38]

A second way in which a critical dimension is introduced is through the *performance of the characters*. The epic is given shape in large part through the words and actions of its characters. What emerges is a cultural grammar—the boundaries that define the culture—from the perspectives of actors as they move about in the world, giving form and meaning to social reality through "dialogue and juxtaposition with a social Other."[39] The contours of these boundaries do not proceed from an "objective" stance outside the cultural world but emerge and are given shape dialogically as characters constitute themselves and their world through language.[40] As Hannah Arendt suggests, in talking about political action, the "specific revelatory quality of action and speech, the implicit manifestation of the agent and speaker, is so indissolubly tied to the living flux of acting and speaking," it can be represented "only through a kind of repetition," or *mimesis*, which corresponds to dramatic reenactment.[41] This has significant implications for how we might approach the epic, for it suggests that though Homeric performance is an act of *mimesis*, it is neither closed nor static. Through dialogue, we come to identify overlapping, and even clashing, "value centers" (to use Bakhtin's term) that underlie how each character uniquely organizes the world "into a complex of values."[42] That is, through the movement of dialogue we see confrontations both within and between boundaries. What this suggests is the possibility of ambiguities, tensions, and even conflict as the Homeric characters constitute themselves and their world by invoking and reinvoking a cultural grammar that organizes and gives meaning and significance to their values, beliefs, and social relations.

Finally, oral performance can play a significant role in thinking about the nature and issues of community organization. As Morris observes, "Any literary form is a functioning part of the society to which it belongs, rather than a passive reflection; and oral poetry, it seems, can play a particularly active structuring role."[43] Helpful for understanding this role is Victor Turner's notion of a "*social drama*." Turner defines a "social drama" as "an objectively isolable sequence of social interactions of a conflictive, competitive or agonistic type" that "may provide materials for many stories."[44] Such social dramas, including the *Iliad*, follow a particular structure in which there is a visible infraction of rules, a crisis following from that infraction, a redressive phase in which there is some reflection on the events leading up to and following the crisis, and finally either reintegration or recognition of the schism.[45] Important for us here is that social dramas do not simply reflect and reproduce a particular "cultural configuration."[46] Rather, a performance can be "reciprocal and reflexive" since it is involved in a "critique, direct or veiled, of the social life it grows out of."[47] Social dramas present breaches in and inversions of accepted norms, actions, beliefs, and social structures, introducing a "performative reflexivity" in which the artist raises "problems about the ordering principles deemed acceptable in 'real life.'"[48] The social drama portrayed in the *Iliad* draws attention to fundamental questions of community organization.

This last sentence anticipates my second claim: that the *Iliad* is political. My argument builds on a growing interest in understanding the social and political context of the *Iliad*. I feel a great debt to the work of Finley and Donlan because I see them as having blazed the trail for viewing the epic as depicting a functioning social system. Where I differ from them, though, is about what is being depicted. Whereas Donlan and Finley argue that the epic portrays a Dark Age society, dating from roughly 850 to 760 B.C., my suggestion is that the *Iliad* is shaped in important ways by some of the considerations and issues that arise with the emergence of the polis in the second half of the eighth century.[49] My argument, thus, builds on a growing body of scholarship (including, I might note, some of Donlan's recent work) that examines the importance of the polis as a backdrop to the *Iliad*.[50]

My interest is less to note instances of polis organization and more to explore the broader question of how the composition, as a whole, is engaged in a reflection on political life. It turns out that developing this argument requires a rethinking of what we even mean by the political. What has often been assumed, and sometimes stated outright, in discussions of the *Iliad* is that political activity is an outgrowth of the polis. That is, we must have a polis to have politics. Thus, action in the epic is seen as either political, to the extent that one can identify rudimentary forms of polis-organization, or "prepolitical" because of the underdeveloped nature of polis institutions at the time.[51] The problem with both approaches is that they conflate an activity—politics—with an institutional form—the polis.

The notion of the polis as a precondition for politics derives in part from Aristotle and in part from an anthropological and political scientific framework, now distilled and interpreted by several generations of classical scholars, that emphasized in its approach to the Homeric epics the analysis of structure and function and the development of taxonomies within political and social systems. What developed over time was a notion of the political that became tied to the emergence of specific structures and institutions in which one could identify functions that were exclusively (or primarily) political. The focus on defining functional relationships in terms of particular structures helps us to understand why questions about the politics of Homeric society are often linked to the emergence of the polis as an autonomous, structural entity. The autonomous polis, it is suggested, contains the necessary institutional arrangements to carry out the political functions of the allocation of resources, the enforcement of values, and the adjudication of disputes.

What I set out in the first chapter is a notion of politics defined neither as a structure nor as a function but as an activity. The activity of politics constitutes what I will call the *political field*, a realm in which questions of community organization are raised, determined, and implemented. Such questions include, but are certainly not limited to, "What do we value and how are these values expressed in the goals of community life and organization?" "What binds us together?" and "On what basis are social relationships, including issues of leadership and authority, organized?" From this perspective, the polis does not provide the conditions for, as much as it provides evidence of, the activity of politics.

A philosophic obstacle looms in our view of the *Iliad* as a work of political thought, as well: namely, our conception of a Homeric cosmology. Politics, as an endeavor in which "people constitute orders within which they live together among themselves and set themselves apart from others," is often viewed as a realm that is freed from the automatic processes of life and nature. Classically understood, "political events and political conditions became subject to the will of the participants and whatever was contingent upon their interaction."[52] The *Iliad*, though, poses a special problem for this understanding of politics because, simply stated, the gods play such a prominent role in the epic as a force originating outside of, and appearing to act on, the human will. Thus, Wolin, in his influential discussion of political philosophy, dates the "invention of political philosophy" with the pre-Socratics in the sixth century B.C. Prior to this time, "man had thought of himself and of society as integral parts of nature, as subject to the same natural and supernatural forces." Only when nature was viewed as something comprehensible was the way "cleared for a rational explanation of all phenomena, political and social, as well as natural."[53]

The second chapter challenges this conception of Homeric action by a rather unconventional route. I look at moments in which the gods intervene most in human affairs—that is, those cases in which human action seems the most subject to natural and supernatural forces. I argue that we can identify a pattern of response of the Homeric characters to the unpredictable, seemingly incoherent, actions of the gods. Briefly stated, the warriors respond to divine interference by seeking to maintain (or, if need be, restore) their status in the community. Divine intervention, thus, reveals both issues of community maintenance and the nature of human agency as individuals, through their deliberative and willful actions, seek to maintain a cultural equilibrium. This approach leads to a more integrated conception of human action: not one in which agency exists apart from divine action, but one in which notions of divinity have a cultural foundation and, somewhat ironically, are integral to and integrated into a conception of human action.

In the next five chapters, I pursue in greater depth some of the interpretive paths laid out in the first two chapters. The argument takes the form of a story of epic thought. What I mean by this is that the conceptual issues I will be addressing, issues such as authority, power, rights, and ethics, are not treated as abstractions but are given form within the context of dialogue, action, and plot. Thus, in chapter 3 I look at how the quarrel between Agamemnon and Achilles broadens from a dispute about war booty into a more fundamental question of authority. Achilles structures the conflict by asking who shall "readily" obey Agamemnon. For Achilles, the exercise of authority consists of the ability to get others to willingly act together. For Agamemnon, however, the exercise of authority lies in the ability to compel obedience, through force if need be. In the first nine books, the *Iliad* traces the implications of Agamemnon's exercise of authority as his actions weaken, and ultimately imperil, the political field. We become witness to the paradox of a leader whose exercise of authority seems only to diminish his power.

In chapter 4, I examine the attempts by the embassy of Odysseus, Phoenix, and Ajax to persuade Achilles to return to the Achaian camp. In depicting himself as treated like a dishonored outsider, Achilles articulates the basis for his withdrawal from the political field and battlefield: he no longer sees himself as receiving the rewards and protections of warrior society. Achilles advances a claim to self-sufficiency, instead, in which he no longer ties his worth to the receipt of honor and glory.

The *Iliad*, I suggest, leaves us with a political problem since both Agamemnon's assertion of might and Achilles' claim to self-sufficiency imperil the survival of the Achaian political community. The military crisis is averted because Achilles reenters battle to avenge the death of Patroklos. But the political question raised by Achilles remains unanswered. I argue in chapter 5 that the issue of authority relations among the elite is revisited in the funeral games. In this pan-Achaian community, we see a process of decision-making that involves the recognition and mediation of contending claims in a public forum. The effective exercise of authority, thus, is not premised on might, or any individual possession, but rests in a collegial space constituted by the elite.

While in chapter 5 I look at how a public field redefines the nature of authority relations among the elite, in chapter 6 I focus on how this public space underlies the relationship between the leaders and the people. This relationship has always posed an interpretive problem because the people appear as something more than subjects but less than citizens. Drawing on Weber, I suggest that we can identify a form of plebiscitary politics in which the legitimacy of the leaders rests, at least in part, on the acclaim or perceived acclaim of the people. This has significant implications for understanding the volatility of the political space, both as it appears in the *Iliad* and as it underlies the historical tension between tyranny and democracy in the development of the polis.

In the final chapter, I focus on how the *Iliad* contributes to a political ethic. Whereas Plato argues that the epic cannot be engaged in a set of ethical questions because it depicts the phenomena, rather than the essence, of human experience, I argue that it is experience that provides the foundation for ethical reflection. Experience does not determine an ethic; rather, it is the way in which the ethical self, as one's sense of the responsibilities and obligations to others, is enacted. Central to the ethical self is the notion of esteem, or *an image of oneself in relationship to others*. In this final chapter, I show how Achilles' image of himself is transformed through his experience of suffering. When stripped of his war prize, Achilles sees himself as *suffering-from* the afflictions of war. He responds by withdrawing from battle, believing that he can impose suffering without suffering himself. With the death of Patroklos, though, Achilles experiences himself as *suffering-with* another. This recognition is critical, since Achilles comes to see not only that his actions affect others in unpredictable and irreversible ways, but also that his own sense of worth is affected by the suffering he has brought to others.

Achilles' stance at the end of the epic has political significance since it answers to the fundamental political problem of how communities can be given endurance when they are made vulnerable by the nature of human connectedness. From the outset, the *Iliad* exposes this vulnerability through the collision between Agamemnon and Achilles. The *Iliad* locates the answer to this vulnerability in the ability and responsibility of individuals to act together to project themselves into a future. In the meeting between Priam and Achilles, the activity of human dwelling is preserved as the *Iliad* ends with a moment of care that is set against the frailty of a world of coming and going.

1

Political Fields

Δάρδανον ἄρ πρῶτον τέκετο νεφεληγερέτα Ζεύς,
κτίσσε δὲ Δαρδανίην, ἐπεὶ οὔ πω Ἴλιος ἱρὴ
ἐν πεδίῳ πεπόλιστο, πόλις μερόπων ἀνθρώπων

First of all Zeus who gathers the clouds had a son,
Dardanos
who founded Dardania, since there was yet no sacred Ilion
made a polis in the plain to be a center of peoples

20.215–17

Though recent work on the *Iliad* has taken note increasingly of the role of the polis in shaping the epic, a persistent, and often unexamined, suggestion remains that action within the epic is "prepolitical." Even those who have made the strongest arguments for the importance of the Homeric polis have often accepted this formulation of the Homeric world as prepolitical. This conclusion derives in part from a tradition of interpretation of Aristotle that identified the "independent city-state as the typical form of *polis*."[1] But these interpretations blend well with an anthropological and political scientific framework, now distilled and interpreted by several generations of classical scholars, that emphasizes in its approach to the Homeric epics the analysis of structure and function and the development of taxonomies within political and social systems.² A notion of the political developed over time that became tied to the emergence of specific structures and institutions in which one could identify functions that were exclusively (or primarily) political. This focus on defining functional relationships in terms of particular structures helps us to understand why questions about the politics of Homeric society are invariably linked to the emergence of the polis as an autonomous, structural entity. The autonomous polis, scholars suggest, contains the necessary institutional arrangements to carry out the political functions of the allocation of resources, the enforcement of values, and the adjudication of disputes.³ I set out in this chapter a notion of politics defined not by structure but by activity. Drawing on the anthropological work of Victor Turner, I argue for an approach to politics as an activity in which questions of community organization are raised, determined, and implemented. This approach will allow us not only to view "the political" in the *Iliad*, but to relate evidence of the polis within the epic to a broader question of how the composition, as a whole, is engaged in a reflection on community life.

STRUCTURE AND FUNCTION: SOCIAL ANTHROPOLOGY AND POLITICS

Even a cursory glance at Homeric scholarship reveals the prevalence of the view that the Homeric epics portray a world that is prepolitical. M. I. Finley, for example, who has argued persuasively for a view of the Homeric world as a functioning social system, concludes, nonetheless, that neither Homeric poem "has any trace of a *polis* in its political sense."⁴ For Finley, "political decisions" must be "binding on the society" and "political units" must have a "governmental apparatus."⁵ For

Posner, the society depicted by Homer is prepolitical because it lacks "a state or government."[6] For Halverson, "no significant political dimension" appears in the epics (in this case the *Odyssey*) because there is neither an organizational nor a psychological dimension to communal life.[7] Hoffmann argues that the impulses of the Homeric heroes have nothing to do with political considerations.[8] Edmunds, in responding to Raaflaub's argument for a political reading of the *Iliad*, suggests that the fundamental situation of the *Iliad* is "not a political one" but a "personal matter" because Achilles' loyalty to Agamemnon and to others is "prepolitical or apolitical."[9] And Scully, in one of the most complete discussions of the role of the polis in the *Iliad*, suggests that though a polis exists that is "distinct from its many oikoi," and though one can identify the emergence of a polis ideology in which ethical decisions may be guided by "the collective needs of a beleaguered polis," the Homeric world remains, nonetheless, prepolitical. What is lacking are institutional forms and roles that emerge later: notions of citizenship, a system of governance, and a "mutually defining process between the individual and the political system" in which politics, as an autonomous sphere, defines human life.[10]

These conceptions of the Homeric world are united by a set of assumptions about the nature of politics, assumptions that enter classical scholarship by way of earlier work in social anthropology. Two schools are particularly important for classicists: that represented by the structural-functional approaches of Radcliffe-Brown, Fortes, and Evans-Pritchard, and that represented by the evolutionary approaches of Service, Sahlins, Fried, and Cohen. Though these schools differ in important ways, they share an attempt to identify, and classify, politics in structural and functional terms. This notion of politics is guided largely by methodological concerns; namely, the interest in developing taxonomies and comparing social systems requires identifiable and discrete units of analysis. Thus, the political could be studied only as distinct institutions and roles emerge with correspondingly distinct functions.

Radcliffe-Brown, for example, writes that the task of social anthropology is "the systematic investigation of the nature of social institutions" that will "enable us to discover the universal, essential, characters which belong to all human societies, past, present, and future."[11] The methodological aim of examining societies in "abstraction" requires that one "mark off a class of phenomena," such as politics, economics, or religion, "which can profitably be made the subject of separate theoretical treatment."[12] Two related directions would emerge for how to define a political class of phenomena: first, one could define politics by particular functions, such as the maintenance of order or the legitimate use of force; or, second, one could define politics in terms of the structure of groups in the political system. Radcliffe-Brown, on the one hand, focuses more on the function of political organization, suggesting that "in studying political organization, we have to deal with the maintenance or establishment of social order, within a territorial framework, by the organized exercise of coercive authority through the use, or the possibility of use, of physical force."[13] Fortes and Evans-Pritchard, on the other hand, emphasize the relationship of status differentials in society to the distribution of power and authority, the roles of government officials, the rights and obligations of subjects, and, in turn, their relationship to government groups.[14] Though originally functionalism was developed as a way to view political relationships in stateless societies, invariably in discussing the execution of these functions, discussion would shift to particular structures (such as a government apparatus).[15] Structure and function were not separate but related since political systems could be compared by the level of complexity: increased structural complexity attended increased role differentiation in society.

Reacting to the abstract formalism of structural anthropology, an evolutionary school of social anthropology emerged, which argued that "general structural and functional resemblances" will often show up in quite different types of society.[16] These critics retained from the earlier comparative-structural approaches the emphasis on the institutional and organizational nature of politics, arguing, though, that the role of structures must be understood within the evolutionary development of societies. In these evolutionary approaches, societies were seen as progressing through stages of political development, with each stage defined by a functional equilibrium between different social groups. At issue in the scholarship was the nature of this evolution: were increasing structural complexity and functional differentiation the result of greater sociocultural integration of groups in response to a more complex environment, the result of competition between groups for scarce resources, or a combination of both factors?[17]

Social anthropology provided Homeric scholarship with a powerful tool for viewing the Homeric world as a functioning social system. In extending the work of Finley, Walter Donlan and Carol Thomas argue that the Homeric poems recreate the "actual economic, social and political institutions of the long Middle Geometric period (roughly 850–760)."[18] To make this argument, Donlan draws primarily on the work of Fried and Service to provide a taxonomic model for viewing Homeric society as a functioning social system.[19] For Donlan, Homeric society corresponds to the stage of a "ranked society," which is an "evolutionary stage between 'egalitarian' and 'stratified' (or 'state') societies."[20] Donlan writes, "Homer's military/political leaders conform to the anthropological types of the big-man and the chief, figures possessing varying degrees of authority, sometimes considerable, but little coercive power."[21] Extending this framework still further, Tandy has suggested recently that the "polis came into existence when a newly institutionalized

political and economic center undertook to exclude the peripheral members of the community from the economic mainstream."[22] Political organization emerged with a "transformation"
in economic organization, and an ensuing crisis in distribution,
caused by the introduction of markets.[23]

Runciman, too, approaches the Homeric social system from
an evolutionary perspective. Drawing on Cohen's systems
approach, in which state origin is viewed as a "multiple feed-
back system" in response to particular pressures, Runciman
argues that the "evolution from statelessness to statehood" rests
upon the fulfillment of "certain initial conditions."[24] In particular, the "critical transition depends on the conditions for a
cumulative accretion of the power available to the incumbents
of prospective governmental roles."[25] That is, there must be an
accumulation of a surplus of ideological, economic, and military power in the hands of future state officials to establish
formal rules and institutional structures over a designated territory. This evolution of the state, which has become synonymous
with the emergence of the political, is characterized by the
"specialization of governmental roles; centralization of enforce-
able authority; permanence, or at least more than ephemeral
stability, of structure; and emancipation from real or fictive kin-
ship as the basis of relations between the occupants of governmental roles and those whom they govern." Using this taxonomy
of state development, Runciman discerns in the Homeric poems
not political structures but "semistates," or communities that
do not carry potential for progress toward a state: there are no
governmental roles beyond "patriarchal domination"; the poleis
appear more as "communities with a residential centre, not
states"; the people are neither citizens nor subjects but more
like "an audience"; and mediation is ad hoc rather than there
being institutionalized "judicial roles."[26]

The "political" question that emerged from the study of the
Homeric epics, as it was guided by this anthropological tradition,

was, not surprisingly, largely a taxonomic one: what type of pre-
state society is reflected in the epic and does this reflection
correspond to an actual historic period (and which one)? Guided
by this anthropological tradition, classicists approached the
study of Homeric society by first identifying formal institutions
or groups within a society and then determining the distinct
functions they performed.[27] Politics, from this perspective,
came to be identified with the emergence of an autonomous
polis and a set of differentiated institutionalized roles and
relationships between rulers and citizens within that polis.[28]
The absence of either a polis organization, as in the case of the
Achaian camp, or formal governmental institutions, almost
invariably led to a view of the Homeric world as prepolitical.

The approach creates a perplexing situation in which institutions are political, but the preinstitutional activity of forming
these institutions is not. Donlan, I think, recognizes this problem when he suggests that the transition to a city-state was itself
a "political process," one defined not by institutionalized roles
but by a "dynamic"—a term suggestive of an activity of community formation.[29] But politics, when conceived within the
evolutionary framework employed by Donlan, also appears
quantifiable. Thus, Donlan claims at one point that with the
integration and institutionalization of roles (and the corresponding decline in "mechanical solidarity" as a basis of leadership), relationships are seen as "more truly 'political.'"[30] The
use of the quotation marks around "political" suggests a certain
recognition of the ambiguity of the term, as referring both to
institutional arrangements and to processes. The difficulty of
structural-functional approaches is that they do not easily admit
into the framework a political process that is not tied to a
particular institutional arrangement.[31] This poses a significant
problem for understanding the politics of the *Iliad*, for "institutions and constitutions and the corresponding terminology had
to be newly created," Raaflaub writes, "and the political sphere

itself had to be discovered and gradually penetrated by thought, understanding, and explanation."[32] A conceptual vocabulary is needed that can locate the political without defining it in relationship to either an autonomous sphere or particular institutional arrangements.

POLITICS AS PERFORMANCE: THE FORMATION OF POLITICAL FIELDS

In developing this language of analysis, I draw on a view of politics that has been suggested by Victor Turner, a cultural anthropologist. Turner has emphasized, from his early attempts to develop a political anthropology to his classic explorations of the metaphor of performance for understanding human action, a notion of politics identified not with static structures but with the "flow" of "social processes": the succession of events, the seeking of goals, the ordering of relations, the emergence of conflict and tensions, the upsetting of norms, the creation of alliances, and attempts at redress and resolution.[33] Politics, from this perspective, appears as an activity in which questions of community organization are raised, determined, and implemented. We will see a change in the unit of political analysis: from a focus on structure and function to what Turner describes as a "field."[34] The political field is not defined by institutional and territorial boundaries but rather is constituted by groups who are engaged in political activity. This adds a certain fluidity to our understanding of politics, since the "political field can expand and contract" as activities move "across group boundaries without necessarily encountering hindrances." This also changes our focus from "examining such groups as lineages, villages, or countries to determine what processes they might contain" to tracing the activity of politics "into whatever groups the processes lead."[35] Political fields appear as arenas in which issues of identity and organization are both addressed and expressed. That is, political fields are not just institutions established to resolve issues but arenas in which communities continually define who they are.

In thinking about what we mean by a *political field*, it might be helpful to imagine a battlefield. A battlefield is not defined by particular boundaries but instead is constituted by the activity. The boundaries of the battlefield can expand and contract and the composition of the field can change as new groups enter and exit. That it is the activity that defines the boundaries of a political field, and not the field that defines the activity, is not altogether different from Alcaeus's words in the late seventh and early sixth centuries, "for warlike men are a city's tower," or Nicias's words to his troops, "you yourselves, wherever you settle down, are a city already."[36]

Through this conception, one might identify a number of activities as political. These would include the raising of questions of authority and legitimacy, the exercise of persuasion and force, the emergence of demands or claims on the community, the appearance of conflict that threatens community organization, and the encounter with ethical questions of our relationship, obligations, and responsibilities to others. These activities are not necessarily directed toward a functional equilibrium, but exist as "a field of tensions" in which individuals may be motivated by interest, by concerns with the public good, and by different outlooks on the goals of community life.[37] It may well be that in the study of such activities we encounter institutions. But these institutions should be regarded as instances of political processes—a particular set of formalized relationships that emerge from, are constituted by, and continue to be altered through political activity.[38]

We can use the metaphor of performance to depict this activity of politics. The image is suggestive of the potential connection between anthropology, classics, and political theory as

it is employed both by Turner in describing social processes as
"dramatic" and by the political theorist Hannah Arendt in her
description of political action.[39] This metaphor has several
implications for our understanding of politics. First, the metaphor of performance connotes a cultural, rather than a natural,
product. This cultural connotation serves as an important point
of contrast with approaches to social systems that draw on the
language of natural processes. Whereas natural systems of
organic growth, development, and evolution "are objectively
given and exist independently of the experience and activity of
men," cultural systems "depend not only for their meaning but
also for their existence upon the participation of conscious,
volitional human agents and upon men's continuing and potentially changing relations with one another."[40] Human meaning—
the question of who "I" am and who "we" are—is constituted
by and with others. Like "performing artists," so "acting men
need the presence of others before whom they can appear."[41]

A second implication of the metaphor of performance is that
it changes our focus from the operation and evolution of
political structures, or what Turner calls "structural time," to a
focus on "historical time" in which politics is given form and
meaning as it is constituted narratively.[42] Arendt is, again,
helpful on this point, as she suggests that through speech and
action, one inserts oneself into a "web of human relationships."
The insertion of oneself starts "a new process which eventually
emerges as the unique life story of the newcomer, affecting
uniquely the life stories of all those with whom he comes into
contact." Because action occurs within this web, "with its innum-
erable, conflicting wills and intentions," action "almost never
achieves its purposes." But what is produced are "stories": stories
of a life disclosed in speech and action and stories of human
action that become history.[43]

The change from structural to narrative time suggests a third
implication of the metaphor of performance, a corresponding

change in methodological orientation. Whereas an emphasis on the examination and comparison of structures across time, as we have seen, leads to a methodological preference for abstract, differentiated, and objectively defined characteristics, an emphasis on the performative dimension of politics gives importance to an analysis of its narrative shape. Since the "specific revelatory quality of action and speech, the implicit manifestation of the agent and speaker, is so indissolubly tied to the living flux of acting and speaking," it can be represented "only through a kind of repetition," or *mimesis*, which corresponds to dramatic reenactment.[44] Whereas political thought, at least since the time of Plato, has often sought to sever the relationship between the constitution and contemplation of political life, what is suggested here is a more fundamental correspondence between the activity of politics and its contemplation. Specifically, a recounting of activity—the telling of a story—can make visible the more fluid dimensions of politics: the formation of communities, the emergence and resolution of conflict, the struggle for authority, the articulation of rights, and debates about the distribution of community resources. My suggestion is simply this: the contemplation of political life does not require thinking from abstraction; rather, contemplation, including critique, may arise through the narrative shape given to the performance of politics.

ARCHAEOLOGICAL SITES AS POLITICAL FIELDS

Before looking specifically at the *Iliad*, I want to turn to the eighth and early seventh centuries, a time in which the *Iliad* is likely to have received its extant form. This period, which is the end of what is often referred to as the Dark Age, was seen, until fairly recently, as a "generally poor and backward age."[45] This conception, though, has come under considerable revision as archaeological evidence accumulates that points to the eighth century as a momentous time of transition and even revolution.[46] The nature of the transformation was far-reaching, including rising population density in settlements, increasing foreign trade and interaction, growing material prosperity, and the introduction of an alphabet.[47] The recent finds at Lefkandi on Euboea, a settlement that flourished in the tenth and ninth centuries, have been nothing short of spectacular. The excavations reveal an unexpected variety and wealth of grave goods, a monumental tomb, molds for casting bronze tripods (a skill assumed to have been lost in the Dark Age), and extensive trade and communication with Attica, Thessaly, Cyprus, at Al Mina in Syria, Italy, and Sicily.[48] Some have interpreted these finds as strong corroborating evidence that Homer is not romanticizing a Mycenaean past, but describing a Dark Age present.[49] So strong are the parallels that scholars have even suggested that the Euboeans might have been the original audience of the Homeric poems.[50]

Scholars have identified in the eighth century, as well, the emergence of polis structures, however embryonic. Though this scholarship has been invaluable in yielding important insights into the structural transformations of the eighth century, we have seen how conclusions about political development have often rested on identifying when the nascent polis acquired sufficient institutional structure and differentiation. The problem is that when we make the appearance of an activity—that of politics— contingent on the appearance of institutional forms, we conflate a process with a form. Rather than searching for institutions, my interest is to use our language of politics to look for evidence in this archaeological record of the emergence of political fields, or sites of contestation and coordination in which questions about the organization and identity of community life arise.

No one piece of archaeological evidence points conclusively toward the emergence of political communities. The reason for this is the incompleteness of the archaeological record. Few sites reveal the spatial configuration of an entire community at any given time, let alone over a period of time. Any number of factors may account for this: a preference among archaeologists for unearthing monumental structures (such as temples) and grave goods; the difficulty of locating structures, such as common dwellings, made of materials (such as mudbrick, thatch, or wood) that do not last; the difficulty of identifying the function of structures (such as an agora); the destruction of past communities through newer construction; or the existence of a new town on top of the ancient town that makes access impossible. The town of Argos serves as an illuminating example. It is one of the most important Dark Age communities, yet excavations have been limited to sanctuary and temple sites and graves because a new town sits atop the old town. Little is known, apart from what can be learned from sonic surveys, of the layout of the community in the eighth century.

For yet another reason archaeological evidence cannot, by itself, demonstrate the development of political communities: archaeological finds provide us with material remains, such as grave sites, pottery shards, buildings, tools, even a written record at times. What is lost, if only because it rarely leaves a material record and thus is so difficult to capture, is the activity that gave rise to these forms. This is a particular problem when talking about politics since the political is not, as we have suggested, reducible to particular institutional forms or functions. Politics is an activity in which questions about the identity and organization of community life arise. The archaeological record cannot portray this activity, but we can find hints and clues about the material conditions that made politics likely and the practices that reflect its presence and suggest its importance.

Of the material conditions that make politics likely, growth in the population and density of settlements in the eighth century seems particularly convincing evidence.[51] Population density was accompanied by increasing social complexity and differentiation. Communities remained overwhelmingly agricultural, but wealth came to be derived increasingly from production of metal goods, pottery, building materials, textiles, and foodstuffs for both domestic and external exchange. Such production and trade raised dramatically the material prosperity of settlements[52] as well as increased social stratification.[53] Increasing wealth, population density, and differentiation placed greater demands on community organization and coordination, and necessitated more refined qualities of leadership and mediation.[54] Organization and coordination would, in turn, foster the growth in both the density and prosperity of these settlements.

Politics, though, is not reducible to a set of material conditions, nor is it simply the expression of material needs.[55] Politics, importantly, is a realm in which people think about themselves, and constitute themselves, as communities. Benedict Anderson talks of "imagined communities" to describe how individuals come to see themselves as bound together.[56] Material needs are certainly important (perhaps even primary) in the formation of communities. But important as well is a shared sense of a past, a common belief system and set of values, jointly enacted rituals, a common sense of a future, and shared responses to new and threatening challenges. The archaeological record does not allow us to know how community life was imagined. But to the extent that the organization, coordination, and mediation of community life became a community activity, and thus political, we would expect to see the activity of politics coincide with the collective definition and organization of space.

The eighth century appears as a time of transition toward a more collective definition and arrangement of community space. The development of hero cults and ancestor cults at this time suggests the emergence of a shared sense of the past.[57] The establishment of civic deities, with corresponding urban and extra-urban sanctuaries, served to provide a common religious identity, symbolically linked town and country, and demarcated the territory of the community from surrounding settlements.[58] Accompanying this rise of city sanctuaries was an increase in votive offerings by a broad cross section of the community.[59] The construction of city walls,[60] the creation of public spaces,[61] and the establishment of common cemeteries outside the town rather than burials close to one's home[62] suggest a more collective definition of community space. The building of monumental temples[63] and public infrastructures,[64] town planning,[65] public works projects, and the relocation of people through colonization[66] point to an increasing ability to organize and direct collective resources. And the construction of interstate sanctuaries, such as at Olympia, Delphi, and Delos, provided for "the establishment of formal relations between communities."[67] Summarizing the growing list of Dark Age developments, though, risks overstating the uniformity of characteristics between communities and the completeness of these characteristics in any one community. To counter this tendency, I will look briefly, instead, at three settlements: Zagora, Dreros, and Corinth. Each of these settlements illustrates different ways in which we can understand the spatial organization of political fields in the eighth century.[68] This will provide, in turn, a historical context for the activity of politics that we see in the *Iliad*.

Zagora: The Enclosing of Space

The first site is Zagora, located on the island of Andros in the Cyclades. The site is an interesting one for archaeologists and historians of the Dark Age because the settlement was abandoned in the seventh century. Without having to contend with new construction on top of the settlement, excavators were able to provide a much more thorough reconstruction not just of the layout of the Dark Age settlement, but of changes in the organization of that layout over time.

One of the striking features of Zagora is the existence of an extensive defensive wall, measuring as much as seven meters thick, that surrounds the entire settlement.[69] Walls are first and foremost functional, since they are constructed in response to unstable environments.[70] This does not mean, though, that walls do not tell us something about the collective definition of space. Walls are the product of decisions. We see in Zagora, and in other Dark Age and Archaic settlements, a different decision in what should be enclosed. Whereas Mycenaean and Minoan practice was to fortify the "palace," leaving the houses outside the wall, the people of Zagora enclosed the houses that made up the town center.[71] The decision to enclose an entire community, if only for defensive purposes, suggests the bounding of a space that is seen as common, shared, and important.

A further organization of a collective space occurs within the walls. The houses appear to be oriented around a demarcated, open-air sanctuary and stone altar at the center of the town. Near the altar is evidence of burning, likely from ritual sacrifices.[72] Though the evidence does not allow us to identify with any certainty who was being worshipped, the location of the sanctuary is consistent with the emergence during the ninth and eighth centuries of community cults. "Common cult," as Sourvinou-Inwood notes, was the way for "expressing communality in the Greek world."[73] The development of a town sanctuary and the performance of community rituals suggests a broader social process of forming a common identity in which the town orients itself physically around the sanctuary, identifies itself with a civic deity, and enacts these relationships through collective rituals.[74]

The residences also appear to follow an organized layout. Instead of the loose collection of apsidal houses that are usually in evidence in early Dark Age settlements, one sees an orderly arrangement of square and rectangular units. A common, continuous wall runs along several units. This common wall was not built all at once but was constructed in six different periods as new units were added. Though it could be argued that an orientation along a common wall was simply the result of architectural efficiency, the same orientation of units is continued where there is no structural connection. This suggests, as the excavators note, a "strong element of planning."[75]

Increased differentiation and stratification also appears within the community. Several houses underwent structural changes, either through subdivision of existing rooms, the addition of new rooms, or the amalgamation of previously distinct houses. One- and two-room dwellings were transformed into four- and five-room structures, with differentiated space for storage, and often a private courtyard.[76] Smaller units were constructed in two other areas in the settlement. These changes are consistent with the growing wealth and social differentiation within the community, a wealth that was likely acquired through trade.[77]

A "rulers' dwelling" may also exist.[78] It is the largest unit (though not by much),[79] contains some fine Attic kraters and Corinthian pottery that would have likely been prestige items,[80] and has a courtyard that opens toward the sanctuary. The excavators note that though the main room is not as comparatively grand as they had originally thought, the "position of the house to which it belongs may have been considered privileged because of its proximity to the sanctuary."[81] This proximity to the sanctuary would be consistent with what some have argued was an early religious role of the ruler in leading and overseeing the performance of community rituals.[82] If we are to take our clues from architecture, it seems likely that some sharing of leadership occurred among the elite (rather than there being a single hereditary leader). No single house dominates the community landscape. And the larger houses, which are all located on the highest ground of the settlement, are fairly similar in size, show signs of sharing in wealth through expansion and the development of storage areas, and seem to emulate each other in organizing their living spaces around a courtyard. In a different context, Antonaccio has interpreted the arrangement of elite graves around the monumental tomb at Lefkandi as a site in which elites contended for legitimacy through their association with, and imitation of, an ancestral past.[83] Similarly, it may well be that the duplication of a more elaborate organization of living space in Zagora manifests both elite coordination (through the sharing of wealth) and elite competition (through the imitation of displays of wealth).[84]

DREROS: COMMUNITY AS PUBLIC SPACE

Dreros, a settlement in what Homer describes as "Krete of the hundred cities" (*Krêtên hekatompolin*, 2.649), presents us with a second type of evidence for community formation: namely, the development of public spaces. This is not to say that such spaces did not exist in Zagora or other communities; they may not have been found or may not be distinguishable in the archaeological record. Dreros is striking because of the eighth-century configuration of a set of public spaces that would appear later in seventh-century Lato and sixth-century Delos. Lying between two peaks in the center of the settlement is a flattened area measuring twenty-three by forty meters that has been identified as an agora. At the southwest corner of the agora are the remains of seven steps that have been built into the natural slope of the hill. This was apparently part of a much more extensive series of steps across the south end of the agora and tapering off as one rounds the corner at each end. "This primitive theatre," suggests Coldstream, "would have been the setting for public assemblies, both religious and political."[85]

Built on the same alignment of the agora, accessible by two paths that lead from the agora, is a temple, believed to be the temple of Apollo Delphinios. There is evidence of cult sacrifices, a display of votives, and goats' horns (which are associated with

Apollo).[86] The significance of this temple lies not only in the development of an urban cult but in its association with public meeting places at such sites as Delos, Delphi, Thermon, and Eretria.[87]

To the southwest of the temple, overlooking the agora, is a building that has been identified (not without controversy) as a *prytaneion*.[88] The *prytaneion* plays an important role in the development of the Greek polis. Whereas in early Dark Age communities the largest building would likely be the residence of the chieftain, with the development of a stronger citizen role in governance the central civic building becomes the public *prytaneion*. It functioned as a location of ritual meals for foreign guests, leaders, and distinguished citizens. It served, as well, as a law court and, with the development of written law, an archive.[89]

Some evidence of early political organization in Dreros is consistent with the centrality of these public spaces. An inscribed stone dating from the mid-seventh century appears as one of the earliest known written laws.[90] The decree is public in two ways. First, like other law codes that would follow, such as at Gortyn, it is displayed publicly. Such display has significance, not only because the law is formalized but because communication of the law no longer rests with a privileged interpreter.[91] The decree is public in a second way, and that is in its origin. It begins, "*Ad' eFade poli,*" or "This has pleased the polis," suggesting that the decree comes from a citizen-body, perhaps an assembly. The decree states that no person may hold the highest office of *kosmos* more than once every ten years, a clear limit on the concentration of power in the hands of a single person. Among the penalties for a person who violates this is that he will be "liable to fines double the amount of those inflicted by him as a judge (*dikaksie*)." This seems to suggest that one of the functions of the *kosmos* was to serve as a judge and issue fines. The inscription ends by requiring that the oath be taken by the *kosmos*, the *damioi*, and the "*ikati oi tas pol[io]s*" or "twenty of the polis."[92]

We do not know with certainty what the different positions were, though Ehrenberg has suggested that the *damioi* were likely the financial magistrates and the "twenty of the polis" served as a council.[93] We cannot know the political forms of the eighth century, but the archaeological record testifies to the formalization of public spaces that provided a forum for an ongoing contestation and negotiation about who shall rule, and under what conditions. These institutional forms did not create politics, but arose from a process of thinking and acting politically.[94]

Corinth: Fashioning a Founding

"Wealthy [*aphneion*] Corinth," as Homer refers to it (2.570, trans. modified), reflects general demographic and economic changes occurring throughout the Greek world in the ninth and eighth centuries. In the late Bronze Age and early Iron Age, settlements in the Corinthia were scattered and limited in size.[95] Evidence points to a reemergence of a more extensive and stable settlement c. 925–875, followed in the eighth century by steady population growth and expansion,[96] expanding sea communication and trade, increasing economic diversification, and a growing material prosperity of the settlement.

A continuing scholarly puzzle has been how to reconcile the "achievements of early Corinth with the site of early Corinth."[97] That is, given the important commercial role of Corinth, where are all the people? Something like an urban center certainly existed in Corinth, but the population that has been discerned from burials is not nearly what one might expect. As Catherine Morgan comments, if we were "to rely on preserved remains alone, the pre-eighth-century population of the Corinthia would at times appear so low as to be barely viable."[98] Increasingly, archaeologists are finding new habitations dispersed throughout the area. Williams has suggested that the availability of different water sources and the extent of fertile plain allowed an "organic arrangement of the communities already established."[99] This would permit the area to grow without placing enormous population pressures, and a corresponding need for urban planning, on the central settlement. But on what basis can we be justified in talking about Corinth and the surrounding area as an integrated community?

The notion of a political field is helpful here because it locates politics not in permanent institutional structures but in a more fluid and ongoing process of negotiation about the collective organization of resources. Such efforts at collective organization appear in a number of guises. First, Corinth followed a pattern not uncommon among early communities in Greece by gradually expanding leadership positions. There is some historical corroboration (though it must be treated carefully) that the form of leadership changed in the mid-eighth century from a hereditary monarchy (which had been the tradition since the founding of Corinth in c. 900) to an elective oligarchy among the Bacchiads.[100] The enlargement of office can be explained most easily as an attempt to lessen factional strife among the Bacchiads, as the family grew through descent.[101] There was also a council consisting of members of the Bacchiads, who elected the officials.[102] And the people may have had some nominal role in an assembly, though any formal powers were likely circumscribed.[103]

Second, evidence points to a growing attention to the organization of community space. During the mid-eighth century, burial practice changed from family group burials within the settlement to common burial places for the town, such as at the north cemetery.[104] The significance of burials, as Morris has argued, is that they can be "treated as the material remains of self-representations of social structure through the agency of ceremony."[105] That is, burial patterns, including the location of cemeteries and who and what is buried in the cemeteries, can tell us something about community relationships and organization.

In contrast to burials around houses, which indicate more segmented relationships, the establishment of cemeteries outside town may indicate the development (and perhaps enforcement) of a sense of both a communal living and burial space. Within the town, the archaeological record indicates an increased prominence of a differentiated commercial space. Though Corinth (and the rest of Dark Age Greece) was still an agricultural and not a commercial society, this evidence suggests a growing attention (and perhaps even direction) to organizing the production process.[106]

Third, Corinth's establishment of a trading post on Ithaca (c. 780) and the colonization of Syracuse (c. 733) and Corcyra (c. 709) indicate a willingness and ability of the elite to organize community resources in pursuit of commercial opportunities. Ithaca, located at the opening of the Gulf of Corinth, likely served as a trading post for developing Corinthian markets to the west.[107] The colony at Corcyra, says Roebuck, "seems to reveal a conscious recognition of the island's importance as a port of call on the route to Italy, as well as of its capacity to offer a livelihood for settlers from its soil." Unlike Ithaca and Corcyra, the colony at Syracuse was likely established both as a remedy for resource pressures at home and as a commercial venture.[108] But this suggests a political response to the economic integration of town and country within the Corinthia. In either case, the surrounding area appears to have acquired sufficient economic integration to stimulate political action. As Roebuck suggests, "the whole enterprise has the character of a regularly organized action by the Corinthian state. There was an oekist [founder], Archias the Bacchiad, and the settlers had been assured of grants of land to be given them on arrival in Syracuse."[109]

And the final evidence of collective organization is the organization of sanctuaries and civic rituals, or what Morgan evocatively calls the "sacral landscape," which is a critical component for the creation of a sense of common identity among a dispersed population.[110] In his classic discussion, de Polignac describes how the emergence of a polis was often marked by an urban sanctuary, located either close to the agora or on an acropolis, and by sanctuaries located on the margins of an inhabited area (a sub-urban sanctuary) and/or well outside town (extra-urban sanctuaries).[111] Corinth provides an interesting case in which the extra-urban sanctuaries seem to precede an urban sanctuary. Morgan has made an argument recently for an early extra-urban sanctuary at Isthmia, located to the east of Corinth, that may have served in the pre-eighth century as a site of regional coordination. Such sanctuary activity "indicates a need (and the organization) to bring together people from a wide area" and "points to the existence of some sort of community of cult" that allowed a cross section of the community, including women, to participate.[112] With the defeat of Megara to the north in the mid-eighth century, Corinth constructed an extra-urban temple to Hera Limenia on the promontory at Perachora, marking the political expansion and control of the territory by Corinth.[113] The array of offerings at Perachora suggests the multiple meanings that may be given to a sanctuary. As Morgan writes, "it seems likely that the foundation of the sanctuary reflected a complex of interests, including celebration of the household, trade, and control of land essential to Corinth.[114]

Four seemingly minor sanctuaries also seem to have appeared in the eighth century: an extra-urban sanctuary at Solygeia, and the urban sanctuaries of Hera Akraia, Athena Hellotis, and Kotyto. Whatever the origins of the cults practiced at these sanctuaries, each of them became connected with a constructed Corinthian myth-history. One set of stories gives Corinth a mythical past by linking the location to the ancient place of Ephyre. This connection integrates into a Corinthian past the legends of Medea, Sisyphos, Bellerophon, and the adventures of Jason.[115] In a second set of stories, the founding of Corinth is associated both with the Dorian invasion and the legendary return of the Heraclidae (the descendents of Heracles). According to the tradition that developed, Aletes (one of the descendants of Heracles) led the Dorians in battle against the original inhabitants of Corinth (the Aeolians). Solygeia became the site of Aletes's victory.[116]

Whereas the cult of Hera Akraia was associated with a pre-Dorian, mythical past of Medea and Jason,[117] the cults of Athena Hellotis, Kotyto, and Solygeia were closely connected to the founding of Corinth by Aletes. The sanctuary at Solygeia appeared on the legendary site of the Dorian conquest of Corinth.[118] The establishment of an extra-urban sanctuary at Solygeia at this time served to tie this outlying area symbolically to the myth-history of Heraclidean founding. The cults (and festival) of Athena Hellotis and of Kotyto were connected by legend to the deaths of Hellotia and Kotyto, daughters of the Aeolian king, brought about by the invasion of Aletes.[119] What the cults of Hera Akraia, Athena Hellotis, and Kotyto have in common is that they emerged as communal expiation for a death. The bonds of community appear both as a recognition of community culpability for a public death and as a community act of ritual cleansing. The development of such community-based cult practices "signaled the emergence of a society that seemed to acquire self-awareness as it retook possession of the past by endowing it with a sacred character, organizing in an increasingly overt fashion collective practices and sanctuaries in which rituals transformed a disparate collection of individuals or groups into a community active and solid in its devotion to a particular cult."[120] Participation, as it was connected to a legendary past, became a civic participation in a founding myth.

CONCLUSION

In looking at Zagora, Dreros, and Corinth, I have attempted to identify from the archaeological evidence the increased prominence of the activity of politics in the eighth century. I have done so not by equating institutional forms with processes, but by seeking evidence of these processes. We have looked for evidence of political fields, or sites of contestation and coordination about collective ends. And we have identified the material basis of politics as connected to the growth in population density and material prosperity. These demographic and economic changes likely placed increased demands on the community to develop processes of mediation, coordination, and distribution. How that looks in the archaeological record, though, varies considerably. The enclosed space of Zagora contrasts with the dispersed settlement pattern of Corinth and the organization of public spaces in Dreros. Each of these images provides partial glimpses into the complex ways in which political fields are constituted. The creation of founding legends, the establishment of sacred boundaries, and the collective organization of space tells us something about the complex ways in which questions of community organization and identity assumed increased prominence.

THE *ILIAD* AND THE DRAMA OF POLITICS

In thinking about the politics of the *Iliad*, scholars have sought to match up references in the epic to this archaeological record. And certainly attestations of this archaeological context appear in the *Iliad*. In fact, there are sufficient mentions of these eighth-century developments to indicate that this backdrop formed part of the common understanding of both the poet and the audience. So, for example, numerous references appear to shrines and altars for public worship that are tied back to civic organization,[121] as when Theano, Athene's priestess who was chosen by the Trojans, goes to Athene's temple "on the peak of the citadel" (*polei akrêi*) to pray to "Athene, our city's defender" (*rhusiptoli*) to spare the city.[122] The practice of hero-cult is suggested.[123] And the *Iliad* alludes to a town layout with streets, an agora, and communal washbasins, and walls that enclose the entire city and demarcate the "flat land" from "the city" (*polios*, 22.456).[124]

Yet, just as we limit our understanding of the political by locating politics solely in systems of formal institutions and groups, so we constrain our understanding of the politics of the *Iliad* by looking for a formalized system. The framework offered here allows us to view the *Iliad* as more than an artifact that testifies to the emergence of polis structures. The *Iliad* appears as a narrative account of the drama of politics. This account is not of already established institutions but of communities in formation, conflict, and transition. The narrative structure of the opening scenes makes clear the political context of the drama of the *Iliad*, as we encounter political fields before we see battlefields. The epic sets out a powerful relationship between political fields and battlefields as the tumult of war works to expose fissures within the community that demand resolution at the risk of community dissolution. In subsequent chapters, I examine how these communities are imperiled, and how this imperiling leads us to reflect on the activity of politics. My interest, in the final part of this chapter, is to show how the *Iliad* provides an account of the initial constituting of these political communities: by the Achaians, on the one hand, and the Trojans, on the other.

The *Iliad* opens with otherwise independent aristocratic households called to assembly (*agorênde*) by Achilles (1.54). The people (*laos*) are assembled in response to nine days of plague that has decimated the Achaians. Alarmed by what would likely doom the Achaians, Achilles calls for an interpreter of dreams to "tell why Phoibos Apollo is so angry" (1.64). Kalchas, the inter-preter, explains that Agamemnon's refusal to accept the ransom of Chryses, a priest of Apollo, for his daughter, Chryseis, has resulted in Apollo sending "griefs" against all the Achaians in the form of a plague (1.96). This opening is significant for several reasons. First, it points to elements of a common identity in that the Achaians seek redress in a public forum for their culpability, in the eyes of Apollo, in the actions of their leader. Kalchas, for example, refers to Agamemnon as a man who "holds great kingship / over the men of Argos, and all the Achaians obey him" (1.78–79). Upon hearing that Agamemnon was the cause of their plight, "Then all the rest of the Achaians cried out in favour / that the priest be respected and the shining ransom be taken" (1.54, 376–77).

Second, the opening makes explicit the public context for the conflict between Agamemnon and Achilles. This context involves issues of the distribution of resources, made explicit when Agamemnon threatens to take, and then does take, Achilles' war prize. Achilles' response is to place Agamemnon's action within the context of the community, declaring that "it is unbecoming for the people [*laous*] to call back things once given" (1.126). But the assembly also serves, as we will see in subsequent chapters, as the context for Achilles to raise a more fundamental issue about the nature of authority, one that will eventuate in the transformation of relationships within that political space.

As the story unfolds, a clearer picture of an interdependent social organization emerges, with its own political assembly, social hierarchy, religious rituals, and demarcated sacred space.[125] In the space constituted by these assemblies, we see the emergence of a broader set of questions about community life in which "the process of decision making is public throughout."[126] References are made, for example, to the role of assemblies in decision-making within the already established territories of the Achaian leaders; to decisions about military strategy; to the administration of "rights"; to the witnessing of judgments involving redress for harm by others; to the communalization and distribution of resources; and to the burial of Patroklos by the community rather than a return of Patroklos to the homeland.[127] Such public assemblies are seen as important to, perhaps even making a claim on, the individual. So Odysseus requests that Achilles consider the effect of his actions on "the other / Achaians" (*Panachaious*) (9.301–302).[128] Furthermore, the assemblies are sufficiently prominent that they are seen as a place where the Achaians "dealt out / rights" (11.806–807) and "where men win glory" (1.490).[129]

The political context for the drama of the *Iliad* is suggested still further by our first glimpse of the Trojans. Though war has been raging for ten years, Homer interrupts this chronology to take us back in time, in effect, to the initial constituting of a Trojan alliance. We first encounter the Trojans as they are "holding assembly [*agoras agoreuon*] in front of the doors of Priam / gathered together in one place, the elders and the young men" (2.788–89). While the Trojans are assembled, the son of Priam watches the Achaians from "aloft the ancient burial mount of ancient Aisyetes," a burial site suggestive of the organization of a community around a cult of heroes (2.793). Iris, in the likeness of Polites, a son of Priam whose name means "citizen," speaks to Hektor of the urgency of the situation: "In my time I have gone into many battles among men, / yet never have I seen a host like this, not one so numerous" as they "advance across the plain to fight by the city" (2.798–99, 801). To defend the city, though, requires that the surrounding communities of Troy, who are "multitudinous" in their speech, be organized (2.804). Iris tells Hektor to "let each man who is their leader give orders to these men, / and let each set his citizens [*polietas*] in order, and lead them" (2.805–806). In interpreting this passage, Qviller suggests that Hektor's speech is a "perfect summary of the process forming the early *polis*" in which "*polites*," or citizen, "acquired a new, a political significance."[130] I am reluctant to ascribe such a transformation to this passage. But, at the very least, the passage points to the constituting of a community in which people of different languages and towns are bound together through a common sense of purpose, which, in this case, is to withstand the onslaught of the Achaians.

Within this interstate confederation, public assemblies are formed whenever important decisions must be made. At times, these assemblies meet within the walls of Troy in a fairly established institutional context.[131] But these assemblies are also called whenever (and wherever) important decisions must be made.[132] So, Hektor holds "an assembly of all the Trojans" in an open space on the battlefield to discuss whether they should rest for the night before continuing their assault on the Achaians (8.489). And the Trojans, in response to Achilles' entrance into battle, also "gathered into assembly" on the battlefield (18.245) to decide whether to return to the "city" (*astude*) (18.255) and defend it from the "market place" (*agorē*), the "great walls" (*astu de purgoi*), and the "gateways" (*pulai*) (18.274–75).

Homer describes here the material organization of a community space: its walls, gateways, and marketplace. These material forms, though, as Homer makes clear, are the expressions of a collective identity, one we see recounted through the legend of the founding of Troy as a political community. The city has divine origins, being able to trace its genealogy back to Dardanos, a son of Zeus, who founded Dardania. But the poet draws an important distinction between Dardania, in which the inhabitants lived in a realm undifferentiated from nature (20.218), and "sacred Ilion," which was "made a city in the plain to be the centre of peoples" (*polis meropôn anthrôpôn*) (20.216–18). The act of founding is one of fashioning a human space apart from nature, an act that is venerated by the dedication of an altar to Ilos, the founder, and is recalled by the gathering of the Trojans at that spot.[133]

The *Iliad* gives narrative life to the archaeological evidence of the formation of a community space and identity. We see not the settled institutional vestiges of politics—a system—but the performance of politics: the creation of one community (the Achaians), and the imperiling of another (the Trojans), by war. In subsequent chapters, we will look at how this political space is threatened, expanded, transformed, and reconstituted as the epic engages in a reflection on the political question of the organization and purpose of community life. Before turning to these issues, though, we must address one philosophic issue that stands in the way of an understanding of the *Iliad* as a work of political thought: namely, whether we can identify in the epic a concept of human agency. That is the subject of the next chapter.

2

Human Agency and the Divine

μὴ μὰν ἀσπουδί γε καὶ ἀκλειῶς ἀπολοίμην,
ἀλλὰ μέγα ῥέξας τι καὶ ἐσσομένοισι πυθέσθαι

Let me at least not die without a struggle, inglorious
but do some big thing first, that men to come shall
know of it

22.304–305

A long tradition in political thought exists, dating from at least Aristotle, that politics exists as a realm free from the automatic processes of life. For Aristotle, politics was a fundamentally different activity from labor. Whereas labor and acquisition answered to the daily needs of survival, politics was concerned uniquely with larger questions of community well-being. The difference, for Aristotle, was one of the nature of the activity. Issues of production posited a means-ends relationship, in which one labored to accomplish a particular end. But politics was valuable in itself because it provided a realm for the exercise of logos: the distinctively human faculty of language and reason. The exercise of reason, which in a political setting included questions of what is just and unjust, required that the individual be free from the dictates of necessity. Beggars, slaves, laborers, and women could not be proper citizens, for Aristotle, because their actions were governed by necessity. Beggars were ruled by hunger, slaves and laborers were instruments of production, and women were ruled by emotions, on the one hand, and the demands of the household, on the other. The result, suggests one scholar in talking about the Greek "discovery" of politics, was "an almost ideal model of the political: political events and political conditions became subject to the will of the participants and whatever was contingent upon their interactions."[1] The development of political thinking, contends Wolin, rested upon a differentiation between phenomena that were ruled by nature and divine laws and activities that were the creation of human association.[2]

Such a differentiation appears to many commentators to be absent in the Homeric world. Simply stated, the gods in the Homeric epics, and the *Iliad* in particular, are everywhere. They watch, take sides, devise plans, appear in dreams, provide counsel, interfere in the physical universe, and even engage in fighting. Early commentators would struggle with the nature of the gods in the Homeric epics, questioning whether they were ethical, allegorical, or mistaken poetic creations.[3] But the contemporary debate has focused much more on the implications of this divine world for human agency. The terms of this debate have been driven, in large part, by a post-Cartesian and post-Kantian formula that has identified agency as resting upon an autonomous will and self-conscious action. From a Cartesian perspective, the self is conceived as a unitary and "volitional" actor in which action is "preceded, and caused, by a distinct and conscious act of will."[4] Given a more ethical cast, the Kantian agent requires the existence of morally autonomous individuals guided by their own rationally determined and freely chosen values. It is a "domain of moral value . . . altogether immune to the assaults of luck."[5] Stated in its most general form, agency rests upon a particular conception of the will, one that is free from such external controls as chance, contingency, or luck. From this perspective, the gods in the *Iliad* act and appear as a force originating outside of, and upon, the human will. We can see the problem immediately. Agency in the Homeric world—and a political realm free from the dictates of external contingency—can be purchased only by a corresponding diminution in, or harmonizing of, the role of the gods.[6]

The purpose of this chapter is to challenge the nature of this trade-off by way of a rather unconventional route: namely, by rethinking how communities understand chance. We can define chance, or luck, as Nussbaum does: that is, as the occurrence of an event that "does not happen through his or her own agency, what just *happens* to him, as opposed to what he does or makes."[7] But defining chance as events that are unforeseen, unintended, and outside human control is incomplete, because it does not help us understand why, from the myriad unanticipated events that occur each day, we single out for attention some but not others. My suggestion is that we can better understand chance as a cultural construction. Which events we pay attention to and the meaning we assign to these occurrences are constituted by the culture in which we live. This will lead us to a notion of chance that does not exist apart from human agency but, as notions of chance and agency are mediated through culture, serve to define the other.

GODS OR MEN: THE SCHOLARLY CONSTRUCTION OF HUMAN AGENCY

Though it is impossible to do justice to the nuances of the different arguments, most scholars have been guided in their thinking about human agency and divine action in the Homeric epics by a post-Kantian and post-Cartesian framework. On one end of the spectrum are those who reject the possibility of

agency precisely because of the prominent role of the gods. For
Dodds, Homeric characters lack any unified concept of the
"soul" or "personality." Absent this innerness, "all departures
from normal human behaviour whose causes are not immediately perceived, whether by the subjects' own consciousness
or by the observation of others, are ascribed to a supernatural
agency, just as is any departure from the normal behaviour of
the weather or the normal behaviour of a bowstring." In one
revealing passage, Dodds articulates what has served so often to
confound Homeric scholars: why did "a people so civilised,
clearheaded, and rational as the Ionians" not eliminate "this sense
of constant daily dependence on the supernatural?" Answering
this question took Dodds into the field of anthropology and the
application of the now well-known distinction between shame
and guilt cultures. In the shame culture of Homeric society,
situations that caused public contempt or ridicule would be
projected to divine agency.[8]

Bruno Snell, in his Hegelian reading of the emergence of
the Greek conception of the self, notes that "in Homer every
new turn of events is engineered by the gods." The result is that
"human initiative has no source of its own; whatever is planned
and executed is the plan and deed of the gods."[9] Indeed, for
Snell, Homeric man is missing consciousness: a realization "that
decisions of the will, or any impulses or emotions, have their
origin in man himself."[10] Snell does argue that conceptions of
the self in the Homeric epics differ from "primitive" views in
that Homeric man is not completely bound by the gods but is
elevated by them; they make "him free, strong, courageous,
certain of himself." But this is not enough to raise Homeric
man to the freedom of human agency; it is only enough to see
in Homer the seeds of human freedom that "founded our
western civilization."[11] In a more recent elaboration of Snell's
argument, Erbse has written that "the activity of humans," as
well as their "wishes and decisions" are possible only through a

framework of divine action. Human action and thought in the epics, suggests Erbse, depend upon the gods for authorship.[12]

Finally, Jean-Pierre Vernant has argued in a series of essays that the tragic sense of responsibility that develops in fifth-century Athenian drama arises at a point in which individuals are developing sufficient autonomy to begin making choices for which they are responsible, but are still tied to an inscrutable divine order that binds, even traps, individuals by their decisions. In the case of the epic, Vernant continues, there is no action since "man is never envisaged as an agent,"[13] that is, as "a responsible and autonomous subject who manifests himself in and through actions that are imputable to him."[14] Only with such autonomy of the will can there be the self-conscious and responsible subject to which Vernant refers.

On the other end of the Homeric scholarship spectrum are those who see in the epic the operation of human agents. Agency is identified, though, only by drastically curtailing the role of the gods. Thus, John Gunnell argues that in reformulating the various myths and legends, Homer carefully limits the powers of the gods to provide a new focus on human action.[15] Adkins, in his highly influential discussion in *Merit and Responsibility*, frames his understanding of human ethics and morality with the suggestion, "we are all Kantians now." Adkins's point is not to make Homer a Kantian, but to show "why the concept of moral responsibility is so unimportant" to the Greeks. Nonetheless, Adkins is able to salvage some notion of agency by separating statements of destiny from the human experience of action: situations covered by Zeus's prophecy, and these same situations that arise from human action, are "events" that are "simply described on two levels which do not intersect." Even at those critical moments in which an event is ascribed specifically to divine action, "the characters still act 'of their own free will,' for the incompatibility of the two statements does not occur to the poet. Common-sense carelessness again preserves individual responsibility."[16] A thoughtful Kantian Homer was not.

In between these two views stands the bulk of Homeric scholarship that seeks to find some balance between the human and divine world. Most often, this balance is struck by viewing the gods as literary devices. Greene, for example, suggests that polytheism has "artistic advantages." The "demand of the story" determines whether the "more abstract" Fate or the "more vividly personified agent" of Zeus is used to "express the cause of events which man is powerless to alter." Fate does not control all aspects of human action, though. The "conflicting wills of the gods" provide a "loophole for a certain amount of human freedom."[17]

Giving further refinement to this artistic element, Burkert, in his classic discussion of Greek religion, suggests that the "double stage of divine machinery" (*Doppelbühne des Götterapparats*) is used in the composition of the *Iliad* to mirror human action to heighten the contrast between the human and divine world. The divine machinery is also used to provide divine motivation for human action.[18] Bremer, in developing the notion of a *"Götterapparat,"* argues that the gods serve as poetic devices in three ways. First, the gods are used to postpone the drama to heighten tension. Second, the gods serve as mirrors that parallel human action, often to show either the magnitude, on a divine scale, of human action and emotion or to contrast the seriousness of the human world with the frivolity of the divine world. And third, the gods appear as focalizers in which their gaze and reaction to human action serve to direct our attention to the mortal world. By placing the gods as spectators, the audience "is invited to share the focalization" of the gods "and at the same time to feel that it is only a partial appreciation of what is going on."[19]

Bremer does not preclude other understandings, including religious understandings, of the gods. His interest, instead, is to argue that the gods do not interfere with—and may even enhance—the narrative structure of the epic. But other scholars take this argument still further, seeking to explain divine action as a literary expression. Mark Edwards treats these interventions of the gods as a device to facilitate "the smooth working of the plot." Through the intervention of the gods, heroes can be saved from unnecessary deaths, the "Greeks can be beaten, without losing too much face, because it is the will of Zeus," and divine assistance "to the stronger man can be direct, and brings him additional honor."[20] Edwards, for example, rescues Achilles' image of Zeus holding up the scales to determine human fate from a dire fatalism by suggesting that the image is "obviously artistic, not religious."[21] Similarly, although careful to emphasize the variable quality of the gods, James Redfield notes that the gods, as literary figures, "are often forced to intervene; they know how the story is supposed to go and have some responsibility for keeping it on course."[22] Eric Havelock suggests that the gods serve as a "kind of shorthand" for inexplicable events. The reason the gods are used this way, argues Havelock, is because the nature of oral composition necessitates more a "syntax of narrative rather than a syntax of analysis" that would seek to explain events in a sequence of cause and effect.[23] Pucci suggests, in looking at key moments of divine action, that "the god does not function as the aggrandizer of a human decision, fury, military prowess, and so on, but as a narrative device, a sort of narratological contrivance to legitimize a textual point."[24] And Hazel Barnes treats the gods as metaphors, even personifications, of inexplicable occurrences that do not render the Homeric characters as "powerless." Instead, concludes Barnes, that the characters believe themselves to be agents despite the intervention of the gods is really no different from the view of ourselves as having free will despite being "dependent on chance events in a world which we cannot control."[25]

One of the problems with literary approaches is that the gods appear to be treated seriously by both the poet and the characters. As Griffin notes, "The Homeric epics are poems about the actions

and doom of heroes, but we see everything in them falsely if we
do not see it against the background of the gods and of the
dead." What emerges in the epic is a contrast between a divine
world, in which "gods can be irresponsible in action and need
fear no disastrous consequences," and the human world in which
men may be god-like in their heroic action but, ultimately, must
die.[26] Seth Schein, too, writes that "Homer was responsible for
the religious view, characteristic throughout the archaic and
classical periods, that emphasized human ignorance and powerlessness in the face of a higher cosmic order even while it made
human beings the subjects and objects of all significant action,
suffering, and speculation."[27]

The contribution of Griffin and Schein is to challenge the
trade-off between human action and divine intervention by
depicting the paradoxical quality of the Homeric world. It is
one in which human action exists within the context of a divine
universe. Less clear from these formulations, though, is how
the Homeric characters understand themselves as agents in a
world in which the gods are so active. In particular, how do the
characters understand their actions in those moments when
they appear, because of the operation of the gods, to have the
least control?

Some of the answer to this question has been provided
already as scholars have sought to reject the trade-off between
agency and chance by challenging autonomy as necessarily
characterizing human agency.[28] So, for example, Nussbaum
argues for an account of human excellence and agency "that is
inseparable from vulnerability" and "values openness, recep-
tivity, and wonder."[29] Less often discussed is the other side of this
trade-off: namely, the notion of chance. Chance is often assumed
to have an objective existence. By that I mean that the nature
of chance is viewed as a universally similar occurrence that exists
apart from human definition. Individuals and cultures are seen
as varying in how they explain or accommodate these chance

events. It is my suggestion that chance is itself a cultural construction, one that does not exist apart from human agency, but is constituted by the cultural environment in which the agent acts. What ties chance to culture is a notion of risk: cultures, as they consist of shared beliefs and values, provide dispositions about what is dangerous, in general, and what is threatening about chance, in particular.

This idea has its origins in the work of Mary Douglas and Aaron Wildavsky, who, in writing about perceptions of risk, argue that "risk taking and risk aversion, shared confidence and shared fears, are part of the dialogue on how best to organize social relations."[30] That is to say, risks are not self-evident nor are they premised on objective observations of the world. Rather, perceptions of risk are the products of social relations in which meanings "are conferred on objects or events through social interaction."[31] As "common values" around which cultures are organized "lead to common fears," cultures will develop their own "risk portfolio[s]," emphasizing certain risks and ignoring others. The organization of social relations, in turn, works to protect the culture from these perceived dangers through prescriptions and proscriptions expressed in customs, rituals, and more formal laws and institutions.[32]

In extending their work, we can understand chance as a form of risk. "Bad fortune," as it affects us in ways for which we cannot fully prepare, points to aspects of life that we see as threatening (or at a cultural level, destabilizing). What counts as risk, as something to be feared and guarded against, is tied to our values and beliefs, for we do not fear what does not matter. As these values are shared, we would expect to see social arrangements that are both premised on a particular understanding of chance and serve to regulate against the ill effects of bad fortune. What counts as "good fortune," on the other hand, is accorded both the status of "good" and "fortune" by the values and expectations of a culture.

This suggests a far more complex understanding of chance than has been generally recognized. Chance itself comes to mean different things in different contexts: one culture's chance is another's deserved rewards. Furthermore, by this conception one does not just "respond to" or "act in the face of" chance, characterizations that are often made. Rather, how one acts is itself tied to perceptions of chance: to the type of danger posed, a danger that is both individually perceived and culturally reinforced.

In the warrior culture of the Homeric world, chance is perceived as having its most pronounced effect, and elicits the greatest reaction, when it disrupts the status hierarchy. Viewing chance as culturally constituted will allow us to identify a pattern of response of the Homeric characters to the unpredictable, seemingly incoherent, actions of the gods. As we will see, the warriors respond to chance by seeking to maintain (or, if need be, restore) their status in the community. Chance, thus, reveals both issues of community maintenance and the nature of human agency as individuals, through their deliberative and willful actions, seek to maintain a cultural equilibrium. This leads to a more integrated conception of human action: not one in which agency exists apart from chance, but one in which chance has both a cultural foundation and, somewhat ironically, is integral to and integrated into a conception of human action. Agency and chance, thus, do not exist apart, but serve to define each other as they are mediated through culture.

HIERARCHY AND HOMERIC SOCIETY

Before looking at the operation of chance in Homeric society, we need to provide some explanation of the dominant cultural system, or way of organizing community life, depicted in the *Iliad*. Though a number of different terms have been used to describe this culture—aristocratic, semi-ranked, status-based—one can detect a general consensus in scholarship about the contours of the culture. What follows is a brief justification for classifying Achaian culture as hierarchical. This discussion is important for several reasons. First, it provides an understanding of the cultural organization of Homeric society for readers unfamiliar with Homeric scholarship. Second, it makes an argument for how different aspects of Achaian culture—its beliefs, social relationships, and cosmology—are related to one another. This provides support for the notion that we can conceive of Homeric society as a functioning social system. The third reason for the discussion is that it will provide a basis for understanding later how Achilles departs from the values and practices of a hierarchical culture.

Hierarchical cultures are characterized by gradations of status with corresponding obligations and roles. Importantly, an individual's identity and sense of worth (or what I refer to in chapter 7 as *esteem*) are defined by reference to this social system, which distributes punishments and rewards for the fulfillment of one's social roles. Finley argues that "status was perhaps the main conditioning factor" in the action of the heroes. "A man's work and the evaluation of his skills, what he did and what he was not to do in the acquisition of goods and their disposition, within the *oikos* and without, were all status-bound. It was a world of multiple standards and values, of diversified permissions and prohibitions."[33]

At the highest end of the status hierarchy are the *agathoi*, or nobles, which serves as a class title for the warriors. One is born as *agathos*, but one who is *agathos* is expected to display *aretê*, or excellences appropriate to his social status. These excellences for a warrior include courage, skill in fighting, good counsel, and strength.[34] But more than simply a set of competencies, *aretê* serves as the basis for receiving honor (*timê*) and glory (*kleos* or *kudos*). The community honors the warrior through

material recognition of the warrior's status and accomplish-
ments, including the distribution of war booty. In the famous
exchange between Sarpedon and Glaukos, Sarpedon describes
how they are "honoured before others / with pride of place,
the choice meats and the filled wine cups" and how they are
given the best land (12.310–11). Whereas honor serves as compensation in this life, glory provides an immortality of remembrance that, in Nagy's words, appears as a "*cultural* negation of
a *natural* process."[35] Perhaps no other warrior more poignantly
expresses this desire for immortality than Hektor. In a pause
between the sorrow of the day's battle and the anticipation of
the renewal of battle in the morning, Hektor expresses this
longing: "Oh, if I only / could be as this in all my days immortal [*athanatos*] and ageless [*agêraos*] / and be held in honour
[*tioimên*] as Athene and Apollo are honoured" (8.538–40). Every
warrior recognizes that immortality is ultimately unachievable,
because mortals die. But, as Sarpedon notes in the conclusion
of his exchange with Glaukos, humans risk death in war "where
men win glory" (*kudianeiran*) precisely because they are not
immortal (12.325). For Hektor, as for Sarpedon, their worth is
closely bound up with glory they will receive. Likewise, the
"greatest disgrace for the warrior class is to get a bad name of
being a coward and lacking ἀρετή [*aretê*]."[36] The honor provided by a community incurs an obligation to fight cour-
ageously in battle, though. To do otherwise, to be "ignoble"
(*akleées*), would invite shame (*aidôs*) (12.318). Without constant
proof of *aretê*, the privileges of *agathos* appear not as a recognition of status by the community but as the demands by an
elite to feed upon the community.

Vernant notes how these gradations of status permeate
Achaian society. Not only does one see a correspondence of
wealth, birth, and qualities of excellence with status, but the
body, too, assumes "the form of a sort of heraldic picture on
which each person's social and personal status is inscribed and

can be deciphered: the admiration, fear, longing, and respect he inspires, the esteem in which he is held, the honors to which he is entitled."[37] One need only think of Homer's description of Thersites, who speaks against Agamemnon. Thersites is punished not because he lies (he actually speaks accurately) but because his lower status does not allow him to speak in this way against the king. To accentuate this lower status, Homer describes Thersites as "the ugliest man who came beneath Ilion. He was / bandy-legged and went lame of one foot, with shoulders / stooped and drawn together over his chest, and above this / his skull went up to a point with the wool grown sparsely upon it" (2.216–19).

Rituals and ceremonies, including gift-giving, were connected to gradations of status. Gift-giving was a widespread practice in Achaian society, serving an important social function of recognizing another's honor or, if necessary, compensating for honor taken from the individual.[38] Importantly, gift-giving was set within the context of a hierarchical social structure: "no one could just give a gift to anyone else. There were rather strict lines of giving, and grades and ranks of objects."[39] As Muellner notes, "The social/cosmic hierarchy is ceaselessly reestablished and redefined by communal divisions, sacrificial or otherwise, because in the society represented in epic there is no notion of value other than relative value and no notion of relative value other than publicly witnessed and approved exchange value such as that defined in a communal division."[40]

The Homeric cosmology serves to justify the careful regulation of social action. The status ranking and prescriptions and proscriptions of a hierarchical culture are predicated on a cosmology that rewards the maintenance of such order and punishes, often severely, its breakdown. We see the elaboration of numerous rituals and ceremonies designed to harmonize, or in Douglas's words, "to make an explicit match between civilization and the purposes of God and nature."[41] So, for example, the performance of hecatombs are attempts to merge godly with human purpose so that the gods will favor one side in battle. We can also read the funeral ceremonies of fallen heroes as attempts to harmonize the earthly with the divine realm as the gradations of status in the community are given permanence in the remembrance of the heroic life.[42] And, as Muellner has argued, we can understand the anger of Achilles, and the disaster that befalls the Achaians, as arising from Agamemnon's violation of a social and cosmic order.[43]

CHANCE IN THE *ILIAD*

Having established the hierarchical nature of Achaian society, we now can examine how the operation of chance is defined by this culture. We must be somewhat cautious in talking about "chance" in the *Iliad* for several reasons. To begin with, no Homeric noun corresponds to "chance." We do see the use of the verb *tunchanô*, which can have the meaning of "happen" or "chance upon," often with the connotation of success or good fortune.[44] Hera provides us with some sense of the word's meaning in one passage in which she resolves to cease fighting with the other gods over the Trojans or Achaians. She tells Athene, "I can no longer / let us fight in the face of Zeus for the sake of mortals. / Let one of them perish then, let another live, as their fortune / wills [*hos ke tuchêi*]" (8.427–30). At first glance, Hera seems to be distinguishing fortune from the intervention of the gods. But this is not the case, as Hera continues to explain: "let him," speaking of any one of the gods of Olympos, "as is his right and as his heart pleases, / work out whatever decrees he will on Danaans and Trojans" (8.429–30). Thus chance does not exist in a realm removed from divine intention.

The relationship of chance to divine action is consistent with the perceptions of the Homeric characters of a cosmos as a personal rather than impersonal one. Divine intention is seen by the characters as infused in every action and outcome. I am not speaking about that characteristic of the Homeric epic referred to as "double motivation" in which we see both divine and human intentions, often contrasted ironically, behind important actions.[45] My observation takes this one step further by suggesting that outcomes that would appear completely random to us, in which intention is irrelevant to the outcome, are seen by Homeric characters as infused with intention.[46]

The choosing of lots in the *Iliad*, for example, occurs against the backdrop of an active and personal universe. In Book 3, lots are drawn to determine whether Menelaos or Paris will cast his spear first. As the lots are being shaken in a helmet, both sides pray to Zeus that "whichever man has made what has happened happen to both sides, / grant that he be killed and go down to the house of Hades" (3.321–22). When the Achaians later draw lots to see who will fight Hektor, again the people pray that the best warriors, those most capable of defeating Hektor, will draw the lot. We might initially see these two prayers as merely self-serving expressions of hope. But in both instances, the lot is not drawn by an individual; rather, the lot "leapt" from the helmet.[47] The prayers, then, appear as more than self-serving wishes. As divine intention is seen as infused in the event, the characters tie a random occurrence (at least it seems so from our perspective) to responsibility on the one hand and capability on the other.[48] This observation is important because it points to how incomprehensible we make the Homeric universe when we attempt to explain away or diminish the importance of the gods. It also suggests the difficulty of applying a modern conception of chance, which rests upon an impersonal universe, to the Homeric world.

When we speak of chance in the Homeric universe, we must limit carefully the discussion to those events that from a human perspective are both inexplicable and unintended. I will not be referring to occasions that can be attributed to psychological phenomena, such as when Agamemnon insists that his actions toward Achilles could be attributed to "delusion" (19.88).[49] Nor am I interested in events that are the result of specific decisions by, or desires of, the individual.[50] Instead, I will look at four occurrences, ones that are inexplicable to, and unintended by, the characters. These examples have been chosen for two reasons. First, they seem to portray different responses by the characters to chance. This is important because of the frustration often expressed by Homeric scholars that gods intervene to change human fortune "by their own logic, which is inscrutable to mortals."[51] Inscrutable, perhaps, but the Homeric characters never seem to be as perplexed as we think they should be. Second, these scenes are immediately recognizable and referred to in other discussions of the role of the gods. Thus, I have sought to formulate my argument on the ground established by others. My claim is for a better interpretive scheme.

FOUR RESPONSES TO CHANCE

I return to Vernant's suggestion that since Homeric characters are tied to a divine and inscrutable order, they attribute their actions and intentions to this other realm. This leaves us with a puzzle: If Homeric characters seek to align their lives with a divine order, how do they respond to those occasions when, in the words of one character, "the divinity cuts across the plan" (*epi mêdea keirei*) of humans (15.467, trans. modified)?[52] We would expect, following Vernant's argument, that Homeric characters would seek as best they could to adjust their human aims to those of the gods. Yet, this does not happen. In each of the four examples to be discussed, the characters attribute chance to divine intention, yet the characters do not always adjust their actions accordingly. Accounting for this will be the initial task of this chapter.

Example 1: In the midst of battle, a lightning bolt (hurled by Zeus) terrifies Diomedes' horses and causes Nestor to lose hold of the reins to his chariot. Nestor, calling out to Diomedes, interprets the bolt of lightning as a sign that "the power of Zeus no longer is with you" (8.140). Nestor's advice is to steer the chariot away in flight since "no man can beat back the purpose [*noon*] of Zeus" (8.143). Diomedes hesitates, concerned that Hektor will say to the Trojans that Diomedes ran in fear, but Nestor is able to convince him of the wisdom of this plan of action. Nestor and Diomedes in this example act in accord with divine intention.

Example 2: In the middle of battle, Teukros's bow breaks just as he shoots at Hektor. This causes his arrow to be "driven crazily sidewise" (15.465). Adding to the unexpected nature of the change in fortune, Teukros even mentions that he had freshly rewound the bowstring that morning. Teukros looks to Ajax and exclaims, "See now, how hard the divinity cuts across the plan [*epi mêdea*] / in all our battle" (15.467–68, trans. modified). Ajax counsels Teukros to "let your bow and your showering arrows / lie, now that the god begrudging the Danaans wrecked them" (15.472–73). But, continues Ajax, Teukros should pick up a spear and continue to hold off the Trojans: "Let them not, though they have beaten us, easily capture / our strong-benched ships. We must remember the frenzy of fighting" (15.476–77). Ajax convinces Teukros to maintain their course of action even when it seemingly conflicts with divine purposes.

Example 3: Hektor, as he faces Achilles alone, miscasts his spear and realizes that Deïphobos, his companion, is not with him. He concludes that he has been deceived by the gods who "have summoned me deathward" (22.297). Though believing now that the gods must have always been against him, he resolves

that since his "death" (*moira*) is upon him, "Let me at least not
die without a struggle, inglorious [*akleiôs*], / but do some big
thing first, that men to come shall know of it" (22.303–305).
The desire for remembrance has been noted often; what has
received less attention is Hektor's expression that great deeds
can be crafted even as they run contrary to the perceived intentions of the gods.

Example 4: During the chariot races in the funeral games, a
succession of accidents occurs. After the chariots have made the
turn and are on the way back to the finish, Diomedes begins to
close the distance to Eumelos, who is leading the race. Apollo
causes the whip to fly from Diomedes' hand, resulting in Eumelos
pulling ahead. Athene, seeing Apollo's "foul play" (23.388),
returns the whip to Diomedes and in her anger smashes the yoke
of Eumelos's chariot. As Diomedes pulls out to a commanding
lead, he sees that Athene has given strength to his horses and "to
himself gave the glory" (23.400). Antilochos, too, in calling to the
horses to run quicker, recognizes that Athene has given spirit to
Diomedes' horses and glory to Diomedes. Antilochos does not
seek to match this speed; he wishes only to catch Menelaos so as
not to be mocked for being beaten by a mare. In anticipating the
return of the horses, Idomeneus believes that Eumelos's horses
must "have come to grief" (*eblaben*) (23.461), since Eumelos can
no longer be seen. Conjecturing about what might have happened to Eumelos, Idomeneus suggests that "it must be / that the
reins got away from the charioteer, or he could not hold them /
well in hand at the goal and failed [*ouk etuchêsen*] to double the
turn-post" (23.464–66). At the conclusion of the race Achilles
attempts to give second prize to Eumelos, who, in actuality,
finishes last. After some debate among the other contestants,
Achilles finally gives Eumelos a separate prize, but one nonetheless dear to the chariot racer. The response to these series of accidents is to neither conform nor act contrary to divine intention
but, instead, to rectify the results created by chance.

Scholarly explanations have been offered for each of these examples. But each explanation seems able to account for the reactions to one incident but leave inexplicable the responses to the other incidents. Wolfgang Kullmann, in drawing a distinction between the reaction of characters in the *Iliad* and the *Odyssey*, argues that the gods serve as "an explanation for the tragic nature of life, not as a force guaranteeing justice." Using Athene's deception of Hektor as an example, Kullmann notes Hektor's "resigned attitude" toward the will of the gods. Unlike the reflectiveness of the characters in the *Odyssey* on the actions of the gods, "In the *Iliad* the heroes accept divine action as something fateful and inescapable."[53] But such an explanation does not account fully for the reactions of the characters. Although Hektor does resign himself to his fate, he expresses an intention to continue to perform some great feat. Furthermore, we see no such fatalism in the example of Teukros, nor does Achilles seem willing to accept completely godly intentions in the chariot races.

Literary interpretations are offered for these instances, as well. Redfield, for example, understands the example of Zeus sending the thunderbolt against Diomedes as a requirement of the plot.[54] The gods, knowing how the story turns out, keep the plot on course. Treating the intervention of the gods as poetic shorthand is questionable, though, because it risks reducing the gods to literary forms devoid of substance. This is problematic for any number of reasons, not the least of which is that even plot devices and literary inventions (if we want to accept them as such) must be plausible to the audience. This means that it is not enough to categorize these godly interventions against human intention as personifications of chance or explanations of the inexplicable; we must, in addition, inquire into how chance or the inexplicable is understood.

Willcock, in his important essay on the Greek gods, goes some way toward addressing this connection between human

action and the infusion of divine intention into chance when he
suggests that although the dropping of the whip and the breaking
of the yoke are "perfectly explicable as accidents in the race,
and we may so rationalize them if we wish," the restoration of
the whip by Athene "is supernatural and not to be explained
without the physical intervention of a god." This intervention,
though, is not the cause of, as much as the explanation for,
success. "The interference of Athene, including the magical
return to Diomedes of his whip, merely achieves what would be
the proper result in any case. The natural victor wins." Moreover, argues Willcock, this alliance of the victor with the gods is
consistent with an archaic belief "that it is not for humans to
command success"; instead, "success implies the help of a god."[55]

There are two aspects of Willcock's argument that lead to an
incomplete explanation of the perceptions or reactions of the
Homeric characters. First, with whom the gods side changes in
the views of the characters, making the category of "natural
victor" something known only after the fact.[56] We can see this
ambiguity arise in the chariot races in which Diomedes is characterized by the poet at the outset of the race as "by far the best
[*aristos*] of them all" (23.357). But Achilles characterizes Eumelos
as the "best man" (*ôristos*) (23.536). This does not do irrepar-
able damage to Willcock's thesis, since it could be argued that
anyone can believe that he or she has a chance of winning.
Striving is fine, as Willcock notes. But since success is a gift of a
god, we might expect a general acceptance of the outcomes of
human competition once the "natural" or divinely sanctioned
result is clear. This is not the case, though. Achilles' statement
comes at the conclusion of the race when it is clear whom a god
has favored.

Second, Achilles' response points to a gap in Willcock's
argument: what happens in cases of bad luck? Though the contestants accept the good fortune that has come to Diomedes—
even Achilles does not tinker with that result—Achilles does not

similarly accept the misfortune that has befallen Eumelos. Even though Eumelos finishes last, he is the "best man" according to Achilles, and Achilles determines to give Eumelos second prize, "as is suitable" (*hôs epieikes*) (23.537, trans. modified).[57] One might well ask in what way second prize is "suitable" to Eumelos since he finished last. And in fact, Antilochos, who finished second, raises this very question, suggesting that Eumelos "should have prayed to the immortal / gods. That is why he came in last of all in the running" (23.546–47). Achilles neither denies that the gods were involved nor does he seek to take away the winner's prize. But Achilles does not seem completely willing to accept the outcome as "natural," either. Achilles does not quite command success, but he does attempt to give success where none was won.

THE CULTURAL CONSTRUCTION OF CHANCE

Achilles' actions are puzzling, not because he seeks to make a companion feel better by allotting a better prize, but because he premises his action on a statement that though Eumelos finished last, he should receive second prize "as is suitable." Adkins laments that this scene presents "a hopeless tangle of values."[58] The rationale for Achilles' position, a rationale that will help us begin to untangle some of these values, can be found earlier in his statement establishing that Eumelos is the "best man" (*ôristos*) (23.536). Second prize is "suited" to Eumelos not because he has done particularly well in the race, but because he is seen by Achilles as *aristos* (the superlative of *agathos*).

The problem that arises for the Homeric characters is that though the gods can bestow *aretê*, as Willcock notes, they can also strip the individual of *aretê*, making beggars and wanderers of the best of men. In fact, my contention is that accident or chance has its most profound effect on one's *aretê.* Contrary to Willcock's assertion that moments of chance serve to confirm one's allotment by allying the gods with the "natural victors,"[59] chance can also serve to disrupt this congruence. In these situations the characters respond by seeking to restore a balance between *agathos* and *aretê.*

This perspective allows us to understand better why Achilles responds as he does to the misfortune that befalls Eumelos. The accidents of the race create for Achilles an imbalance between Eumelos's status as *aristos* (the superlative of *agathos*) and the communal recognition of his excellences. To add to this imbalance, Eumelos is portrayed not simply as losing the race but as arriving at the finish line with the skin from his elbows torn and his mouth, nose, and forehead lacerated. Eumelos's youthful countenance is despoiled, his "springing [*thalerê*] voice ... held fast within him" (23.397). As Vernant has argued in another context, the desire to defile the body of the enemy is born of a desire to strip the enemy of his outward signs of *aretê.* One's *aretê* is closely tied to what Vernant calls "the beautiful death" in which the heroic body is remembered for the beauty and splendor of its youth.[60] In acting out these rituals of war in the funeral games, Eumelos returns despoiled. Achilles' act, then, appears as one of restoration of Eumelos's *aretê,* since he provides to Eumelos the public recognition of his excellence. Read from this perspective, Achilles is not saying that Eumelos really deserved to take second in the race; rather, giving a better prize would be suitable or in proportion to Eumelos's status. In this way, the community (with Achilles as distributor of the prizes) restores an equilibrium of status and recognition of one's excellences that is momentarily disturbed by the intervention of chance.

We can understand the responses of the characters in the other three examples as a similar attempt to maintain a balance between status and the community's recognition of one's excellence. So, from Hektor's perspective, the bad luck he has encountered, including the vain casting of the spear and his mistaken belief that his companion was with him, does not change his destiny (*moira*) as much as bring it to fulfillment. This much is always accepted by the warriors and, it would seem, is what Kullmann refers to as the tragic notion of life portrayed in the *Iliad*. But Hektor is unwilling to accept that the change of fortune will result in a permanent loss of *aretê*, a loss that will cause him to die in disgrace. Hektor, thus, does not act to change his *moira* but to correct the imbalance between his status as a warrior and his *aretê*. Hektor determines to perform some last great deed, not to win, but to be remembered by his community. Hektor, like Achilles when he intervenes on behalf of Eumelos, looks to the community, rather than the gods, to restore the balance between his status and excellence.

When Teukros's bow breaks, Ajax urges him to keep fighting. The appeal appears driven, at least initially, by the necessity of survival. And, in fact, there is some suggestion of that when Ajax exclaims to the Argives that "here is the time of decision, whether / we die, or live on still and beat back ruin from our vessels" (15.502–503). But the reason Ajax gives for continuing to fight, even if the Achaians cannot win, is that it is "Better to take in a single time our chances of dying / or living" than to run from "men worse than we are" (*kheiroteroisin*) (15.511–13). To flee without a fight from one who is inferior is disgraceful, undermining one's *aretê*. One must fight despite the change in luck, not to alter one's portion or *moira*, but to retain one's excellence and honor.

The final example, in which Nestor advises Diomedes that they align themselves with the intentions of Zeus and flee, differs dramatically from Hektor's decision to keep fighting. But the difference actually provides confirmation of our thesis. When Nestor suggests that they turn back, Diomedes protests, concerned that Hektor will boast to the other Trojans that Diomedes ran in fear. In this we see the counterpart to Hektor's desire to perform one last deed: namely, Diomedes' fear that if his last deed is that of running, he will be remembered as lacking courage. To get Diomedes to follow his advice, Nestor must convince the young warrior that no one will ever believe Hektor if he "calls you a coward and a man of no strength" (*kakon kai analkida phêsei*) because of all the Trojans Diomedes has already "hurled in the dust in the pride of their manhood" (8.153, 156). The exchange again suggests the role chance plays in creating an imbalance between status and reputation. Only in this case, the response to bad luck is to accept it for now, but only because the loss of *aretê* is not sufficient to require rectification.

Relating these examples back to our earlier discussion of how the perception of and response to chance are conditioned by cultural values and social interactions, we can see how the Homeric notion of chance appears to reflect a cultural concern with the destabilization of hierarchical gradations of rank. Though chance can give one *aretê*, more critically it can undermine *aretê*, creating an imbalance between one's rank and recognized excellences. This poses a particular problem for a hierarchical society because the lack of *aretê* threatens the class privileges and status claims of the warriors. Neither the individual nor the community simply accepts the results of chance but seeks, instead, to manage chance by restoring *aretê* to accord with one's status. The response to chance, thus, serves as a reaffirmation of the status ranking of Achaian and Trojan society.

If notions of chance are culturally constituted, as we have suggested, it seems appropriate to contrast how chance is constituted in another kind of culture, one characterized, in Douglas's and Wildavsky's terms, by competitive individualism, or liberal individualism.[61] Liberal individualism is characterized by a belief in individual economic and political liberty. In the case of liberal individualism, chance threatens to undermine the notion of individual equality upon which individualist economic and political structures, such as competitive markets or equal protection under the law, are premised. This understanding of chance enters into the argument of John Rawls in his influential theoretical work on the foundation of social justice. Rawls posits at the start a hypothetical original position in which no person knows "his fortune in the distribution of natural assets and abilities." Essential for Rawls's argument is that principles of justice be formulated upon a foundation of equality to ensure "that no one is advantaged or disadvantaged in the choice of principles by the outcome of natural chance or the contingency of social circumstance."[62] Whereas chance in a hierarchical culture is viewed as disruptive of natural differences or inequalities, it is seen in liberalism as creating undeserved inequities. Chance violates the prescriptive rules of status differentials in hierarchy; it infringes on the procedural rules of equal opportunities in a liberal society.[63]

Such a Rawlsean original position, though, cannot be maintained: chance happens. Some individuals are advantaged, others disadvantaged, by the operation of chance. We would expect, then, that liberalism would provide a cultural response to chance that confirms its individualistic, competitive social and economic structures. Indeed, since chance is seen as random and impersonal, bad luck is understood more as a temporary phenomenon that may become good luck with continued effort. In a culture of entrepreneurial individualism, we see certain stories downplayed, such as those in which misfortune eventually drives a person to destitution. On the other hand, we see the validation of rags-to-riches tales in which the individual invariably meets at some point with bad luck. With the continued taking of risks, though, hard work eventually pays off and one reaps the rewards of effort.[64] The struggle for riches takes place in a competitive, individualist culture against the backdrop of a benign universe, one that does not actively frustrate human intention and effort. As portrayed in the *Iliad*, however, chance never works in such a way that one who is not *agathos* suddenly gains *aretê*. Individuals may fall, but upward mobility, even by chance, is not presented as possible.

CHANCE AND HUMAN AGENCY

The notion of Homeric characters managing chance, or at least the consequences of chance, should strike us as interesting for a number of reasons, not the least of which is Snell's claim that Homeric individuals lack a consciousness of themselves as being able to struggle against necessity.[65] That is, one aspect of agency is an ability to recognize when one's actions are circumscribed by events that are out of one's control. Such necessity, though, does not in turn constrain human intention. As Vernant writes, "In action the agent is recognized as preeminent; the human subject is assumed to be the origin and efficient cause of all the actions that stem from him." Furthermore, "In his relations with others and with nature, the agent apprehends himself as a kind of center of decision, holding a power that springs neither from the emotions nor from pure intelligence" but from the "indivisible power" of the will "to say yes or no, to acquiesce or refuse."[66]

And in fact, in large part because of this metaphysical tradition we ask, "Are the Homeric characters free?" The answer to the question is invariably filled with qualifiers as we recognize that such notions as free will and determinism are later categories that fit only partly into the Homeric world. The problem is that in framing the question this way we import a notion of the relationship between human agency and what might be called contingency that requires that we either diminish the role of the gods, treating them as less than serious actors in the world, or restrict the possibility of action as an expression of the human will. I have sought to confront this dilemma by highlighting incidents of chance that are seen by many as the clearest examples of utterly capricious gods imposing their intentions on the human world. Yet, I want to advance the somewhat ironic claim that it is in these moments of chance that we can see created a "space of action,"[67] a space that is itself culturally constituted. By returning to each of the four examples we can begin to reconceptualize the meaning of Homeric agency, one in which the beliefs of the agent are grounded in this Homeric space rather than a Western metaphysical tradition. This will help us understand not only the nature of human agency in the *Iliad* but how the agent's quest for glory is tied to and supportive of the hierarchical needs of Homeric society.

In rejecting Bruno Snell's argument that Homeric characters lack "innerness," Bernard Williams suggests that "there is surely enough of the basic conceptions of action for human life: the capacities to deliberate, to conclude, to act, to exert oneself, to make oneself do things, to endure."[68] And a look at the four examples in this chapter provides strong support for this contention. In the scene in which Nestor suggests to Diomedes that they retreat since Zeus now appears to be against them, both accept Nestor's formulation of Zeus's purpose, yet they still engage in a debate about which course of action, retreating or fighting, would be better. Furthermore, the debate moves from an exchange between two characters to a debate within one character, Diomedes.[69] When Nestor more adamantly insists upon retreating, Diomedes "pondered between two ways" (*diandicha mermêrixen*) (8.167, trans. modified)[70] and "three times in his heart and spirit he pondered turning" (*tris men mermêrixe kata phrena kai kata thumon*) (8.169). This sort of conscious deliberation, born purely of neither the emotion nor the intellect but of the heart and spirit, is, even by Vernant's standards, characteristic of human agency.

So in the example in which Teukros's bow unexpectedly breaks, Ajax tells Teukros to lay down the bow "now that the god begrudging the Danaans wrecked them" (15.473). Recognizing this, though, does not seem to inhibit action. Ajax, instead, tells Teukros to fight with a spear to protect the ships and ends his statement with "We must remember [*mnêsômetha*] the frenzy of fighting [*charmês*]" (15.477). It seems difficult to understand Ajax's injunction without a notion of agency, for though Ajax enjoins Teukros to fight, it is an injunction that appeals to the internal quality of an agent, the memory of battle.

The scene continues with Ajax speaking to the other Achaians, providing his assessment of the increasingly bleak situation. The choice facing the Argives, according to Ajax, is "whether / we die, or live on still and beat back ruin from our vessels" (15.502–503). Ajax then calls upon his companions to think about the consequences of failing to fight: "Do you expect [*elpesthe*], if our ships fall to helm-shining Hektor, / you will walk each of you back dryshod to the land of your fathers?" (15.504–505). Ajax suggests, instead, that they continue fighting in close combat, claiming that "there can be no design [*noos*], no plan [*mêtis*], better than this one" (15.509, trans. modified). Even in the chaos of war, Ajax provides a view of agents as the center of decision, their deliberation counting in matters of life and death.

Intimations of this notion of action appear in the other two examples, as well. We see in Hektor's last moments a determination to undertake one last struggle even though he knows he is doomed. This incident serves as an important counterexample to Adkins's claim that in Homeric society "intentions are almost irrelevant."[71] We cannot make sense of Hektor's actions if outcome is all that matters, for Hektor ties the hope of remembrance to his struggle, not his success. His last deed is to try and for that he is remembered.[72]

We can gain perhaps the best visual image of the space of action as Achilles attempts to find a just distribution of prizes after the chariot races, an effort made necessary by the intervention of the gods. It is a space that does not stand opposed to the gods but one that is conditioned by a particular cultural understanding of and response to the gods. We do not have free-floating human agents seeking to assert their "freedom" in the world; instead, action, as it is constituted by Homeric culture, occurs within the realm of one's allotment.[73] But it is a realm in which the characters nevertheless, as in the chariot races, argue (23.542), judge (23.574), appease and are appeased (23.606).

We can see easily how other examples of divine action provide a context in which Homeric characters debate, decide, and act. Athene appeals to Achilles not to stab Agamemnon, asking "but will you obey me?" (*ai ke pithêai*) (1.207). Agamemnon responds to a deceptive dream planted by Zeus by unwisely revising the dream as he tells it to his men (2.5–141). Athene is portrayed as persuading, rather than commanding, Pandaros's foolish heart to break an oath and shoot at Menelaos (4.85–126). Athene steers the arrow away from killing Menelaos, but it nonetheless hits him, at which point Agamemnon has Machaon summoned to heal his brother (4.189–219). On a number of occasions, warriors fight even when they sense that the gods have turned against them (11.317–19, 16.101–29, 17.421–22). When Idomeneus suggests that "no man is responsible [*aitios*] for this," Poseidon (in the likeness of Thoas) responds, "may that man who this day wilfully hangs back / from the fighting never win home again out of Troy land, / but stay here and be made dogs' delight for their feasting" (13.222, 232–34). And even when Apollo stuns Patroklos by hitting him in the back, Euphorbos and then Hektor must decide to strike Patroklos for him to die (16.784–850).

Two examples suggest how the gods, themselves, limit their interventions to preserve a realm in which mortals can act. When Ares engages physically in killing mortals, he is characterized by Hera as fighting "out of due order" (*ou kata kosmon*) (5.759). The concern is that such direct carnage by the gods would soon doom the mortal world. For this reason, Athene intervenes (by

way of Diomedes, and with the approval of both Hera and Zeus)
to prevent Ares from further killing. In the second example,
Zeus encounters the opposite situation. He must decide whether
to restore his son, Sarpedon, to life. Hera speaks successfully
against this action, suggesting that if Zeus were to bring
Sarpedon back to life, then the other gods might well do the
same (16.440–49). Where Ares threatens the space of human
action by dooming those who should live, Zeus threatens this
space by restoring those who should die. In the first case, human
action is futile since earth becomes the realm of the dead; in the
second case, as Sarpedon himself notes, human action becomes
unnecessary when all are made immortal (12.322–25).

Part of the reason Snell and others have rejected a notion of
agency in Homeric society derives from an assumption that the
will is an ethical will in which action is guided by the moral
determinations of an autonomous self. Williams agrees with this
moral assessment, to an extent, suggesting that Homeric notions
of action "did *not* revolve round a distinction between moral
and nonmoral motivations."[74] Homeric characters are praised,
for example, for their endurance or resourcefulness even if
these actions are guided by circumstances and not by a sense
of an absolute duty to a higher law. But, as Williams notes,
through this attention to circumstance we can begin to understand how Homeric decisions are guided by ethical determinations. This is not an apology for a Homeric ethical conception but an assertion of a notion of ethics that takes account of
psychological motivations within the context of community
roles and practices. As I will argue more fully in the final chapter,
the ethical self emerges as a participant in society—conscious
of roles and expectations, possessing a memory of past actions
of society, and able to reason about potential responses to
situations.

In developing this notion of action, we are not left, as is Adkins,
with explaining how the "competitive values" he associates with

areté do not pull the community apart. Adkins gives us every reason to believe that such a competitive scheme will exert an extraordinary strain on the community, not only because the claims of an *agathos* can ultimately override all other claims of the community, but because Homeric society lacks any organization to mediate conflicting claims of an *agathos*.[75]

We can now see how Homeric society constructs the notion of action in such a way that the excellences to which Adkins points are tied to an issue of community maintenance. Homeric society is not kept together by well-developed political institutions that serve to mediate a competitive ethos.[76] Rather, what underlies Homeric society is how this ethos is, itself, defined within the context of a hierarchical society. This is no small issue, for it tells us that although excellence appears to create a competitive individualism, it is an excellence carefully tied to the internal gradations of status and obligation within the community. In this context we can better appreciate A. A. Long's critique of Adkins that "the language used to decry an ἀγαθός [*agathos*] for some deficiency is often used to condemn him for some excess."[77] Such cultural constraints work because they become internalized as part of Homeric intentional action. When chance results in the loss of *areté*, the restoration of the warrior's reputation becomes both a product of individual intention and community interest, whether we are speaking about how deeds will be remembered, as is Hektor's concern, or of the active recognition on the part of Achilles on behalf of the community for the excellence of Eumelos. We must posit a notion of agency that is itself tied to the cultural context of Homeric society, a society in which one's allotment serves not to oppose but to define the realm of action. To do otherwise, to demand a notion of metaphysical freedom, requires us to entangle the Homeric characters in a language they do not understand.

Power, Force, and Authority

πῶς τίς τοι πρόφρων ἔπεσιν πείθηται Ἀχαιῶν

how shall any one of the Achaians readily obey you

1.150

Authority in the *Iliad* has been understood frequently by placing its expression in the context of an already
formed system of relationships. From this perspective, authority
in the *Iliad* does not appear political since there are not yet any
formalized polis institutions. Authority, instead, is viewed as
prepolitical, since it derives, according to Finley, from the
institution of the household. In his influential discussion of
Homeric social structures, Finley argues that authority appears
as "might," a household form of "power" that "depended on
wealth, personal prowess, connexions by marriage and alliance,
and retainers."[1] Loyalty is more "concentrated in a narrow
sphere of kin and followers" than in the larger community, justice is a "purely private matter," and political institutions, such
as the assembly, point "less to the reasons than to the decision
itself, and hence to the power of authority."[2] As Edmunds
argues, in this same vein, the conflict in the *Iliad* is a "personal

matter, not a political one" because Achilles' loyalty to Agamemnon and to others "is based on the principles of φιλία
[*philia*], a kind of friendship." Stated slightly differently, the
nature of the conflict is personal, for Edmunds, because it is
located in an established system of personal relationships. Even
about the scene in which Achilles throws his scepter to the
ground, a scepter that in Achilles' own words is used by the
"dispensers of justice" (*dikaspoloi*) who "administer the justice
of Zeus" (1.238–39), Edmunds remarks that this use of the
scepter demonstrates the nonpolitical nature of the conflict.
The conflict is nonpolitical, in his view, because it is about "the
division of spoils amongst warriors," which is "not an institution of the polis."[3] In short, the nature of the conflict derives
from its location in a system—in this case, a system of personal
rather than institutional relationships.

There have been, to be sure, attempts to locate this conflict
within a political framework. Luce cites the term *dikaspoloi* as
evidence of "familiarity with formalised legal procedures."[4] But
he does not attempt to show how the issues raised by the words
and action of the scene, themselves, might be political. We can
make this linkage comprehensible by viewing politics as dynamic,
in which a field is constituted by, and does not determine, the
nature of the political activity. I will suggest that the conflict
between Agamemnon and Achilles is at first a public discussion
of how the community should respond to Apollo's plague, a
discussion that itself constitutes a political field. Within the
context of this public discussion, the conflict between Agamemnon and Achilles appears as a social drama. The conflict
begins as a breach of norms when Agamemnon decides to take
back the war prize that had been given to Achilles. But the conflict quickly escalates from a specific breach to a broader crisis
of authority that threatens the stability (and even the survival)
of the community.

VIOLENCE AND THE FRAGMENTATION OF THE POLITICAL FIELD

The political aspects of the conflict between Agamemnon and Achilles are immediate. The dispute takes place in a public arena: among the people (*laos*) called to assembly (*agorê*) by Achilles (see 1.54). Though the initial issue is divisive enough—whether Agamemnon should ransom back Chryseis—this conflict escalates quickly when Agamemnon suggests, and then declares, that he will seek compensation by taking Briseis, Achilles' war-prize. Achilles' response is one of anger, but he quickly structures the conflict as raising a broader, and overtly political, question about the nature of Agamemnon's authority.[5]

Achilles inquires of Agamemnon, "with your mind forever on profit, / how shall any one of the Achaians readily [*prophrôn*] obey [*peithêtai*] you" (1.149–50)? Achilles concedes that Agamemnon has what Finley would describe as "might." But leadership requires more than might. Leadership requires authority, or a willingness of others to obey. In Homeric society, such authority rests both on ascribed characteristics, such as one's birth into a noble family, and achieved characteristics, such as one's prowess in battle. For Agamemnon to maintain authority, particularly over other powerful leaders assembled for war, he must not only possess these ascribed and achieved characteristics, but be able to use them to get others to support him.[6] Achilles warns that if Agamemnon continues with his practice of sending his warriors into battle and taking the best of the war spoils for himself, Agamemnon will not be able to engender active support for his leadership. Thus, Achilles adds the modifier *prophrôn*, broadening the issue from obedience to the demeanor of those asked to obey. This is significant, for not only is the question of leadership extended beyond the household, but Agamemnon's understanding of the "power of authority," to use a phrase from Finley, is directly challenged.[7] For

Agamemnon, the power of authority is demonstrated by his ability to compel obedience, by force if need be. For Achilles, though, the leader's power depends on the readiness of others to "go on a journey or to fight men strongly in battle" (1.151).

From the opening of the *Iliad*, Agamemnon's association of the power of authority with the ability to compel obedience through force is made clear. When Chryses, a priest of Apollo, attempts to ransom back his daughter from Agamemnon, the Achaian people cry out in favor of the proposal. But Agamemnon, displeased by the supplication, drove away the priest harshly, (*kakôs*), warning him that harm would come to him if he ever returned to the Achaian camp (1.25–32). The priest, in terror (*eddeisen*), obeyed (*epeitheto*) Agamemnon's command. That Agamemnon strikes terror in an enemy, even a priest of Apollo, should not necessarily alarm us, except that Agamemnon then turns this terror on his own people. When Achilles summons Kalchas, a seer, to explain the plague, Kalchas, at first, expresses his reluctance to speak truthfully about the cause of the plague because he fears he will "make a man angry who holds great kingship / over the men of Argos, and all the Achaians obey [*peithontai*] him" (1.78–79). Even though Kalchas does not explain why the Achaians obey Agamemnon, what is clear is that, at least for Kalchas, Agamemnon's ability to command obedience rests on a fear of retribution.[8] As Kalchas continues, "For a king when he is angry with a man beneath him is too strong" (*kreissôn*), and even if he swallows his wrath (*cholon*) for one day, he will keep his bitterness (*koton*) until he can pay back the slight" (1.80–83).

Although fear can create compliance, even for a fairly long time (as the experience of the former Soviet bloc suggests), it does not lead to a corresponding readiness to comply once that fear is removed. Obedience, in the case of Kalchas, becomes a question of silence, of not speaking against the king.[9] Fear is not an adequate substitute for authority. The reason is that the readiness to obey vanishes once the fear is neutralized, which is what Achilles does when he guarantees protection from anyone who would seek to injure Kalchas, even Agamemnon. For those, like Achilles, who do not fear Agamemnon, his authority is not the object of awe. Thus, Achilles, in agreeing to protect Kalchas, refers to Agamemnon as one who "claims [*euchetai*] to be far the greatest of all the Achaians" (1.91), suggesting in this context a boast that lacks substance.[10]

Having shown the limits of fear as a basis for authority, Achilles sets his sights on a much more formidable target: Agamemnon's inheritance of wealth and the scepter as a basis of his kingship. On numerous occasions this inheritance is claimed, both by Agamemnon and by Nestor, as suitable in itself for the title of "kingliest." Nestor, for example, early on chastises Achilles for attempting to match his strength with the king since he is "greater who is lord over more than you rule" (1.281). For Achilles, though, this inheritance creates only an illusion of kingship, not a sufficient reason to listen to or obey Agamemnon. Achilles, instead, derides Agamemnon for never having earned his authority through acts of courage. "Never / once have you taken courage in your heart to arm with your people / for battle, or go into ambuscade with the best of the Achaians" (1.225–27). Agamemnon, according to Achilles, hides behind his might, using it not to help his people but to devour them through his greediness (1.231).

Agamemnon recognizes that Achilles' statements go far beyond a particular grievance or breach of custom to a more fundamental question of who shall govern. At this point Nestor, the elder, seeks to temper the anger of the disputants by drawing upon a more conventional understanding of political relationships, pointing to Achilles' importance on the battlefield and Agamemnon's might, as "the "sceptred king" and "lord over more than you rule" (1.279, 281). Although Nestor on other occasions is able to get his way by judiciously deflecting the issue, in this case Agamemnon sees clearly the implications of Achilles' argument. "Yes, old sir, all this you have said is fair and orderly. / Yet here is a man who wishes to be above all others, / who wishes to hold power [*krateein*] over all, and to be lord [*anassein*] of / all, and give them their orders, yet I think one will not obey [*peisesthai*] him" (1.286–89).

Agamemnon, thus, seeks to demonstrate the power of his authority by showing Achilles his might. By taking Briseis, he attempts to make clear "that you may learn [*eidêis*] well / how much greater I am than you, and another man may shrink back / from likening himself to me and contending against me" (1.185–87). In commenting on this passage, Pucci suggests that "Agamemnon does not deny Achilles the right to speak; he denies him the same weight, the same commanding power, the same authority of speech that he enjoys." As the word *eidêis* suggests, by seeing the might that Agamemnon can wield, Achilles is to learn to show him honor, to recognize the proper order. And indeed, according to Pucci, Agamemnon's ability to compel obedience is never contested. As Pucci argues, "It is sufficient for Agamemnon to say, 'I am the stronger,' and it is so, because this command word both embodies and gathers the deference and the acquiescence of the others. Being and word coalesce, and the identity between the authority of the king and that of the community is guaranteed. That is why he is *anax andrôn*."[11] To punctuate the force of his command, Agamemnon tells his guards: "Go now / to the shelter of Peleus' son Achilleus, to bring back / Briseis of the fair cheeks leading her by the hand. And if he / will not give her, I must come in person to take her / with many men behind me, and it will be the worse for him" (1.321–25). For Pucci, as for Finley, power, authority, and force coincide in the person of Agamemnon, and that coincidence is never contradicted.

But does Agamemnon's display of strength demonstrate his power and successfully turn back Achilles' challenge? Though

Agamemnon is able to claim Briseis as his own, in the ensuing books of the *Iliad* the "neat equation between word and power," as Pucci maintains, is dramatically undermined.[12] Through the first nine books, the *Iliad* traces the consequences of Agamemnon's leadership, revealing a seemingly paradoxical situation in which Agamemnon's exercise of authority leaves him without power.

The first suggestion that word and power do not coincide is made by Achilles, who describes the actions of a "cruel king" (*basilêos apêneos*) (1.340) who "uttered his threat [*êpeilêsen*] against me" (1.388). Agamemnon's actions are not only violent but deceptive, as Achilles claims that Agamemnon, and the community, have taken back what they have promised (1.126). It is in this vein that Achilles later speaks to Odysseus: "I detest that man, who / hides one thing in the depths of his heart, and speaks forth another" (9.312–13). The sense of being "cheated" (*êleten*) (9.375), as Achilles describes the feeling later, precipitates initially a violent reaction by Achilles as he reaches for his sword (1.194). Ultimately, Achilles withdraws from the public space, proclaiming his refusal to become one of Agamemnon's nonentities: "So must I be called of no account [*outidanos*] and a coward / if I must carry out every order you may happen to give me. / Tell other men to do these things, but give me no more / commands, since I for my part have no intention to obey [*peisesthai*] you" (1.293–96). Achilles' withdrawal is expressed symbolically by his throwing to the ground the scepter used in the administration of justice (1.245, 238). But his withdrawal points to more than the discontent of one warrior; it suggests the limits of force. Agamemnon can intimidate Chryses and Kalchas, and can take back Briseis, but he cannot make Achilles fight. In fact, as Achilles suggests, the resort to force will slowly deplete Agamemnon's ranks since the only people who remain, who will submit to Agamemnon's leadership, are "nonentities" (*outidanoisin*), those who no longer speak or act (1.231).

With Achilles out of the way, Agamemnon calls an assembly to test precisely what Achilles claimed was lacking: the ready obedience of the Achaian troops. In developing this scene, Homer carefully sets out the basis of Agamemnon's authority, namely his inheritance of Zeus's scepter from his father:

> Wide-ruling Agamemnon
> stood up holding the sceptre Hephaistos had wrought
>   him carefully.
> Hephaistos gave it to Zeus the king, the son of Kronos,
> and Zeus in turn gave it to the courier Argeïphontes,
> and lord Hermes gave it to Pelops, driver of horses,
> and Pelops again gave it to Atreus, the shepherd of the
>   people.
> Atreus dying left it to Thyestes of the rich flocks,
> and Thyestes left it in turn to Agamemnon to carry
> and to be lord of many islands and over all Argos.
>   (2.100–108, trans. modified)

The recounting of a divine genealogy to rule is particularly salient since Zeus has just sent a false dream to Agamemnon (that he will soon defeat Troy), a dream that Agamemnon further falsifies by telling the assembly of warriors that Zeus has said they will not win the war. Leaning upon his scepter, the emblem of his inherited authority, Agamemnon recounts the difficulties that have been faced in nine years of battle and concludes: "Come then, do as I say, let us all be persuaded [*peithômetha*]; let us / run away with our ships to the beloved land of our fathers / since no longer now shall we capture Troy of the wide ways" (2.139–41, trans. modified). There is a cruel irony in Agamemnon's first assertion of his leadership after Achilles' challenge, for his advice is enthusiastically embraced by the people. But his power is almost dissolved as the order of the assembled Achaians gives way to "tumult": men flee the assembly, shouting to one another to drag the ships down to sea (2.149–54). The public field fragments since there is neither the will nor the desire to act together in war.

The fractured field is reconstituted by Odysseus, not by the willing compliance that Achilles mentions, but by force. Odysseus threatens the other leaders with the anger of Agamemnon, who might do "some harm to the sons of the Achaians" (2.195). And he physically strikes others (2.199). Odysseus, too, speaks on behalf of an inherited tradition of kingship, proclaiming to the warriors, "Surely not all of us Achaians can be as kings here. / Lordship for many is no good thing. Let there be one ruler, / one king, to whom the son of devious-devising Kronos / gives the sceptre and right of judgment, to watch over his people" (2.203–206). The irony of Odysseus's statement is immediate: although speaking ostensibly on behalf of Agamemnon, Odysseus is the one in possession of the scepter, having taken it from Agamemnon. In upholding Agamemnon's authority as the one king, Odysseus is actually the only one at this point acting as a king. Agamemnon's powerlessness is evident as he stands by helplessly while his scepter is used to violently reassert his authority.[13]

This is where I think scholars are incorrect in suggesting that Odysseus successfully restores Agamemnon's power.[14] Easterling, for example, argues that by reading "the way the narrative develops," we can see that Odysseus's emphasis on Agamemnon's power culminates in the king's "rousing speech" and approval by the other leaders.[15] And Russo suggests that we see in the narrative design of the epic the "triumph of the normative over the deviant."[16] From the perspective offered here, Odysseus can restore order, stopping the people from fleeing. But in restoring order, Odysseus does not necessarily restore Agamemnon's power. For what holds the political field together now is not people acting together, but force.

By the ninth book, the implications of Agamemnon's acts of force and deception toward Achilles have now become clear. Although Agamemnon maintains his authority as leader of the Achaians, his power is now imperiled: the Achaian community faces imminent destruction. Agamemnon, himself, seems to recognize how inextricably his power is tied to the maintenance of his own people.[17] He laments that now Zeus "bids me go back / to Argos in dishonour having lost many of my people" (9.21–22). Having realized he has been deceived by Zeus (the source of his scepter), Agamemnon calls the dispirited troops into assembly and reveals to them that it is Zeus's desire that they return without honor. Agamemnon then repeats a phrase whose formula we saw in Book 2: "Come then, do as I say, let us all be won over" (9.26). As in Book 2, Agamemnon then states, "let us / run away with our ships to the beloved land of our fathers / since no longer now shall we capture Troy of the wide ways" (9.26–28).

Interpreting Agamemnon's actions charitably, one could argue that he senses that the gods have turned against the Achaians and that he seeks only to release the warriors from any further obligation to fight against these increasingly insurmountable odds. Certainly, by the tenth year the original purpose of war has become considerably less pronounced in the minds of the warriors and other issues of individual pride and glory have become more prominent. Yet, even at this potentially generous moment, the assembly does not rise up in eagerness to flee (perhaps remembering Odysseus's intervention in Book 2), nor does it otherwise affirm Agamemnon's gesture, but stays "stricken to silence" (9.29).

Diomedes finally breaks the silence, exclaiming that he will not listen to Agamemnon's "folly" (9.32). Diomedes, no longer silently in awe of Agamemnon (4.401), inserts himself into the political field by pointing out that it is his "right" in the assembly to speak out against the king. Whether or not Diomedes is pointing to a more formalized right to speak in the assembly or merely pointing to what is customary is difficult to determine (and will be explored in chapter 5). But what is clear is that Diomedes, once having established this right, launches into a critique, interestingly enough, of Agamemnon's power and a defense of his own courage, reminiscent of (and perhaps emboldened by) Achilles' argument in Book 1. The young warrior points out that he has been a victim of Agamemnon's unwarranted recriminations, and notes that although Zeus gave to Agamemnon the scepter that gave him "honour beyond all," Zeus "did not give you a heart, and of all power [*kratos*] this is the greatest" (9.38–39). Agamemnon's vestige of authority— the scepter—remains, but the ability to use that authority to engender power is sadly lacking. The incompleteness of Agamemnon's power is evidenced in the reactions of others. Unlike Achilles who refuses to obey Agamemnon by removing himself from battle, in this case Diomedes indicates his refusal to obey by stating that he will remain to fight even if Agamemnon goes home.

We can, perhaps, dismiss Agamemnon as a crude stereotype of bad (or irrelevant) leadership, as many scholars have done.[18] Focusing less on the character of Agamemnon and more on the implications Homer seems to draw from Agamemnon's actions, though, we have begun to identify a larger question of the nature of political power. For Agamemnon, power appears as a possession, like strength or might, that he can use to compel others to obey. But his use of force seems only to weaken his power, since he must admit, at the point at which the community is imperiled, that he is unable to do anything to help them. Agamemnon is powerless because power is located not in a person but in the political field. Power originates when people speak and act with each other and enables groups to act together to pursue particular goals. The power of a leader, as

Hannah Arendt suggests, is an empowering by "a certain number of people" within this field "to act in their name."[19] The mechanisms of empowerment, in general, are complex, ranging from election to inheritance, from formal law to unwritten tradition. What is important is that power rests on recognition by the group to act on its behalf. So Agamemnon's power to lead the confederation of Achaians depends, as Achilles notes, on the willingness of others to go along with him to win back both his and Menelaos's honor (1.158–60). And Agamemnon's power to distribute war prizes is seen as a power that is carried out on behalf of the people. However great may be his resources of land and wealth, Agamemnon's power exists only as the Achaians constitute themselves together. And his power will dissolve the moment it is not actualized by people appearing together.

The greatest threat to power, then, is a breakdown in the public relationships between people. "Power is actualized," writes Arendt, "only where word and deed have not parted company, where words are not empty and deeds not brutal, where words are not used to veil intentions but to disclose realities, and deeds are not used to violate and destroy but to establish relations and create new realities." Deception and violence prevent the development of power by denying the condition of power: namely, people acting and speaking together. Fraud and violence, on the contrary, foster the conditions for isolation, rendering in people either a weakness and passivity or a "self-sufficiency and withdrawal from the world."[20] In Kalchas we find the former; in Achilles the latter.

The opening of Book 9 appears as an attempt by the Achaians, however desperate, to explore how power can be restored, even if authority was never in question. Diomedes' distinction between Agamemnon's authority and power is telling, as is Nestor's attempt to explain how the maintenance of a strong following requires that the leader elicit counsel. As Nestor states, "It is yours therefore to speak a word, yours also to listen, / and grant the right to another also, when his spirit stirs him / to speak for our good" (*agathon*) (9.100–102). Nestor seeks deftly to balance Agamemnon's claim to be greater than (*pherteros*) Achilles, a claim of excellence that carries considerable weight in Greek society, with the good (*agathon*) of the community. But beneath this balancing act is a substantial challenge to Agamemnon's understanding of his authority. Nestor suggests that as a king Agamemnon should not only listen to others but facilitate (*krêênai*) these expressions of different views (1.100–101). Nestor in an important sense picks up on Achilles' argument by suggesting that the criterion for effective leadership is not the silence of nonentities but the ability actively to engage different, even opposing, views. By doing this, Nestor tells Agamemnon, "all shall be yours" (9.102). What emerges is a view of authority that rests, as scholars have suggested, on power. But it is a notion of power that arises from the constituting of a political space through the engagement of others. The intrusion of violence or deceit threatens this public space since it provokes either a reaction of violence or a retreat into silence. It is the nature of this retreat, as exemplified in the reaction of Achilles, to which I now turn.

Self-Sufficiency

Φοῖνιξ, ἄττα γεραιέ, διοτρεφές, οὔ τί με ταύτης
χρεὼ τιμῆς

Phoinix, my father, aged, illustrious, such honor is a thing
I need not.

9.607–608

In the previous chapter, we saw how Agamemnon's substitution of force for power precipitates a more general crisis that threatens to fragment the political field. Achilles' reaction is not simply one of anger toward Agamemnon, but of a more general disillusionment with the Achaians who remain silent as Agamemnon takes Achilles' prize. In this chapter, I examine Achilles' relationship to Achaian society when he withdraws from battle. In explaining this relationship, scholars have often suggested that Achilles either enters some extra-cultural, semidivine world,[1] or never really leaves and continues to uphold fundamental Achaian values.[2] The problem with these choices is that Achilles is seen either as remaining a part of the Achaian warrior culture, even as he refuses to participate in it, or as rejecting Achaian culture and entering some noncultural, unearthly realm, even as he continues to occupy earthly space and interact with others.

One can identify in Achilles' words, though, a more ambiguous relationship with the Achaians, one that requires that he neither enter the realm of the gods nor comply with warrior practices. Some of this ambiguity is conveyed when Achilles exclaims that Agamemnon brought disgrace (*asuphêlon*) on him by treating him as if he were "some dishonoured *metanastên*" (9.648, also 16.59). *Metanastês* is a difficult word to translate. It derives from *naiô*, which is the verb "dwell" or "inhabit," and *meta*, which in this case means "among."[3] The word conveys both a transitional quality, as someone who has changed his or her home, and a more stable quality, as someone who (having changed homes) now lives among others.[4] Arieti translates the term as "alien," but then suggests that the land that Achilles "comes from is the country of the gods; he is an alien in the world of man."[5] Through this interpretation, though, we lose track of the social and political context of the word, a meaning that is quite consistent with Achilles' invocation. Lattimore translates the term as "vagabond," though that language has some contemporary connotations of impoverishment that may not fit Achilles' circumstance. Hainsworth sees Achilles as referring to himself as a "'refugee,' obliged to beg for his bread and abused by the more fortunate."[6] And Gschnitzer reveals some of the difficulty of translation when he creates a word, "*Mitwohner*," to capture the sense of a person who lives with, but is not completely a part of, the community.[7]

I follow Gschnitzer in translating *metanastês* as something like "migrant" or "outsider," to connote a foreigner who lives among others but does not receive the protections of that community. In citing this passage, Aristotle notes that a *metanastês* was excluded from the civil privileges of the polis.[8] And the word is related etymologically to a later word, *metoikos*, or foreign settler, and to the Athenian technical term *metic*, which refers to a foreigner who pays taxes but does not enjoy civil rights.

We cannot reconstruct the possible references that *metanastês* would have had for an eighth- or seventh-century audience. Neither a developed notion of citizenship existed, as there was for Aristotle, nor was there a technical language of inclusion and exclusion. But the notion of a *metanastês* as an outsider who would not receive the protections of the community would be consistent with both archaeological traces and epic allusions. Archaeological evidence points to a fluid Greek world, marked by wars, colonization, and expanding trade and commerce. Migration may have occurred for any number of reasons, including fleeing from invaders, escaping punishment for one's crimes, or seeking economic opportunities.[9] Nestor makes a reference to one who is driven out of his land, consigned to wandering: "Out of all brotherhood, outlawed, homeless [*anestios*] shall be that man / who longs for all the horror of fighting among his own people" (9.63–64). Phoenix must flee his land after sleeping with his father's mistress. And the *Odyssey* refers both to beggars (*ptôchoi*), who wander uninvited, and *demiourgoi*, or craftsmen and specialists, who would go from town to town as their skills were sought (*Od.* 17.382–87). Though begging and impoverishment may be one consequence of such an outsider, more central is the lack of standing of the *metanastês* within the community. Among the gods, Hephaistos, the craftsman to the gods, is "envied, admired, and ridiculed at the same time.[10] And Phoenix's wandering ends when Peleus takes him in and restores his social and political status within the community (9.447–84).

Deprived of his war prize, Achilles sees himself treated not as a warrior, in which his heroic deeds are reciprocated by the receipt of tangible, social rewards, but as something like an outsider who labors hard but has no protection against being cheated. Achilles' rather unheroic characterization of himself as having "laboured" (*mogêsa*) greatly for Agamemnon is revealing, as he now sees his compensation denied (1.161–62). Achilles even suggests that this asymmetrical relationship has been ongoing. He claims to do all of the hard fighting, "but when the time comes to distribute the booty," Agamemnon's "is far the greater reward, and I with some small thing / yet dear to me go back to my ships when I am weary with fighting" (1.166–68). The phrase Achilles uses, "and with some small thing, yet dear to me" (*oligon te philon te*), appears in the *Odyssey* in a begging context (see *Od.* 6.208 and 14.58).[11]

Achilles' point seems clear: he is not being paid the social rewards due a warrior; instead, he is treated like one who must labor without protection or, in Achilles' more exaggerated state, one who must beg. Withdrawal from fighting appears to him as his only alternative to "disgrace" (*asuphêlon*): he will no longer suffer for the scraps he receives (9.647). Achilles' response to the breach of norms is to refuse to participate in the practices of society. But he does not return to Phthia. Instead, he suspends himself between home and battle, entering what Turner would characterize as a "liminal" realm, or literally "threshold" (*limen*), between normal patterns of social interaction.[12] Achilles is not antisocial, as there are relationship with others. But these relationships no longer appear governed by the ordering principles of society.[13] Instead, Achilles articulates a notion of autonomy, or self-sufficiency, in which he defines his own happiness apart from the mediating structures of warrior society.[14] More than just a refusal to be abused, Achilles' statements carry a much stronger implication: social prescriptions and proscriptions do not meaningfully bind us to others.

ACHILLES AND THE CLAIM OF SELF-SUFFICIENCY

Our first encounter with Achilles after his withdrawal from battle occurs when he is visited by the embassy of Odysseus, Ajax, and Phoenix in Book 9. Beside his ships, removed from, yet able to watch over, the Achaian camp, he is "pleasuring his heart" by playing a lyre and "singing of men's fame" (9.185–89). The verb "pleasuring," from *terpô*, is used in several other scenes. It appears later to describe how Patroklos cares for the injured Eurypylos: Patroklos "had been entertaining [*eterpe*] him with words and applying / medicines that would mitigate the black pains to the sore wound" (15.393–94). Pleasuring is seen again in conjunction with comforting when several of Achilles' comrades attempt unsuccessfully to comfort the grieving Achilles after Patroklos's death (19.313). The term can also suggest getting one's fill, often in the context of lamenting. Thus, Achilles says that "when we have taken full satisfaction from the sorrowful / dirge [*tetarpômestha gooio*], we shall set our horses free, and all of us eat here" (23.10–11).

The connection of *terpô* to lamenting and comforting suggests a continuity between Achilles' "pleasuring" his heart through singing and the last time we saw Achilles—in Book 1 in which he "weeping went and sat in sorrow apart from his companions" (1.349). Achilles' singing appears not so much as the beginnings of the "search for the dignity and the meaning of the self," as Whitman suggests, but as a means of comfort for this sorrow felt from his separation from Achaian society.[15] Interestingly, this comforting or healing is not coming from someone else, as when Patroklos comforts Eurypylos, nor does it take place within the context of communal grieving, as with Patroklos's funeral. Instead, Achilles in Book 9 is comforting himself, an indication that he is not so much isolated (he is, after all, with Patroklos in this scene) as he is no longer integrated into a corporate bond that would provide such support. Achilles must rely on himself for healing from his sorrow.

More than just providing solace for himself, though, Achilles seems to distance himself from the norms of valuation in his response to the embassy. The embassy appeals initially to Achilles' sense of esteem by offering to restore his honor, through the

offer of gifts, and his glory, by saving the Achaians in their time
of need. As Phoenix states, if Achilles accepts the gifts, "the
Achaians will honour you as they would an immortal" (9.603).
The importance of this material recognition by the community
is reinforced when Phoenix concludes that if Achilles does not
take the gifts, even if he returns to battle, then "your honour will
no longer be as great, though you drive back the battle" (9.605).

Achilles would certainly have agreed earlier with Phoenix
that the meaning of the heroic life is defined by the receipt of
honor and the promise of glory. But now "such honour is a
thing / I need not" (9.607–608). He is, in fact, "honoured already
in Zeus' ordinance," a suggestion that his honor is no longer
mediated through social structures. These measures of worth
no longer appear operative to Achilles since they can no longer
be trusted.[16] Absent *charis*, the gratitude (in material recognition)
given by a community to the warrior for fighting and risking
his life (9.316–17), the struggle of battle now appears simply as
suffering. Like the mother bird who "brings back / morsels" for
her young, "but as for herself it is suffering" (*kakôs*) (9.323–24),
so Achilles determines that "nothing is won for me, now that
my heart has gone through its afflictions [*algea*] / in forever setting my life on the hazard of battle" (9.321–22).

Not only is nothing won for Achilles in setting his life on "the
hazard of battle" but nothing can be won. Possessed of the
knowledge that he will die if he fights at Troy, and no longer
possessed of a sense of worth that is tied to the receipt of
immortal glory, death presents itself in its finality to him. When
Achilles says that "Fate [*moira*] is the same [*isê*] for the man who
holds back, the same if he fights hard" (9.318), he is not departing
substantially in words from Hektor's earlier statement that "no
man yet has escaped [fate] / once it has taken its first form,
neither brave man nor coward" (6.488–89). Achilles differs so
dramatically from other warriors because of how he comes to
define the meaning of that death. There is an irretrievability to

death, unlike any material rewards that can be bestowed upon an individual. Possessions can be won and lost. But "a man's life cannot come back again, it cannot be lifted / nor captured again by force, once it has crossed the teeth's barrier" (9.408–409). Achilles' exclamation that "a man dies still if he has done nothing, as one who has done much" (9.320) is a statement about how life is defined by death rather than how a life, through the performance of great words and deeds, defines a death. Achilles understands his own life as being carried by his two fates toward his end in death (*thanatoio telosde*) (9.411). He can either fight where his death will come quickly and everlasting glory (*kleos aphthiton*) will be his (9.413), or return home where "there will be a long [*dêron*] life / left for me, and my end in death will not come to me quickly" (*oude ke m' ôka telos thanatoio kicheiê*) (9.415–16).[17] When Achilles comes to define the worth (*antaxion*) of his life by its end in death (9.401), nothing the community can offer will suffice.

The embassy appeals to Achilles' sense of worth not only by offering to restore his honor and glory, but also by suggesting that it is not like him, nor is it like a hero, to have a pitiless (*nêlees*) heart (9.496–97). That is, the embassy compares an ideal image of Achilles, as one who has compassion for his comrades, with his actions. The appeal has two components. First, Odysseus asks that even if Achilles still hates Agamemnon and his gifts, "at least take pity [*eleaire*] on all the other / Achaians, who are afflicted along the host" (9.301–302). Odysseus's distinction points to one aspect of the operation of pity that Aristotle will later describe: pity arises from the sight of pain that befalls one who does not deserve (*anaxiou*) it.[18] In this case, even if Agamemnon deserves to suffer, Odysseus's reasoning goes, the rest of the Achaians do not. Second, Odysseus attempts to implicate Achilles in the suffering of others. He tells Achilles that "it will be an affliction [*achos*] to you hereafter, there will be no remedy / found to heal the evil [*kakou*] thing when it has been done" (9.249–50). The suggestion here is that pity functions when, in Aristotle's words, the pitier expects that the evil may come to oneself or one's friends.[19] That is, pity rests upon some vulnerability to suffering. The appeal to pity by the embassy should not surprise us since, as Zanker has demonstrated, pity functions in warrior society as a motive for "cooperative behavior." Zanker suggests that the appeal to pity fails because Achilles is thrown back on the "impulses of emotion."[20] This formulation is too general, for the emotions play a part both in Achilles' rejection of the appeal to pity in Book 9 and in his later responsiveness to Priam's appeal to pity in Book 24. The question is why the same appeal results in two different impulses. The answer, I will suggest, lies in how Achilles sees his esteem at stake in these encounters.

When Agamemnon takes Briseis, Achilles sees himself treated as though he lacks value or worth. This slight (*oligôria*) precipitates a pain that expresses itself as anger.[21] Anger appears as a desire for revenge toward those implicated in the slight. Achilles, thus, seeks to restore his worth by humiliating those who brought this pain. His anger is directed most immediately toward Agamemnon. But he desires to use all the Achaians to avenge himself on Agamemnon since he holds the other warriors culpable for allowing Agamemnon to take back the prize (see 1.126 and 16.17–18). As Achilles swears to Agamemnon, upon departing the camp, "some day longing [*pothê*] for Achilleus will come to the sons of the Achaians, / all of them. Then stricken at heart [*achnumenos*] though you be, you will be able / to do nothing, when in their numbers before man-slaughtering Hektor / they drop and die. And then you will eat out the heart within you / in sorrow [*chôomenos*], that you did no honour to the best of the Achaians" (1.240–44). Whereas the suffering of a fallen comrade often elicits a pity that serves as an impetus for another warrior to fight harder and win more honor (see 5.561, 5.610, 13.346, 17.352), in Achilles' case the suffering of his comrades without his fighting only serves to heighten his sense of honor. This honor, though, comes from Zeus, who ensures the fulfillment of Achilles' oath of vengeance (9.608).

The appeal to pity also fails because Achilles no longer sees himself as vulnerable to suffering because he no longer attaches his worth to dying for others. Rather, he retreats precisely to remove himself from the thankless suffering that he had earlier experienced. In this realm, he comes to define the possibilities of his life—whether to return home to his father and live a long life or win glory and have a short life—as unaffected by the actions of others. As Achilles replies to Ajax, "I shall not think [*medêsomai*] again of the bloody fighting" until the Trojans have arrived and set fire to the ships of the Achaians (9.650–53). His own ships, as he points out, will remain safe (9.654–55). In this solitary stance, Achilles defines the happiness of his life as one in which he can inflict suffering while not, in turn, suffering.

Achilles' statement of autonomy—that he does not define his worth through the mediating structures of Achaian society— plays itself out in his valuation of social relationships. When the embassy first arrives, Achilles greets them, exclaiming, "You are my friends [*philoi*] who have come, and greatly I want you" (9.197, trans. modified).[22] And he hosts his guests in Book 9 in a seemingly traditional way by providing food and drink. Achilles calls to Patroklos to begin making preparations "since these who have come beneath my roof are the men that I love best [*philtatoi*]" (9.204). Friendship, or *philos*, as Benveniste suggests, is associated with "a complex network of associations, some with institutions of hospitality, others with usages of the home, still others with emotional behaviour."[23] The sentiment of friendship in ancient societies contained a corporate element in which the term was associated with an awareness of membership in, and a corresponding sense of obligation toward, a particular group.

But Achilles seeks to separate this sentiment of friendship from the mediating structures of Achaian society. This is suggested by his change of mood with the completion of Odysseus's speech. After Odysseus relates Agamemnon's offer of gifts, Achilles refers to Odysseus as *polumêchane* (addressing him in the vocative), an epithet for Odysseus that, among other things, suggests contriving (9.308). Achilles proclaims his distaste for "that man, who / hides one thing in the depths of his heart, and speaks forth another" (9.312–13). He not only points out early in his reply that he will not be persuaded, but makes explicit in his discussion of Briseis his awareness of the connection between Agamemnon's persuasion and deceit: "Now that he has deceived [*apatêse*] me and taken [*heileto*] from my hands my prize of honour,/ let him try me no more. I know him well. He will not persuade [*peisei*] me" (9.344–45). Agamemnon's offer of gifts, particularly the gift of his daughter in marriage, only reinforces Achilles' sense that if he returns he will still be treated as a *metanastês*. As Donlan has argued, such a gift was "a form of marrying-up, typically reserved for wandering adventurers and impecunious suitors."[24] As a friend who has dropped by, Odysseus is beloved; as he is linked back to Agamemnon, though, he becomes deceitful.

Similarly, Achilles attempts to affirm an intimacy toward Phoenix that is untarnished by social roles. After Phoenix and others have implored Achilles to accept Agamemnon's offer of gifts and a return to battle, Achilles refuses the offer but requests that Phoenix stay the night. Achilles qualifies this request twice: first, by pointing out that any decision Phoenix makes should be as he "chooses" (*ethelêisin*, trans. modified), and then by concluding with the statement, "but by force [*anagkêi*] I will not lead [*axô*] him" (9.429, trans. modified). In sorting out this seemingly contradictory stance on the part of Achilles, Stanley has argued that this passage is indicative of Achilles' inability to "translate this new apprehension" of internal rather than external value "into consistency either of mood or of reasoning."[25] Arieti suggests that this passage, too, points to a transition in Achilles' thoughts as he moves to a new logos that emphasizes the will rather than societal honor.[26] My point here is that Achilles' statement is entirely consistent with his position. The point of consistency, though, is not so much that Achilles is articulating a new notion of the will that is internal, but derives, rather, from Achilles' unwillingness to bind himself to others. We see in this passage a recollection and rejection of a notion of leadership, as exemplified by Agamemnon, that is premised on force. This passage, "but by force [*anagkêi*] I will not lead [*axô*] him," recalls the force that Agamemnon, as leader, exercised over Achilles in taking the war prize. Thus, Achilles ends the passage not with a statement about Phoenix's will but with an expression of the spontaneous gathering of intimates.

It has been suggested that Phoenix misses Achilles' point and even that Phoenix inadvertently provides the fuel for Achilles' fire by recalling the story of Meleager.[27] But Phoenix's speech makes sense as a response to Achilles' claim of self-sufficiency. Whereas Achilles seeks to distance himself from coercive social relations, ending on the note that Phoenix can stay with him if so desired (9.429), Phoenix immediately reminds Achilles of their inextricable social bond. Phoenix has raised Achilles, caring for him as a child and instructing him to be a "speaker of words and one who accomplished in action" (9.443). Achilles, according to Phoenix, cannot withdraw from Achaian society without, in some sense, rejecting that which made him who he is. Phoenix makes the argument rather pointedly: "I made you all that you are now" (9.484). The importance of this for Phoenix is that there is a bond that cannot be severed, a bond that imposes certain obligations on both parties. Thus, from Achilles' perspective Phoenix's decision to stay with him is entirely voluntary; for Phoenix, however, there is no such choice. Given their bond, Phoenix states that he "would not be willing / to be left behind," not even for renewed youth (9.444–45).

When Phoenix pushes the issue, Achilles responds: "Stop confusing my heart with lamentation and sorrow / for the favour of great Atreides" (9.612–13). Though it has been suggested that this speech reveals Achilles' confusion in coming to terms with his own position,[28] what it suggests, in fact, is a separation by Achilles of the intimacy of friendship from the bonds of Achaian society. Achilles dislikes how Phoenix seems to play upon their love by tying this love back to Achilles' acceptance of Agamemnon's gifts. At this point, Achilles draws the line: "It does not become you / to love [*phileein*] this man, for fear you turn hateful to me, who love [*phileonti*] you" (9.613–14). Achilles loves Phoenix, but it is a love that is endangered to the extent that it is allied with Achaian society.

This distancing of relationships from Achaian norms of valuation is expressed, as well, in Achilles' statements about Briseis. Only there is a problem. To say that he no longer values Briseis is to deny the reason for his anger. But to continue to value her risks implicating him in the exchange relationships that he now rejects. Briseis was originally a war prize valued by Achilles as a social reward. His original relationship to Briseis is defined solely by social convention. When Achilles explains that he now loves Briseis "from my heart," he carefully distances this new, more intimate relationship from his original valuation of her when he concludes, "though it was my spear that won her" (9.343).

I choose the Briseis episode because it is often used by those who ascribe qualities to Achilles that derive less from his character and more from a twentieth-century metaphysical tradition. Whitman, for example, places Achilles' attitude toward Briseis in the broader framework of Achilles' search for and discovery of an essential and absolute inner dignity. Whitman suggests that Achilles' love for Briseis is an example of "an absolute assertion of the importance of another person."[29] Yet such an assertion seems beyond the reach of the textual evidence. Achilles says nothing about the character of Briseis; he only distinguishes a different basis for his valuation of her. Before she was a war prize won by coercion; now he actually loves her even though she was won by coercion.

Whereas Whitman places the statements about Briseis early in Achilles' development, when Achilles has an intuition but not yet a realization of his search for dignity, Arlene Saxon-house suggests that Achilles' statements about Briseis are born of an already developed recognition of his "community with all mortal men." This notion of community seems to have two components: a recognition of "the fundamental equality of all men in death" and a movement "beyond the community of the Achaeans to pity all men."[30] That is, Achilles enters a transcendent, universal community premised on equality and pity. But the notion of equality pronounced by Achilles is an equality of individuals stripped of social artifice: alike, but not necessarily connected. That is why Achilles can watch as his comrades are slaughtered by the Trojans, an act inconceivable by one who pities all humans. Furthermore, his advice to the Achaians is not to forge new bonds but follows on the rejection of social artifice: "sail back / home again" (9.417–18), retreat from the rigors of battle and forego the heroic death.

THE SHIELD AS ARTIFACT OF TRANSITION

In the context of a social drama, Achilles' response to the embassy provides a contrasting voice about the organization of community life. Previously, Achilles saw himself as bound to the other warriors through a system of reciprocal obligations in which one received honor and glory for one's struggles in battle. With the perceived breakdown of this system, Achilles sees himself more as an outsider, laboring without reward. Refusing to suffer such dishonor, Achilles withdraws from battle and refuses to be bound to others. While the first half of the *Iliad* provides a compelling argument for Achilles' dissent, Homer as quickly shifts the ground beneath us, making us question what we might have so enthusiastically endorsed. After introducing the voice of autonomy, Homer retreats, exposing the inadequacy and painful consequences of the claim.[31]

Aristotle, in his *Politics*, provides just such an interpretation of the cultural implications of the *Iliad*. In arguing that humans are by nature political animals, Aristotle quotes Nestor's words that the man "who by nature and not by mere accident is without a state, is either a bad man or above humanity; he is like the 'Tribeless, lawless, heartless one,' whom Homer denounces— the natural outcast is forthwith a lover of war." Though humans, with their faculty of logos perfected, are the "best of animals," the individual who is outside the polis "is the worst of all," capable of "the most unholy and most savage" of acts. The reason for this has direct bearing on our discussion of Achilles. Such extremes of savagery, to which Achilles succumbs as he avenges the death of Patroklos, occur when individual passions are no longer tempered by the conventions of society, when the individual is "separated from law and justice." For Aristotle, justice is "the bond of men in states" and "the administration of justice, which is the determination of what is just, is the principle of order in political society."[32] The paradox of Achilles' position from this perspective is that he seeks to right the injustice done to him by separating himself from the realm in which justice is administered. Achilles' separation from coercive social structures ultimately results in a disordered realm, one marked by a boundless wrath.

Aristotle, thus, places Achilles' claims to godlike status in a cultural perspective. Achilles can make these claims, not because they are true or deserved, but because from his self-sufficient stance there are no cultural limits—neither prescriptions nor norms—on what he can demand. There are, similarly, no cultural limits on his actions: his cruelty is boundless, his anger causes him to actually challenge the gods, he refuses any oath with Hektor, he momentarily desires to eat raw flesh as would an animal, and he even seems to forget the time-honored custom of burying Patroklos. When Aristotle says that the individual who is outside laws and justice "because he is sufficient for himself [*autarkeian*], must be either a beast or a god," his reference fits the self-sufficient Achilles who acts as both.[33]

In drawing out the implications of these final books, scholars have largely followed Aristotle's lead, looking for a reassertion of the norms of Achaian society, even if Achilles' reintegration is imperfect.[34] Werner Jaeger, for example, sees the *Iliad* as a form of *paideia* for the early Greek aristocracy, one in which "nobility of action" was "united" with "nobility of mind." Whitman suggests that by the end of the epic, Achilles has moved toward "a real communion with his human fellows." Redfield argues that the *Iliad* serves as a form of ritual purification in which the culture of the Achaians is reaffirmed, even as culture in the meeting of Priam and Achilles "is overcome." And Saxonhouse argues that Achilles returns to the community, having learned the virtue of moderation.[35]

In the encounter between Achilles and Agamemnon in Book 19, we do see a public end to the strife as both Achilles (19.56–73) and Agamemnon apologize (19.78–144), and Agamemnon provides gifts in compensation (19.138–44) and offers an oath that he never slept with Briseis (19.258–65).[36] Achilles cannot remain in this liminal world after the death of Patroklos. But the importance of Achilles' liminality in the context of a social drama is that it allows society, in Turner's words, to "take cognizance of itself." Achilles' liminality not only stands in contrast to Achaian norms, but also places these norms in the larger context of the cosmos. As Turner notes, liminality offers the possibility of obtaining an "approximation, however limited, to a global view of man's place in the cosmos and his relations with other classes and visible and invisible entities."[37]

   In this context we can begin to develop an interpretation of
Achilles' shield, a shield that is crafted for him by Hephaistos
upon Achilles' reentrance into battle. What has often puzzled
commentators is the apparent disjuncture between the vision of
a balanced and stable communal existence depicted by the
shield and the private, destabilizing anger of Achilles. Scholars
have emphasized different aspects of the shield to reconcile
these seemingly disparate narrative moments, though often by
abstracting the shield from narrative action. Whitman suggests,
for example, that the "intention of the Shield is wonder. It is
the miracle of cosmic diversity focused into formal unity and
order, as the proper adornment of the unified heroic will." By
the time the *Iliad* is over, suggests Whitman, Achilles "lives up
to the fullness of its classic implications—passion, order, and
the changeless inevitability of the world as it is."[38] For Schadewaldt, the shield is a work of Homer's poetic imagination that
exists as a metaphor for the epic portrayal of the world as
ordered by the principle of antithesis or opposition (*Gegensatz*):
of day and night, earth and sea, old and young, gods and men,
words and action, and life and death.[39] Achilles is given this
vision of a "comprehensive whole" (*allumfassenden Ganzen*), as
crafted in the shield, when he decides to avenge the death of
Patroklos and accept his own death.[40] Even more abstractly,
Reinhardt views the shield as a timeless and nameless "glance
at the continuity of life" (*zum Blick auf die Kontinuität des Lebens*)
that removes the audience from the linear flow of events.[41] For
Atchity, the shield presents "an idealized" image in which "past,
present, and future become indistinguishable."[42] And Schein
suggests that the shield provides a view of war and Achilles'
action in an "explicitly artistic perspective of generalized human
life that makes them seem not only heroic but also tragic." The
shield reveals the "terrible disparity between the full range of
human life and the transcendent yet pathetically limited
heroism of the hero who carries the shield into battle." The

shield works, like the rest of the epic poem, to transform human suffering into a "sublime art" of wonderment by the audience.[43]

I find considerable insight in these approaches, and agree that the shield provides a moment of perspective for the audience. But it is a perspective achieved not at once through a transcendent detachment but through the establishment of a narrative relationship between the audience and Troy. The shield, I suggest, provides a vision of healthy community life, a vision given salience by its depiction of what was rather than by what "might be."[44] That is, the shield links the audience to a Trojan past. The linkage is empathetic in that the scenes, in their generality, depict activities that are shared by all communities. The linkage is historical in that the scenes recall images of Trojan life that have already appeared in the epic. And the linkage points to a future in which these images appear later in the epic, transformed at that point by the imminent destruction of the Trojan community. The shield, thus, is not suspended from action but appears as an artifact of transition and transformation since it, like Achilles, enters both the Achaian's and audience's world. The shield does invite reflection and contemplation, not as a transcendent moment but as its generality is related to, and comes into tension with, the particulars of action within the epic.

The shield appears as an artifact of transition in two ways. First, the shield is crafted for Achilles as he enters back into battle to avenge the death of Patroklos. Importantly, this is not a moment of complete integration but of transition as Achilles continues to stand apart from the Achaians, neither mixing with them (18.215) nor participating fully in the rituals of community. Second, the narrative construction of the shield scene is suggestive of this transition as it moves from the cosmos (18.483–89) to a divine depiction of the human realm and finally to Achilles arming himself for battle.

The shield, though, points to a moment of transformation as well. The shield brings into the epic a perspective that is at once grand—as it depicts the sweep of human community within the cosmos—and intimate, as it portrays a daily existence that was once known by the Trojans and Achaians alike. The audience peers down at the human realm as they occupy a perspective like the gods on Olympos or like Achilles perched on his ship. What has often been seen as a problem, namely that no picture could capture the scenes that Homer describes, is, I would suggest, precisely the point. While for Becker there is an attention to the "visual" apart from the verbal,[45] I would argue that the "visual" that Becker has in mind is, and can only be, a construction of the imagination. I say this because the shield portrays an interconnectedness in time: a temporal flow that cannot be depicted but can only be imagined through a memory of the past and an anticipation of the future.

Let me describe briefly how the shield creates this temporal relationship. The inner circle portrays the enduring elements of the immortal world: the earth, sky, water, sun, moon, and constellations. Placed around these immortal elements are the artifacts of human habitation of this world. In the second circle are "two cities of mortal / men" (*poleis meropôn anthrôpôn*) (18.490–91). In the first city, there is both a wedding procession and a dispute in the marketplace. At the very least, the scenes depict fundamental activities of the *oikos* and the polis, both of which are jeopardized in the second city, the city at war. In the first city, the *oikos* is united as husband and wife join together. In the second city, however, the *oikos* is divided, and the polis endangered, as the wives and children stand on the city wall looking down at their husbands in war (18.514). Surrounding the cities are further acts of human habitation, acts guided by the rhythms of the seasons: tilling, the harvesting of wheat on a king's land, the preparation of a feast, the harvesting of grapes, the raising and herding of cattle and sheep, the fending off by herdsmen and dogs of an attack on the herd by lions, blacksmithing, and a festival, complete with men and women in finely spun clothing.

The shield is connected to the epic most obviously as it recalls, in a more general form, specific images and events that have occurred to this point. There is the portrayal of the division of a warrior counsel about whether to sack the city or ransom it that recalls not only the divisions in counsel at the opening of the epic but also the division between Hektor and Poulydamas about the fateful decision of whether to storm the Achaian camp or retreat behind the walls (18.243–313). The women and children who are standing at the rampart resemble both Achilles standing at his ship watching the battle and the women, children, and elders of Troy watching the Achaians (6.431–34). The anticipation of an ambush (18.513) relates back to several scenes: the contention by Achilles that Agamemnon does not participate in ambushes with the men (1.227), the recollections of ambushes by Nestor (4.392) and Hippolochos (6.189), and the suggestion that the women return to the homes and light fires to watch for an ambush (8.520–22). Strife, Confusion, and Death appear both on the shield and throughout the epic,[46] creating bodies soaked in blood (12.423–31) and efforts to retrieve fallen comrades (see 7.423–32), most immediately that of Patroklos (17.412–22). We see, as well, the precinct of a *basileus* both on the shield (18.550) and in Troy (6.242–50), and images of countryside (16.455), shepherding (13.493), and weaving (3.125, 6.490–93). The depictions on the shield of the attack by lions on the herd and the reaping of wheat are disturbingly transformed in the epic as images of human destruction: bestial images of humans attacking others as prey,[47] of reaping as the cutting down of men (11.67–71), of property disputes among farmers as an image of proximity of battle (12.421–24), and of the scales used by women for selling wool as the balance of fate in battle (12.432–35).

But the shield does not simply recall images from the epic. It recalls for the audience, as it creates, images of a healthy community life that likely would parallel Troy before the siege. The

creation of this Trojan past provides the basis for a repetition of
these images that reveals the dramatic changes exacted upon
the Trojans by the Achaians. The pastures of Troy (20.225–26)
will not be ploughed (20.184–85). The "wheat-bearing plain"
outside the walls of Troy becomes the scene of Hektor's flight
and then death (21.602–603). The springs for washing, which
were used by the women of Troy "when there was peace, before
the coming of the sons of the Achaians" (22.156), are now
deserted. And we see not the *anticipation* of the people of the
city who stand at the wall, as depicted on the shield, but the
horrifying *realization* of doom as the women and elders of Troy,
including the family, watch the slaughter and then desecration
of Hektor (21.526, 22.34–35, 85, 460).

The shield, thus, works to extend the narrative time of the
epic by giving us some sense of the transformation in the lives
of the Trojans exacted by the Achaians. Within the context of
a social drama, the shield appears at a point of transition between
Achilles' liminality and his reentrance into battle. The shield, fit-
tingly, reveals at the most general level the notion of intercon-
nection that Achilles has experienced at a personal level. The
perspective offered by the divinely crafted shield, though, cannot simply be assimilated into the community. This is suggested
by the reaction of the other warriors as they avert their eyes, as
well as by the tensions that inhere in the shield: we are made
sympathetic to the Trojan loss by the very artifact that will be
used to inflict this loss. The shield does not resolve this tension;
rather, it depicts human experience in its generality while it is
used for human experience in its particularity—Achilles'
slaughter of Hektor. The point here is that Achilles, like the
shield, is simultaneously outside and within the community.
The result is initially a series of incongruous moments. Even
though Achilles returns to battle, he declares that he does not
yet want to "be among men" (18.91). He expresses indifference
to Agamemnon's offer of gifts (19.147–48). He ignores eating

rituals (19.156, 162–70, 213–14) and casts oaths of fidelity as unimportant (19.191). He forgets norms of ransoming as he kills the unarmed and supplicating Lykaon (21.74–96). He rejects oaths between warriors when he refuses to return Hektor's body (22.261–67) and, in fact, he desires to eat Hektor raw (22.346–48).

Liminality, in the context of a social drama, provides a realm in which everyday reality is suspended and, as Turner writes, "people are allowed to think about how they think, about the terms in which they conduct their thinking, or to feel about how they feel in daily life."[48] Agamemnon's deception and threat of force lead Achilles to suspend himself from the normal processes of Achaian community life, notably assembly and battle, and to ask instead whether the community can bestow anything that is trustworthy or worth his suffering. The shield, as an artifact of Achilles' transition from liminality, provides the most general view of what it is that the community can offer. But it is a view that Achilles, now pulled back into the Achaian community by the death of his dear friend, has yet to translate into action. Just such a translation occurs in the final two books of the epic.

5

Elite Relations

Ἀτρεΐδη, σοὶ πρῶτα μαχήσομαι ἀφραδέοντι,
ἦ θέμις ἐστίν, ἄναξ, ἀγορῇ

Son of Atreus: I will be first to fight with your folly,
as is my right, lord, in this assembly

9.32–33

       In chapter 4, I suggested that Achilles' claim of self-sufficiency was unsustainable because it denied the inextricable relationships that bind humans to one another. No less threatening to the relationships that constitute the political field is Agamemnon, who, as we saw in chapter 3, fragmented and enervated this space through deception and the threat of force. Homer has left us with a political problem. As both Agamemnon and Achilles threaten the foundations of community life, neither provides a suitable answer to how the exercise of authority can engender political power—the willingness and ability of people to act together. Throughout the *Iliad*, Homer brings into question the traditional answers: wealth, heredity, even prowess in battle.[1] None of these attributes, though, necessarily translates into successful political leadership.

In answering this political problem, Homer points to a more complex understanding of the relationship between authority and power. A leader's power is not composed simply of a set of characteristics that one possesses, whether the achievements of Achilles' prowess in war or the ascriptive properties of Agamemnon's genealogy.[2] Nor is power derived from the rewards that one can distribute.[3] Though such rewards may be a necessary aspect of leadership, they are not, as Achilles' refusal of Agamemnon's offer of gifts suggests, a sufficient condition. What emerges, instead, is a notion of power that rests on relationships that make up the political field.[4] In this chapter I explore how political power depends on a recognition of *themis* as a public claim to political rights by the elite. In the next chapter, I examine how political leadership derives its power from a broader appeal to the people.

CONCEPTIONS OF *THEMIS*

An immediate objection to the claim that we see the constituting of a public notion of rights in the *Iliad* is that nothing in the epic resembles a notion of political rights as formalized principles or protections. Indeed, I am not suggesting that we can somehow conflate a contemporary with a Homeric notion of rights. The differences are real and, as it turns out, instructive in our own thinking about rights.[5] But *themis* is a richer and more complex political concept than has been recognized generally in Homeric scholarship. In developing my argument, I depart from two general approaches to the interpretation of *themis*. First, I differ from views that place *themis* within the context of the coercive power of the *basileus*, or leader. This connection is supported, it is argued, by the divine nature of *themis*, which is transmitted through the scepter to the *basileus*. The result is an "ideology of kingship" in which the king leads by personal prerogative through a claim to divinity.[6] Against this notion, I will suggest that *themis* appears as a condition of politics as it establishes relationships within a public space. I depart from a second framework of interpretation, this one holding that *themis* does not possess the attributes of a right. Certainly, we do not see a set of formalized principles. But the conclusion that follows—that *themis* lacks any conceptual substance and, thus, appears as incoherent and inconsistent in its application—conflates a philosophic formalization of rights with the historical process of the constituting of rights. The result of this conflation is to render invisible how rights are given form through human enactment. By viewing rights as enacted, we can understand how the *Iliad* portrays the constituting of *themis* as an aspect of the political.

THEMIS AND DIVINE KINGSHIP

A long-standing interpretation exists of *themis* as an expression of divine kingship. Though the arguments vary, the claim is premised most often on the identification of some continuity between the Mycenaean (c. 1400–1200) and Homeric world of the eighth century. Evidence for historical continuity is provided by etymological relationships between such Homeric words as *basileus, anax,* and *demos,* and the Mycenaean words *qa-se-re-u, wa-na-ka,* and *da-mo.* The Homeric leader, or *basileus,* appears as an heir (at least in name) of a Mycenaean official. Credible arguments have been made, most notably by Gschnitzer, that in Mycenaean times the *qa-se-re-u* was a subordinate local official who reported to the *wa-na-ka.* The *wa-na-ka* was the leader (often translated as "king") of a centralized administrative system (often referred to as a "palace" system). With the collapse of the central administrative system (c. 1200), the local officials became the autonomous leaders of the now isolated and much smaller communities.[7]

The argument for sacred kingship takes this view one step further. The contention is that the *basileus* inherited not just the name, but the vestiges of sacred authority. Scholars holding this view have sought to develop their case by identifying etymological associations between the *basileus* and the divine. Most notably, this association is seen in the privileged position of the *basileus* as holder of the scepter of Zeus and interpreter of sacred *themis*. Power, from this perspective, flows downward, from Zeus, to the *basileus,* to his followers. Not surprisingly, this has led to an emphasis on the coercive aspects of kingly rule and the expected obedience of the people. For Glotz, "*themistes* formed a sacred and mysterious code of family justice (*themis*)." The leader exercised "absolute power" since he received with the scepter "knowledge of the *themistes,* infallible decrees that a superhuman wisdom revealed to him through dreams and oracles, or suggested to his inner conscience."[8] For Bonner and Smith, too, *themistes* were "pronouncements of the king indicating in an authoritative fashion what is right and proper (*themis*) in a particular set of circumstances." For both Glotz and Bonner and Smith, the gods "transmitted" *themis* to the leader who then "summoned meetings of the whole people before whom he made known his decisions."[9]

The association of sacred kingship and personal prerogative is not simply a relic of now discredited Homeric scholarship but remains a feature in contemporary discussions. Benveniste, whose suggestive etymologies are highly influential in Homeric scholarship, sees kingship as connected to the divine because of the association of the *basileus* with *themistes* and the scepter. *Themistes,* for Benveniste, are of "divine origin" and are interpreted by the "head of the family." Since the *basileus* is, for Benveniste, the "chief of the *génos*," then *themis* "is the prerogative of the *basileús.*" Furthermore, the scepter has an almost "mystical notion" attached to it. Originally, suggests Benveniste, the scepter was associated with the staff of the messenger who had authority to deliver a message. The Homeric king is a messenger, as well, imbued with the symbolic authority of Zeus.[10]

Similar associations between the sacred basis of kingship and claims of personal prerogative are reached by a number of other scholars. For Köstler, the king appears both as the interpreter of *themis*, which is a "divine justice" (*himmlische Recht*), and as the holder of Zeus's scepter. The sacred origins of the scepter are seen as a continuing source of the claim to power by the *basileus*. The proximity to Zeus justifies the singular power of the king. The scepter, for example, appears as the "symbol of his power" (*Zeichen ihrer Macht*).[11] As a result, the king rules by personal prerogative.[12] Jones notes that from the beginning *themis* "was seen as given by someone, prince or priest, specially endowed with the insight needed to express the divine will."[13] Deger-Jalkotzy sees the scepter as symbolizing the sacred authority of the Homeric king to interpret the *themis* of Zeus.[14] And Easterling, in drawing on Benveniste's etymologies, suggests that the scepter marks the "sacredness of Agamemnon's royal authority."[15]

Two more extended arguments are instructive because they reveal the reliance upon etymologies for positing a notion of sacred kingship. Lenz has argued for an "ideology of kingship" in which the king, as holder of the scepter, interpreter of *themis*, and descendant of Dark Age priests, claims to be ruling by divine favor. Supporting evidence for the divine basis of kingship includes noting that "*wa-na-ka*" (which becomes "*anax*," a general word for leader in Homer) was probably used in Mycenaean times to refer both to kings and gods; the probable use of the scepter by the Mycenaean "high priest"; and the association of *temenos*, the allotment of land to a *basileus*, with its original meaning as a precinct sacred to the gods.[16] And Mondi, arguing against a secularized form of leadership, claims that Homeric social belief centered around a notion of "divine kingship." In words reminiscent of Glotz, Mondi writes that the king appears as "an exceptional, supra-human figure, believed to possess a certain divine power or efficacy, and treated by the rest of his society with a reverence and devotion otherwise reserved for the celestial deities." The scepter, for Mondi, is a symbol of the ability of the king to "exercise his will" through force. As corroborating evidence of divine kingship, Mondi also looks to the etymologies of words associated with kingship. *Geras*, the gifts given to the *basileis*, appear as evidence of divine kingship because the term also describes offerings to the gods. Thus, "the interaction between man and his king in the Homeric poems is often the same as that expressing the relationship between man and god." *Krainein*, as it is used by Nestor in association with Agamemnon (9.96–102), is interpreted by Mondi as denoting sacred association. Mondi draws upon the "oldest meaning of the verb" as employed by mortals who seek a "favorable divine response to that prayer."[17] Given this meaning, Nestor's use of the term suggests that Agamemnon embodies an earthly Zeus to whom men pray. For Mondi, as for others who view the Homeric *basileus* as a form of sacred kingship, leadership operates as an act of personal prerogative that is sanctioned by divine authority.[18]

Associations with the divine are likely aspects of these terms. But there is a danger when we read a vocabulary of a Mycenaean past, about which we know very little, into the political relations of the Homeric world.[19] This leads to some interpretive peculiarities. For example, the resort to force necessary to restore order is seen as affirming Agamemnon's claim to divine kingship, even though Zeus—the basis of such a claim—has deliberately deceived Agamemnon.[20] Achilles' throwing the scepter to the ground is interpreted as "affirming" royal authority.[21] And *themis* is understood by Benveniste as family law even when it is specifically linked to activities of the Achaians in the agora (11.806–807, 16.387), is related to debate within assembly (9.33), and is specifically connected to the role of the king in speaking, and allowing others to speak, for a good that includes different leaders from different communities (9.102).

But etymology is not destiny. Though the origin of words can certainly be both helpful and enlightening, origins are not presumptive evidence of meaning. Words take on new and revised meanings as they are used in different contexts, creating a layering of different, often overlapping, and sometimes inconsistent, meanings. This multivocality, as it is called, ties words not to their past but to a continually changing social, political, and religious present. Even Mondi, for example, recognizes that *geras* becomes "vulgarized" to include such meanings as a gift to a slave. Mondi maintains the claim to divine kingship, though, by suggesting that this vulgarization begins with the *Odyssey*.[22] Similarly, *krainein* loses its exclusively sacred connotation and comes to simply mean "rule."[23] Scepter is broadened to include simply a walking stick, hardly suggestive of divinity. Hephaistos uses his scepter as a cane, rather than as a sign of authority (18.416). The scepter, in participle form, is also used in the *Iliad* as a "stick to lean on" for a warrior as he "trudges down into Death's house" (14.457). And in the *Odyssey*, the scepter serves as a beggar's cane. *Basileus* no longer has any connection to an administrative center, but comes to have as much a political, economic, and military function as a religious function.[24] And *demos*, which in the Mycenaean context (as *da-mo*) appears as a local administrative division of palace rule, develops a more "all-inclusive" meaning in referring to "the whole population or the whole territory of a given named people."[25]

When Homeric leadership, and terms associated with this leadership, are placed in the context of action, a more complex picture emerges. To take one example, by looking at how the scepter is used and invoked in the *Iliad*, scholars have come to see the scepter as having a public, and not just sacred, meaning. Raaflaub argues for the scepter as indicative of public justice. Ulf suggests that the scepter carries with it a trust of the people. Gagarin sees the scepter as a symbol of "public authority." Griffin identifies the scepter as a reflection of the "authority of the community." And Nagy suggests that the scepter appears as a "thing of nature that has been transformed into a thing of culture."[26]

My interest in this chapter is to continue in this vein by placing *themis* in the context of an emergent understanding of relationships that constitute a political space. In understanding this relationship, we cannot view *themis* in a contemporary context as an individual and inalienable possession. Rather, I will argue for a notion of *themis* as constitutive of a political space. *Themis* appears as a notion of reciprocity among political actors that makes possible the existence of the public space. This poses a challenge to the "ideology of kingship" since it inverts the relationship of the leader to *themis* and to the public space. Instead of the king, imbued with divine *themis*, making possible a human council and assembly, we see a shared public space (whether an assembly or council), as it is constituted by a recognition of *themis*, that makes possible the activity of leadership. The personal prerogatives of the king, in which reciprocal exchange is an act of largesse, become unsustainable in this new context of "equal aristocrats."[27] *Themis* is no longer a personal claim of the king to exclusive knowledge, but a public claim of reciprocity. A condition of kingship, then, is the recognition of these claims by others. These claims transform the leader's scepter from a symbol of personal prerogative derived from Zeus to a symbol of political judgment that is exercised in a gathering of people in assembly (*agorê*) and aristocrats in council (*boulê*). That there remains a head of the council is not the point. There is similarly a prime minister and a president in Western democracies. The point is that there is a change in the understanding of the activity of leadership. Leadership and decision-making occur within a collective space of political actors.

THEMIS AND CONCEPTIONS OF RIGHT

I am addressing two interpretive strands that make difficult any understanding of *themis* as a political right. One strand, which we have just encountered, associates *themis* with sacred authority. The implication of this argument is that *themis* becomes the basis for the exercise of personal prerogative by the *basileus*. I have suggested, though not yet demonstrated, that *themis*, as it appears in the *Iliad*, is not a personal claim of the king but a public claim of the elite. A second view posits that *themis* lacks the conceptual attributes of a right. This claim rests upon identifying rights by their formal characteristics. These characteristics may be formal attributes of rights, such as their universality or their inalienability as aspects of our humanness. Or rights can be identified by their formal conditions, such as equality, consent, or codification. Or, finally, rights can be characterized by their formal content, such as the right to free speech, the right to bear arms, and the right to vote. There is nothing necessarily wrong with identifying rights by their formal characteristics, but there is a danger that we will read as absent what, in fact, may simply not fit into these typologies.

Most often, *themis* is simply translated as "custom," which serves for many to distinguish it from the more formalized characteristics of a right. Finley, for example, distinguishes between "formal rights," which consist only of the king having the "power to decide, alone, and without consulting anyone," and *themis*, which could be understood as "custom, tradition, folk-ways, *mores*, whatever we may call it, the enormous power of 'it is (or is not) done.'" Since *themis*, as it turns out, is used in association both with the decisions of a king and with public actions, what makes one invocation of *themis* formal, and the other not, is not entirely clear. We can perhaps understand this distinction as resulting from a view that rights require government institutions for their enforcement. For Finley, political rights must necessarily devolve from government. But the defense of *themis* in the epic is a "purely private matter."[28] Posner, too, in noting the lack of formal governmental institutions in Homeric society, suggests that *themis* is not a right but more like a social custom that is "adhered to over a long period of time" because it satisfies "a social need." In contradistinction to lawmaking as a governmental function, in which there is an "explicit mechanism for changing rules," in Homeric society one sees a "formal statement of the rule" coexisting "with the new and inconsistent practice."[29] And Benveniste argues that *themis* "designates family law," as opposed to *dikê*, "which is law that holds good among the families that make up a tribe."[30]

The most distinctive critique of *themis* as a right comes from Havelock, who places *themis* in an oral context. For Havelock, *themis* is "oral law," or what he refers to in other places as "formularies"[31] or "Precedent,"[32] which are protected by officials and may be invoked by different parties in judicial proceedings. Justice does not involve "principles" but appears as something, almost like a "quantity," that arises through a "process of exchange" between two parties. Justice is "not a set of preexistent principles or a set of rulings imposed by judges in the light of such principles." Rather, it is a rhetorical activity, "a symbol or a process achieved through oral persuasion and oral conviction."[33]

Placed in the context of the *Iliad*, the operation of justice serves a "didactic" purpose.[34] What occurs in the epic is a "collision" and then a "restoration" that depends "upon the application of a set of rules recognized by the community present in the story, and recognizable by the modern reader, as a form of 'justice.'" Such a restoration occurs, suggests Havelock, when Agamemnon publicly compensates Achilles and swears an oath that he never slept with Briseis. "The terms of Homeric justice, honored in the breach when the feud erupted, have emerged as decisive, pronounced in the settlement over which they may be said to preside as symbols of what has happened." The nature of justice as an act of public negotiation is reinforced in two other scenes: the shield scene in which the disputants appear before elders in the agora, and the dispute between Menelaos and Antilochus in the funeral games, an episode that "conspicuously dramatizes the settlement of a dispute carried out orally in public and rendered effective because it is witnessed by the community acting as a body."[35]

I agree with much of this formulation. But Havelock seems to posit a sharp epistemological break between the status of rights in an oral culture (as exemplified in the epic) and the status of rights in a literate culture. To use Havelock's own image, justice passes from its "shadow" in the epic "to substance" in Plato.[36] Most obviously, the image draws on a Platonic contrast between the shadows of phenomenal experience and the reality of a rational apprehension of the Forms. Important for Havelock is the advent of writing, which allows for the formulation of principles in two ways. First, writing provides a storage device for rules to be recalled and applied. Second, and this goes to the heart of Havelock's argument, the advent of literacy gives rise to a different way of thinking. A linguistic system that allows for statements that express permanence, Havelock argues, is necessary for one to think theoretically (i.e., for us even to be able to think of something like the Platonic Forms).[37] Most critical for the ability to think theoretically is the verb "is," "the only verb needed in any language designed for theoretic purposes to describe the system as such."[38] Simply stated, one cannot ask "What is justice?" without there being an "is" to express the concept in the "timeless present" that expresses permanent relationships. In contrast, an oral consciousness can express experience only through narrative: as the "acts of persons and the happening of events" rather than the existence of ideas.[39] As Havelock suggests, "oral societies are innocent of principles systematically stated by which the inconsistencies common to ordinary life can be judged." That is, absent in Homer are formalized principles of right and just. We see, instead, something like a "rule of propriety embedded in action."[40]

Havelock overstates the degree of this epistemological break between an oral and literate consciousness in two ways. First, he diminishes the conceptual aspects of the Homeric vocabulary. Guided by his framework of interpretation, Havelock empties *themis* of any substance, arguing, instead, that the customary rules are rules of procedure.[41] Judgments, or the application of *themis*, are not guided by principles but by a "pragmatism" in which behaviors that appear to be "puzzling, bizarre, or even illegal" may all be accepted as the necessity of the situation dictates.[42] This argument leads to a series of interpretive difficulties with reading the *Iliad*. For example, in interpreting the passage in which Zeus inflicts harm on the people who "adjudicate *themistas* crookedly / and drive out justice (*dikê*)," Havelock suggests that the "justice" to which Homer is referring is not a concept but an individual who, having received "an adverse ruling based on precedents incorrectly used," is "physically removed" from the agora.[43] But procedures are themselves statements of principles. "Due process," for example, is a procedural guarantee that rests upon principles of equality and fairness. Furthermore, procedures do not exist in a vacuum but require the application of something, such as customary rules of conduct. Without substance, we have procedures for debate with nothing to argue about.

Adkins, in responding to Havelock, has argued quite persuasively that "Homeric man possesses the linguistic resources to express a system as an abiding state of affairs." One sees in the epic the use of a timeless "is," as when Zeus states that "of all the creatures that breathe and move on the face of the earth, nothing is [*einai*] more miserable than a man" (17.446–47). Furthermore, there is also the perfect tense, as in the statement "All things are divided into three" (15.189). Adkins argues that "the claim rests on a systematic apportionment of different parts of the universe; and though the apportionment resulted from the actions of deities, it is now conceived as existing over against those deities, as a permanent state of affairs."[44]

Havelock draws too great of a distinction between oral and literate thought in a second way. Not only does he understate the conceptual aspects of *themis* in the epic, but he also ignores the narrative aspects of the conceptualization of rights in a literate culture. A quickly accumulating scholarship examines the literary and rhetorical constructions of thought. More important for my argument is what I understand to be the performative dimension of the framing of rights. Rights are not born of philosophy nor, for that matter, of contracts. Such a view fundamentally misinterprets the performative aspects of social processes, both oral and literate. Simply stated, the rules of a society, whether we are speaking about customs or about the institutionalization of custom in law, do not simply appear but are themselves the products of ongoing negotiated relationships.[45] That does not mean that negotiations are equitable; it means only that cultural norms develop as individuals define and enact their relationships to one another. What gives a culture its dynamism is the tension between the formalized processes of laws and rituals, which are attempts to create stability and durability, and the indeterminacy that arises because individuals must interpret, enact, and give meaning to these processes. Human enactments are not simply restatements or repetitions of form but a continuing response to changing situations, concerns, and interests. This is not to say that every enactment becomes ratified by a culture, as the rebuke of Thersites' action suggests. Instead, culture depends on human enactment, and those enactments can serve to raise issues that require a reinterpretation or redefinition of relationships within the culture.

I am arguing for a view of the framing of rights as "itself a process or a set of processes."[46] Drawing on Turner, we can identify two processes in the development of rights: the process of regularization and the process of situational adjustment. Whereas the first process, in which we see the establishment of rules and institutions, derives from an attempt to create stability, the second process derives from the interpretation and redefinition of rules to cover new situations or to create new relationships. Rights, from this perspective, are not restricted to codified or abstract expressions. Rather, rights are defined by, and in turn define, a set of enacted relationships between actors within a public field.

THEMIS AS PUBLIC ENACTMENT

I have suggested that etymologies and identifications of specific uses of *themis* are important, but only take us so far. This is because such approaches often assume a fundamentally static employment of a term. Change, thus, appears as incoherence, inconsistency, or vulgarization. Ultimately, we must look at the word in the context of the enactment of relationships within the epic. Through this approach, the invocation of *themis* appears not as the incoherence of custom or oral culture, but as an aspect of regularization in which *themis* is stated as a public claim.

To understand this transformation, we do not have to invoke a theory of development in which organizations follow their own evolutionary logic. Rather, organizational relations can change through a process that Weber describes as "rationalization," in which, in response to environmental factors, political actors may seek to accommodate more efficiently an increasingly complex environment.[47] During the eighth century, a number of environmental changes may have placed pressure on the political organization to make issues of leadership increasingly public. These pressures included increasing population density that heightened demands on resource usage;[48] the rise of other

communities that created security concerns;[49] the intrusion of
a market that placed pressure on resource allocation and control;[50] the consolidation of an aristocratic identity that increased
claims on the resources;[51] and the emergence of self-conscious
dêmos that further heightened demands on the political system,
leading to either integration or suppression.[52] Weber suggests
that this process of rationalization, as community decisions are
placed in a public space, transforms the earlier traditional and
charismatic aspects of leadership. In the next chapter, I will
examine how these charismatic elements are transformed in
the relationship between leaders and led. In this chapter, I will
explore how traditional authority, by which authority relations
are personal and customary, is transformed among the elite
into what Weber describes as "collegiality." An important part
of maintaining one's leadership position rests on "consultation
with formally equal members."[53]

Some historical corroboration exists (though evidence is
both scarce and unreliable) for the development of collegiality
in eighth-century Greece.[54] In Corinth, leadership may have
changed in the mid-eighth century from a hereditary monarchy
(which had been the tradition since the founding of Corinth,
c. 900) to an elective oligarchy among the Bacchiads.[55] The
enlargement of office can be explained most easily as an attempt
to lessen factional strife among the Bacchiads, as the family
grew through descent.[56] There was also a council consisting of
members of the Bacchiads, who elected the officials.[57] At the
end of the eighth century, the leader of Athens may have been
replaced by what eventually numbered as nine annually elected
archons.[58] And Legon considers it likely that aristocratic rule
replaced the Megarian chief in the eighth century.[59]

Though the principle of collegiality has been recognized by
a number of scholars as operating in the *Iliad*,[60] how collegiality
alters authority relations has not always been fully appreciated.
A tendency exists, particularly among those who see the *basileus*

as a form of a king, to view collegial relations through the lens of personal prerogative that operates in earlier forms of traditional organization. Lenz, for example, writes that whether we talk about kings or chiefs, "both are types of personal rule characterized by the presence of a unique individual at the head of a hierarchical social and political structure." This "ideology of one-man rule still prevailed" even when the *basileis* "came together, in a process of state-formation."[61] Certainly, important aspects of leadership remained traditional, if we mean that legitimacy of action was tied to an appeal to custom. But the importance of the principle of collegiality is that it may deprive "any type of authority" of its "monocratic character" or claim to singular, unchecked power. Through this notion of leadership, a separation occurs between public responsibilities and "private affairs."[62] That is to say, we see a departure from acts of leadership as acts of largesse.

A number of mentions of such collegiality appear in the *Iliad*.[63] My interest is to show how *themis* is tied to the notion of a collegial space when *themis* is expressed as a public claim. When Agamemnon threatens to take Achilles' war prize, Briseis, Achilles initially appeals to what is likely the customary expectations about the action of the king. In part, these reciprocal arrangements may derive, as scholars have noted, from the need for the leader to attract and maintain a loyal following.[64] Achilles, in this case, seems to appeal to specific customary limitations on the excesses of a king. Suggestive of the nature of these limitations on abuse are Near Eastern law codes that restricted the king from taking the possessions of others.[65] In this case, Achilles characterizes Agamemnon's taking of Briseis as an instance of just such kingly excess. The customary nature of this reciprocity is suggested when Achilles points out that it is "not fitting" (*epeoike*) for a king or a people to "call back things once given" (1.126, trans. modified).

This much has been noted by others. But Achilles speaks not just to the action but to the motivation of the king. Achilles

continually invokes a language of venality to characterize Agamemnon's actions, a language that suggests a separation between
private and public actions. He describes Agamemnon as the
"greediest for gain of all men" (*philokteanôtate pantôn*) (1.122),
as his "mind forever on profit" (*kerdaleophron*) (1.149), as using
others to "pile up" (*aphuxein*) his own "wealth" and "luxury"
(1.171), as vindictive in taking away the gifts of anyone who
speaks against the king (1.230), and addresses him as "King who
feed on your people" (*dêmoboros*, 1.231). Kalchas, too, describes
his fear of the "bitterness" of a king who will eventually show
his anger. And Thersites, no friend to Achilles, will echo Achilles'
accusation that Agamemnon uses the other warriors to accumu-
late his own wealth (2.226–33).

Ultimately, Achilles fails in his appeal to custom. He fails
because Agamemnon sees judgments of *themis*, ultimately, as a
prerogative of the king. Even Nestor, who seeks to temper the
positions of both Agamemnon and Nestor, suggests that "Zeus
has given into your hand / the sceptre and right of judgment
[*themistas*], to be king over the people. / It is yours therefore to
speak a word, yours also to listen, / and grant the right to
another also, when his spirit stirs him / to speak for our good
[*agathon*]. All shall be yours when you lead [*archêi*] the way"
(9.98–102). At first glance, Nestor's argument goes some distance toward establishing elements of reciprocity between the
king and the people. But, at bottom, Nestor's argument is that
it may be beneficial for a king to listen to the counsel of others
and not to abuse the position, but, ultimately, such decisions
rest with those who have might. This notion is confirmed in a
story Nestor tells of his father who, "angry over things said and
things done, / took a vast amount" of spoils "for himself, and
gave the rest to the people / to divide among them, so none
might go away without a just share" (11.702–704). In this case,
according to Nestor, the justice of the people was preserved.

But the danger of *themis* as a prerogative of the leader arises when he is unable to separate his private desires from public claims to the distribution of resources. This is, in Achilles' mind, precisely what happens with Agamemnon. So, in responding to Achilles, Agamemnon claims that the Achaians must either give him a "new prize / chosen according to my desire [*thumon*]" or "if they will not give me one I myself shall take her, / your own prize, or that of Aias, or that of Odysseus" (1.135–38). Similarly, in offering seven cities to Achilles, Agamemnon portrays the relationship of Achilles to these new cities as one of might: they will "fulfil [Achilles'] prospering decrees underneath his scepter" (9.156). The notion of might continues in Agamemnon's language toward Achilles as he suggests that through this act of largesse in giving gifts to Achilles, the warrior should "give way" (9.158) and "yield place to me, inasmuch as I am the kinglier / and inasmuch as I can call myself born the elder" (9.160–61).[66] The political space becomes subject to the whim of the leader.

Scholars have recognized that Agamemnon's actions breach norms. They have less often granted any conceptual status to this breach. Since the customs appear as "proprieties of behavior" that are "assumed and followed," scholars explain these conflicts not as moments of critique and difference but as the result of the "self-motivated arrogance of personal decision or desire, anger or ambition, or even mere eccentricity," the breaking of rules, or the misapplication of rules. The form of the conflict in the epic is, itself, "told in a way and with a style that will continuously provoke" the reinforcement of the "compendium of social and personal conventions." And the outcome of conflict is seen as always "restorative" and "corrective" in that the epic describes "how the mores are abrogated" and thereby describes "also the means and manner whereby they are restored."[67] The picture here is of the epic that reproduces itself and its culture with each repetition.

When Achilles throws down the scepter, though, he does not simply point to the abrogation of a set of norms. He shows the untenability of *themis* as a prerogative of the king. In the opening scene, Achilles points to one aspect of *themistes*, namely, the public apportionment of resources. Though *themis* is seen as deriving from Zeus, such divine origins are used to justify *themis* as a public enactment, symbolized by the placement of the scepter in the political space of the assembly. Achilles' claim is that Agamemnon has violated his role as carrier of the scepter, a scepter that "the sons of the Achaians / carry . . . in their hands in state when they administer [*dikaspoloi*] / the justice [*themistas*] of Zeus" (1.234–39). Achilles is not speaking of a leader's prerogative but of the empowerment of a leader by the people to act on their behalf. Rather, Achilles communalizes these actions. When Agamemnon suggests that another prize should be found for him, Achilles responds that it is "unbecoming for the people [*laous*] to call back things once given" (1.126). The previous line suggests what makes the people culpable: the booty taken from the cities "has been distributed" (*dedastai*) (1.125). Property taken in war is communalized, and then apportioned in public and on behalf of the people. Thersites, too, seems to interpret the apportionment of prizes, even to Agamemnon, as a public act when he exclaims that Agamemnon has received his choice of bronze and women "whom we Achaians / give [*didomen*] to you first of all whenever we capture some stronghold" (2.227–28). As van Wees suggests, the apparent existence of a procedure for the collection and then redistribution of war booty "indicates a considerable level of organisation and centralisation."[68]

Diomedes, later in the epic, points to another aspect of *themis* as a public enactment when he seems to claim his right to speak in assembly. Responding to Agamemnon's suggestion to retreat, Diomedes says that he "will be first to fight with your folly" and phrases his argument with an unconditional "is": "as is my right, lord, in this assembly" (*hê themis estin, anax, agorêi*) (9.33). This claim is noteworthy because it reflects a change in Diomedes' own understanding of a political space. Before this point, Diomedes is silently compliant in his reactions to the prerogatives of Agamemnon. Diomedes shares with the other warriors the moniker of a "nonentity," since they say nothing when Agamemnon takes Achilles' prize. This prior silence of Diomedes is made even more explicit when he is portrayed as standing silently "in awe [*aidestheis*] before the majesty of the king's rebuking" (4.402). By Book 9, however, Diomedes, like Achilles earlier, suggests that *themis* is not a prerogative of the king. Rather, there is a collegiality exhibited here in which shared rights to speak by a group of leaders inhere in the constituting of the political field. Power is no longer a possession of the *basileus* that is then exercised over others. The *basileus*, as the administrator of *themis*, is imbued with the public duty of protecting the rights of others. The power of the *basileus* becomes tied to the maintenance of this collegial space.

We can find support for the close connection between *themis* and the maintenance of a political field in several other occasions. Patroklos, for example, is depicted as running toward the ships "where the Achaians had their assembly [*agorê*] and dealt out / rights" (*themis*) (11.806–807). We have here an explicit statement of the public nature of *themis*. The assembly is portrayed as the space in which the Achaians, and not simply the king, distribute rights. To be sure, *themis* continues to be associated with a natural order.[69] But the nature of that association is supportive of the notion of *themis* as constitutive of a political space.[70] Among the gods, Themis is in charge of summoning "all the gods into assembly" (*agorênde*) (20.5). Among mortals, we see Zeus portrayed as punishing those "in violent assembly" (*agorêi*) who "pass decrees [*themistas*] that are crooked" (16.387).[71] Importantly, and suggestive of the constitutive nature of *themis* for a political field, the assembly is dissolved at the point at which *themistes* are not observed.

If I am correct that we see articulated a public notion of *themis* as a challenge to the prerogative of the king, then we would expect to see, not a restoration or a return, but a further elaboration of this notion. And in fact, such an elaboration occurs in the funeral games. While evidence exists for the public nature of *themis* in the previous books of the *Iliad*, we see in the funeral games how the leader should act in this new space.

THE FUNERAL GAMES AS POLITICAL ENACTMENT

There is good reason to look to the games for a discussion of important community issues. Games are not simply about play, as suggested by the intensity (almost to the point of death) with which the participants engage in the contests. The games are "the outstanding, ritualized, non-military expression of a value system in which honour was the highest virtue." These games, because of their centrality in religious celebration and their unifying force of "the politically fragmented and often warring Greeks," serve frequently in Greek literature as forums for discussions of the political activity of the era.[72] Certainly Homer's discussion does not appear in the critical form of later elegiac verse; but even for Homer the games, as they mirrored society, served as an important avenue for examining that society.[73]

In looking at the funeral games as a customary form of community remembrance, scholars have often seen them as both a ritualized enactment by which a "wounded and disordered" community can reassert "its structure and its vitality"[74] and as a means for the gradual reintegration of Achilles into the social order.[75] Farenga, in viewing the *Iliad* as a form of a funerary narrative, suggests that the poetry served not just to reaffirm what is old, though, but also to lay the groundwork for a "cognitive revolution" in the eighth century. Through themes of pity and grief, poetry "opened the door for participation in a communicative action fundamental to forming an 'isonometric' citizen class in the nascent polis." Poetic performance, as it engages the audience in a lament for equals, establishes the communicative basis for how individuals could "negotiate a universal understanding of how to act, judge, and speak effectively and fairly within a shared sense of the natural, social, and personal worlds."[76]

Though Farenga does not talk about the funeral games, I think we can usefully see how the performance of the games enacts a notion of community. The games are undertaken to honor and mourn for Patroklos. But throughout the games, the community revisits the still unsettled issue of authority raised in the beginning of the *Iliad*. Played out in the games is a departure from Agamemnon's notion of distribution as an act of largesse. Achilles, to recall, sets the context for this transformation by making the question of *themis* a public one. By doing this, the distribution of material rewards, contrary to the suggestions of Finley and Edmunds, becomes an issue of "political justice."[77]

What indications do we have that the funeral games appear as an enactment of political community? First, we have the performance of Patroklos's burial rites by the Achaians as a whole. Though it is still Achilles' responsibility to see to Patroklos's burial, Agamemnon (and not Achilles, as the head of the Myrmidons) gives the orders "for men and mules to assemble from all the shelters / and bring in timber" (23.111–12). The people are depicted as "mourning" for Patroklos (23.153). And Achilles requests that the "leaders" (*agoi*) remain behind, leaders whom Achilles associates with the "close mourners" (23.160, 163). The scene is suggestive of a community consciousness in which the people identify with a hero and the leaders appear as "social equals."[78] This burial in which all the Achaian leaders are involved contrasts with the normal practice of burying the warrior in the homeland.[79]

Second, Patroklos is buried, and a tomb created, in what becomes the "wide assembly" (*eurun agôna*) for the games (23.258). As burial "in the city market place or even in the council chamber becomes the unique, honorific exception" with the development of the polis, the placement of Patroklos's tomb is suggestive of a hero cult around which communities would unite.[80] The funeral games organized around hero cults would eventually become institutionalized in the pan-Hellenic games, which served as a "temporary but recurrent, community" in which "citizens" are "gathered for a few days of a polis in replica."[81]

Third, in announcing how the prizes will be distributed, Achilles makes the apportionment a public activity instead of a private matter. This, in principle, is no different from Agamemnon's role in Book 1. What is different, as we will see, is how each of the leaders responds to public challenges to the apportionment. Whereas Agamemnon treated the distribution of war booty as a private activity, an act of largesse on his part, Achilles seems able in the funeral games to recognize the legitimacy of public disagreement about the apportionment of the property. Such "communalization" of property, albeit one limited to select groups of society, is important as it reveals "an ideology basic to the polis."[82]

Fourth, we see in the funeral games more formal institutions for adjudicating disputes. Phoenix is made an "umpire" (*skopon*) (23.359, my trans.) with specific responsibilities: "to mark" (*memneôito*) the running so that it can be later recalled (in case of dispute) and to "bring back a true story" (*alêtheiên apoeipoi*) by being able to attest, impartially, about who was winning at the turning point (23.361). Such a role is reminiscent of the polis scene on Achilles' shield in which an "arbitrator" (*histôr*) is sought to resolve a dispute by speaking "the straightest opinion" (*dikên ithuntata*) (18.501, 508). The warriors in the funeral games will look to the leaders of the Achaians, as well, as ones who can "judge" (*dikassate*) between two disputants impartially (*mêd' ep'* *arôgêi*) (23.574).

Finally, Zeus is invoked in overseeing the orderly apportionment of the prizes (see 23.584–85), a role for Zeus associated with the development of the polis.[83] This role of Zeus appears another time in the *Iliad* in which Zeus is portrayed as punishing those "in violent assembly [*agorêi*] [that] pass decrees that are crooked" (16.387).[84]

I will focus on how the issues of distribution and leadership are raised in the first event, the chariot races, considered the most honorable of the funeral games. Achilles announces that he will not compete since everyone knows that his horse is the quickest. This statement is often understood as a sign of Achilles' continuing detachment from the Achaian community. But Achilles' outsider status has evolved into a healthier stance. Before, Achilles stood apart from the community, watching their slaughter. Now, he occupies a role within the community. Initially, he plans to be the distributor of the prizes, but, ultimately, he becomes an arbiter of disputes. Achilles anticipates none of this, however. The distribution of prizes is assumed to be a fairly straightforward act: there are a graduated series of five prizes, with the best horseman receiving the top prize.

Achilles' role quickly expands as he encounters a rather trivial quarrel between Ajax and Idomeneus about which of the horsemen is winning. Initially, Idomeneus called upon Agamemnon to serve as the witness for which horseman is ahead. Strange, though, is Agamemnon's silence. The audience cannot help but remember how poorly Agamemnon had handled earlier conflicts, most notably with Achilles. The argument becomes more heated and "the quarrel between the two of them would have gone still further, / had not Achilleus himself risen up and spoken between them" (23.486–98). Achilles counsels patience, telling them that in time they will be able to see the first and second place horses. Achilles is able to persuade Ajax

and Idomeneus to be patient by getting them to imagine themselves as another warrior watching such a quarrel. "If another
acted so," suggests Achilles, "you yourselves would be angry"
(23.494). This ability to place oneself in another's position stands
in dramatic contrast to Agamemnon's inability to place himself
in the position of the other warriors, a point made by Achilles
(1.149–51) and Nestor (1.272–74).

Achilles' skills at mediation are extended even further with
the completion of the race, an expanded role for Achilles that
is often overlooked because his initial statements of noninvolve-
ment are seen as conclusive.[85] The contest is illustrative of the
contingency and unpredictability of human action. Diomedes
loses his whip and then has it restored. Eumelos's chariot is
destroyed and Antilochos drives recklessly. Distributing the prizes
poses a special problem for Achilles, as we saw in chapter 2,
since "the best man" (*ho aristos*) in Achilles' estimation, Eumelos,
finishes last (23.536). To rectify this seeming imbalance between
recognition by the community and the excellence of the man,
Achilles proposes giving Eumelos second prize. In making this
offer to Eumelos, Achilles appears to reject as well his own earlier
claims to self-sufficiency: namely, that he does not need the
honor or the gifts of others. For Achilles now, it is not enough
that Eumelos be the best man; the community must honor him
sufficiently.

What to do for Eumelos poses a dilemma for Achilles, since
in upholding the centrality of community recognition of excellence he risks a replay of the agonistic notion of honor that
divided him and Agamemnon in Book 1. Indeed, though there
is initially general approval of Achilles' gesture, Antilochos, who
finished second, quickly challenges the decision. Echoing
Achilles' appeal to Agamemnon in Book 1, "And now my prize
you threaten in person to strip [*aphairêsesthai*] from me," Antilochos asks, "You mean to take [*aphairêsesthai*] my prize away

from me" (1.161, 23.544). Though it may be that Eumelos "himself is great," what counts, according to Antilochos, is the outcome of the race (23.543–47). And more importantly, what counts is that he receive *the* prize apportioned for second place. Antilochos does state that another prize may be given to Eumelos from Achilles' own shelter, a prize that may even be greater than the second prize. But important in this statement is an implicit distinction Antilochos draws between communalized and still personal property. Achilles may dispose of his own property as he wishes; but once that property is offered for public competition, be it in the games or in war, it becomes subject to public claims and rules, whether implicit or explicit, that may conflict with the desires of the distributor. One such rule, as stated earlier by Achilles, is that it is improper for the leader, when acting in the name of the people, to take back a reward (1.126). So adamant is Achilles about this principle that when it is violated, he almost, but for the intervention of Athene, strikes Agamemnon. Similarly, Antilochos vows to fight whomever might take the mare.

Achilles' response to Antilochos stands in dramatic contrast to Agamemnon's earlier statements about his prerogatives as leader. Agamemnon is never able to separate his private desires from the norms of public distribution, responding to Achilles that the Achaians must either give him a "new prize / chosen according to my desire" or "if they will not give me one I myself shall take her, / your own prize, or that of Aias, or that of Odysseus" (1.135–38). Achilles, on the other hand, responds not with "might" but recognizes Antilochos's public claim to the property and awards a separate and private gift to Eumelos "that will mean much to him" (23.562). The sequence of scenes that makes up the opening field of conflict, a conflict that is silenced by force, provides the context for a repetition of this sequence. Only this time we see a different culmination to these scenes. Force may secure compliance, but the cost may be the fragmentation of the community. Ready obedience ultimately entails a process of public decision-making, in which contending claims are made and must be mediated.

As often happens in politics, though, solutions to conflict turn out to be temporary. Antilochos, previously the victim, now becomes the accused when Menelaos protests Antilochos's reckless horsemanship. Menelaos appeals to the leaders to judge (*dikassate*) between the two of them to arrive at justice (*themis*) (23.574, 581). Just as quickly, Menelaos proposes, instead, that Antilochos swear an oath to Zeus that he did not cheat. Antilochos gives in, offers Menelaos the mare he had won and anything else Menelaos may want from Antilochos's home. Menelaos, won over by the supplication, gives the mare back to Antilochos.

In interpreting this episode, Finley has argued that this dispute between Menelaos and Antilochos "was a purely private matter" between two households in which the aggrieved party could choose the suitable remedy.[86] But there is an important difference in the resolution of this dispute: all of these actions are carried out in a public forum, even if they contain remnants of older forms of private resolution. Thus, Menelaos appeals to both the leaders (*hêgêtores*) and the counselors (*medontes*) of the Argives to judge impartially between the two. Achilles, if we are to follow earlier illustrations of such deliberations, would likely have acted as an arbiter, deciding whose judgment was the straightest.[87] Menelaos opts, instead, for Antilochos to swear an oath to Zeus, still in front of the people, that he had used no trickery in the race.

What gets replayed here is how private disputes, whether the personal antagonism that drives the conflict between Agamemnon and Achilles or this particular quarrel, invariably spill over into the public realm since they involve issues of distribution. Their resolution, Homer seems to suggest in this scene, rests ultimately on an ability of individuals to give up something:

whether it is to relinquish their vendetta and be ruled by the judgment of another party, as is first proposed, or to recognize the inevitability of mistakes in judgment and, thereby, give up some of one's anger. It is this latter course that the dispute ultimately takes as Antilochos responds to Menelaos that his youthful "mind is the more active but his judgment is lightweight" (23.590). Antilochos asks that Menelaos's "heart be patient" (*epitlêtô*, 23.591). The patience that Antilochos requests has as its root *tal-*, which is tied to notions of suffering and enduring (*tetlêôs*) as well as balance (*talanton*). In a theme that Achilles will articulate more fully in Book 24, suffering appears as a necessary consequence of living among others since one's actions affect, often in unanticipated and unfortunate ways, the lives of others. The patience of the heart is a response to such suffering, both as an ability to endure the pains caused by others, and as the capacity to forgive, or release someone from the consequences of their action.[88] Menelaos responds that he "will be ruled by" this "supplication" and will even give to Antilochos "the mare, though she is mine, so that these men too may be witnesses / that the heart is never arrogant [*huperphialos*] nor stubborn [*apênês*] within me" (23.609–11). In doing so, a balance is restored both personally, as Menelaos is recognized for his excellence, and communally, as the remaining prize can be distributed.

Achilles completes the distribution of the prizes by awarding Nestor, who does not compete, the unclaimed fifth prize. Throughout the *Iliad*, Nestor is the central critic of claims to self-sufficiency, suggesting instead that "the gods give to mortals not everything at the same time" (4.320; see also 11.761–62). This is an important action of Achilles in that he recognizes, and pays honor to, the centrality of diverse contributions to the survival of the community. Achilles' act is a recognition not only that no mortal is complete but also that Nestor, even though he is no longer the best horseman, is still to be honored by the community for his counsel.[89] This seems like a particularly relevant offering given the importance of a shared public space, one in which, as Diomedes comments to Nestor at one point, decisions about what is best are made with others and not by "a man by himself" because that man "still has less mind in him than two, and his wits have less weight" (10.225–26).[90]

Although Achilles pays honor to Nestor and seems to have taken Nestor's advice of the necessity to listen to counsel, the leadership required by Achilles goes beyond that articulated by Nestor. Importantly, as we have seen, Nestor understands the basis of leadership in a more traditional way, as one of "might." Nestor's role throughout the *Iliad* is that of an elder whose advice invariably involves the voice of experience.[91] This role is played out in the funeral games, as well, as Nestor advises Antilochos about how he can compensate for his slower horse with greater skills (23.306–48). This is important in understanding the position Nestor occupies in Achaian society. His age brings him deference and his arguments are grounded in a time that predates the memory of others. The result is that Nestor's role as an advisor is rarely even indirectly challenged, though it may be, as in the first book, outright ignored.

Achilles, in the role that he assumes in the funeral games, occupies a very different vantage point. In resolving the conflicts, Achilles does not appeal to some distant past, nor does he claim (as does Agamemnon) a personal prerogative born of divine support. The solution Achilles proposes rests, instead, on what works in this circumstance. Furthermore, whereas Nestor is able to pronounce a final judgment on a particular situation, Achilles finds himself immersed in a politics born of contending (and not easily resolvable) interests in which decisions give rise to new problems. Achilles' initial decision as to the distribution of the prizes is challenged immediately, leaving him to cast about for a new solution. Achilles must be able to recognize, and in turn respond to, claims made by others. Within this political

field, as constituted by others, we arrive at the answer to Achilles'
question of who shall readily obey. Ready obedience derives
from the recognition by leaders that they act in a space constituted by others.

6

Leaders and Led

ἑσταότος μὲν καλὸν ἀκούειν, οὐδὲ ἔοικεν
ὑββάλλειν. χαλεπὸν γὰρ ἐπισταμένῳ περ ἐόντι.
ἀνδρῶν δ' ἐν πολλῷ ὁμάδῳ πῶς κέν τις ἀκούσαι
ἢ εἴποι; βλάβεται δὲ λιγύς περ ἐὼν ἀγορητής.

it is well to listen to the speaker, it is not becoming
to break in on him. This will be hard for him, though he
is able.
How among the great murmur of people shall anyone
listen
or speak either? A man, though he speak very clearly, is
baffled.

19.79–82

The funeral games address one aspect of political
relations by showing how the ready obedience of the elite rests
on a recognition that decisions arise from a space constituted
by others. The flight of the people in Book 2 should remind us
of the centrality of the rest of the people to the maintenance of
a healthy political field. But what is the relationship between
leaders and led? The *Iliad* seems to point in contradictory directions. The people do not initiate action, but they are not

simply quiet, either. The leaders appear at times to be interested in the tide of "public" opinion, while at other times willing to violently suppress the expression of this opinion. And though there is an assembly of the people in which leaders present courses of action, the leaders appear free to follow or ignore whatever might be the expressed sentiment. Difficulties of interpretation are exacerbated both by the nature of epic poetry, which seeks to tell a story rather than convey history or social change, and by the paucity of knowledge about the nature of politics in the ninth and eighth centuries B.C.

To fill in some of these gaps, scholars have often sought to locate Homeric society either by looking back to a Mycenaean past or by looking forward to the emergence of a polis. There is a danger, though, in reading into Dark Age community organization either the residue of earlier forms of monarchy or the evolutionary telos of later polis development. As Donlan points out, in talking about attempts to locate Homeric community in a Mycenaean past, "we know almost nothing about the social organization of the Mycenaeans, and nothing at all about the social structure of the 'Dorian' newcomers."[1] Furthermore, polis development does not follow a neat evolutionary trajectory, as suggested by the widespread emergence of tyranny in the seventh and sixth centuries. Any model of Homeric politics, then, must be able to explain the importance of the developing role of the *dêmos* without, in turn, assuming an evolutionary trajectory from kingship to polis.

Three models, in particular, have been important in framing scholarly understandings of relations with the people. First, there is the royal model that we saw in the previous chapter that views Homeric political relations as developing out of earlier forms of monarchy. In this approach, the Homeric *basileus* appears as a king who rules by personal prerogative over quiescent subjects. Second, there is a class model. We see not a quiescent people but the emergence of an increasingly self-conscious economic and social class. In this model, the epic is placed in the context of class conflict in which the poem appears as an ideological tool of the elite to legitimate the exploitative relations of power. Finally, there is an integrationist model, with its origin in structural-functional anthropology.[2] From this approach, the *basileus* appears as either a chief or a big-man who, through gift-giving, enters into a network of reciprocal obligations. Like the class model, this approach sees the emergence of a distinct, and increasingly self-conscious, people. Integrationist approaches note aspects of stratification and competition in society, but place more emphasis on the increased recognition and integration (albeit unwillingly, at times) of the people into political association.

Though each of these models points to important elements of the Homeric world, none is complete for understanding the relations between leaders and led. Both the royal model of kingship and the model of an elite counterreaction to the emergence of a people rest on an incomplete understanding of authority relations in the *Iliad*. In particular, too much emphasis is placed on the coercive aspects of rule and insufficient attention is paid to how the emergence of a public space alters the claims to authority made by the elite. I am more sympathetic to the suggestions that there is, both historically and in the epic, an increased assertiveness of the people. I do not think, however, that we can understand these relations solely within the context of a big-man or chiefdom form of organization. Instead, I want to supplement these discussions by suggesting that authority relations between leaders and led can be understood as a form of *plebiscitary* politics.

Plebiscite has many denotations, not the least of which is the practice of a direct form of voting in affirmation or rejection of a leader or a policy.[3] But that is not the only form of a plebiscite. Plebiscitary politics, as described by Max Weber, can be conceived of more generally as a system in which the decisions of leaders derive at least part of their legitimacy from the acclaim, or perceived acclaim, of the people. We do not see a principle of voting in the Homeric world. We do see decisions "enacted" in a public space. These enactments may take a variety of forms: consultation with the people before a decision is made, the appeal by a leader for approval of a decision, and even debate between leaders before the people. The term *enacted* is useful because it draws attention to the public aspects of the activity without claiming that there is a formalized or democratic process. The notion of plebiscitary politics is helpful in making sense of what may otherwise appear in the epics as inconsistent or incoherent relationships between the leaders and the people.

THE EMERGENCE OF THE PEOPLE

The previous chapter introduced the kingship model in which the Homeric *basileus* is associated with the divine. Arguments for divine kingship are noteworthy, though, for their silence about the role of the people. This can be attributed, in large part, to an understanding of authority and power as flowing downward: from the gods, to the kings, and exercised over the people. The people recede into silence as the role of the people becomes one of obedience.[4] I do not want to completely discount associations of the *basileus* with the divine, though. Rather, as I will argue, these divine elements can be understood as charismatic aspects of leadership that are subject to public interpretation.

A number of scholars have taken note of the role of this public. Most significantly, the *basileus* has come to be seen by a growing number of scholars as an anthropological type of big-man or chief in which authority rests partly on ascribed aspects of birth and partly on achieved characteristics of personal prowess.[5] The maintenance of authority, as we have seen, depends upon the ability of the *basileus* to develop and maintain a following, whether by creating reciprocal obligations through the redistribution of goods to followers[6] or, as we saw in the previous chapter, by joining with other *basileis* to share in decision-making. Whereas authority flows downward with a conception of divine kingship, authority now appears as an ongoing (and often unstable) negotiation among the leaders and between the leaders and the led.

Two quite different interpretations are offered for how we can understand this relationship between leaders and led in the Homeric epics. Both approaches place the epic in the context of an emergent, and increasingly self-conscious, people. One argument, influenced by a Marxian notion of class competition, posits an increasing division and conflict developing in the eighth century between an exploitative aristocracy and an exploited, but increasingly resistant, *dêmos*.[7] In this context, the epic appears as an ideological tool to buttress elite control. For Morris, the epic is an "ideological device" that legitimates the "class interests" of an exploitative aristocracy. At a time "of tremendous tension, when the whole structure of society was in a state of flux," the poem presents a view of elite domination as "natural and unchangeable." The *basileis* are "glorified" and the *dêmos* are "ignored" almost "to the point of total exclusion."[8] Tandy claims that the epic appears at a time in which there is widespread social upheaval caused by the emergence of commercial markets across Greece. The appearance of markets poses a challenge to elite hegemony in two ways. First, markets threaten elite control over the distribution of resources. Second, markets threaten elite claims to status by providing a means for the accumulation of wealth by a class of merchants, producers, and traders. Against this social backdrop, the epic becomes an elite tool to "establish and support a self-conscious aristocratic class."[9] The epic does this by affirming aristocratic values and by excluding challenges to those values. Thalmann suggests that we should read the epic as an aristocratic strategy to legitimate the aristocracy's economic and political position. The textual strategy of the epic, as it is "composed for and conditioned by the interests of a military and landowning elite," is to show how challenges to an aristocratic ideal lead to social disruption that can be repaired only by a restoration of hierarchical bonds.[10] The community functions best when the people are most quiet.

Terms like *exploitation, class competition, social control,* and *hegemony* all point to the extraordinary ideological, economic, and political power of an elite. But these claims often rest on overly simple conceptions of authority relations. Tandy, for example, argues that the *absence* of markets in the epic is an elite device that "diverts attention from a primary cause of the social upheaval that has spread through Greece." The claim that the epic is a form of social control rests on a notion of epic production as controlled by the "big man" as benefactor. Though Tandy makes a nod toward an interaction between big-man, singer, and audience, his model ultimately depicts a form of social control that flows from the big-man to the singer and then to the audience. To avoid an oversimplified model of audience control, Tandy does suggest that there is interaction between singer and audience. But any interaction is mitigated by Tandy's claim that the audience, too, is predominantly aristocratic.[11] We end up with an odd form of social control in which the real subject of the epic (the market), and the audience to be controlled by the message (the people participating in the market), are both absent.

Thalmann's recent class analysis of the epic faces similar difficulties. Thalmann argues that we see in the epic the ideological construction of class. But Thalmann's conclusion seems to point in two directions at once. On the one hand, he suggests that the textual strategy of the epic is to show how challenges to an aristocratic ideal lead to disruption and, ultimately, a restoration of hierarchical bonds. The power of the *basileus,* from this perspective, appears to rest on "birth and personal prowess" that "work together to establish position and maintain it." On the other hand, Thalmann suggests that the "conditioned power" of the elite is now "subjected to scrutiny, and therefore a new form of consciousness." The result is that "elite power and hierarchical forms generally were opened to question and conflicted with an emerging citizen ideal."[12] How we are to understand authority relations in the *Iliad* is ultimately unclear. To the extent that there is an emergent citizen ideal, the authority claims of the *basileus* would seem to be altered substantially by the placing of any set of community decisions in a larger public context.

These Marxian approaches have been curiously undialectical in presenting a view of society, and social production like the epic, as governed by elite manipulation of an exploited people.[13] This conception of authority relations is not easily supported by a reading of the epic. Decision-making in the epic occurs both among the elite (in the counsel of *basileis* or *gerontes*) and in a public space of the assembly that includes the people (variously referred to as the *laos*, *dêmos*, and *plêthos*).[14] The people, through the assembly, do not vote and do not make binding decisions.[15] But neither are they compliant, inert, absent, or silenced. In taking account of the role of the people, a second group of scholars has sought to articulate an understanding of a more interactive political authority.

Raaflaub, for example, focuses on how the people and aristocracy develop alongside each other. There is, during the eighth century, the consolidation of an elite ideology aimed at maintaining its privilege.[16] But the "commoners" also "play a significant role in the community."[17] Most notably, an assembly of people listens to debate, expresses "their approval or dissent," and shares "responsibility for the outcome."[18] One sees, suggests Raaflaub, that the "three determinants of citizen status, known from later centuries (land ownership, military capacity, political participation), although not formalized, are already in place."[19] Raaflaub explains the emergence of the *dêmos* through an "interactive model" of *polis* development.[20] Writes Raaflaub, "As the *polis* evolved, the men who owned the land fought in the army to defend the territory of the *polis* and sat in the assembly to participate in its decisions." From the beginning, the *dêmos* is "politically integrated all along, to the extent possible and normal at the time."[21]

Donlan, too, argues that the *dêmos* possesses "a highly refined sense of its collective character as *the* land and *the* people." The *dêmos* is "always portrayed as the populace at large, expressing a common will or experience," such as gathering for a collective activity or dividing spoils. A *dêmos*-consciousness emerges in which the *dêmos* "represents the outermost limit of belonging," a belonging that is associated with the space of the polis.[22] There is not only an identity but a voice. As Donlan suggests, "The evidence of Homer is overwhelming that in the long run the *dêmos* has the final say."[23] A "special kind of reciprocity" develops between the leaders and people, one that evolves into "a quasi-formal contract" that expresses the "mutual rights and obligations of the abstract 'people' (*demos/laos*) and the abstract 'figure of the leader' (*basileus*)."[24] In this chiefdom form of society, leaders are separated from the *dêmos* by "unequal power and status," but do not yet possess significant coercive power.[25] There are traditional, ascribed aspects of the office since the chiefdom's position is often a hereditary one. But the lack of coercive power places a great deal of emphasis upon the personal (or charismatic) qualities of the leader to attract and maintain a following.[26]

To understand these political relationships, Donlan extends Sahlins's notion of "balanced reciprocity"[27] into a political context. From this perspective, the relationship between a *basileus* and the people appears as one in which the people give both "material and symbolic" gifts of support while the chief, in return, gives "material donations" like feasts and, most importantly, "leadership and direction."[28] Where the gifts to the *basileus* are "more obviously and openly dues," his gifts are acts of "largesse." What keeps a chief from becoming too ungenerous is that these transactions occur within a competitive exchange system. The *basileus* develops power through giving but is always subject to the challenge of rivals who may offer more and better gifts to his subordinates.[29]

Though Donlan has provided a useful extension of the idea of reciprocity, there remains an ambiguity in these formulations. Some sense of this ambiguity is suggested in an article by Donlan entitled "The Relations of Power." Donlan's question is simply why, if not out of "force or economic compulsion," did the "*laoi* heed and obey the *basileis?*" In answering the question, Donlan identifies three different forms of legitimacy, all operating at various degrees. Drawing from Weber, Donlan argues that there are elements of "traditional authority" by which the *basileus* maintains authority because the office was seen as an "ancient institution," aspects of "charismatic authority" in which authority depends on the personal qualities of the individual to maintain a following, and even elements of "legal-rational authority" by which the *basileus* is imbued with protecting the *themistes* of Zeus.[30] Donlan has certainly identified the overlapping of authority relations in a politics in transition.[31] However, we need to explain not just that different aspects of authority inhere in leadership, but how, in the epics, these different elements combine. My suggestion is that the interaction of these elements, like a chemical reaction, creates a different (and quite volatile) form of authority relations, one that Weber describes as plebiscitary. In this plebiscitary realm, the charismatic aspects of authority rest in a broader public space.

PLEBISCITARY POLITICS

Weber's discussion of plebiscitary leadership provides a suggestive parallel for understanding the people in Homeric society
as something more than subjects but less than citizens. He points
out that in a charismatic organization, the "basically authori-
tarian principle of charismatic legitimation may be subject to
an anti-authoritarian interpretation." The validity of charismatic
rule rests on recognition by the ruled of a leader's claim to
some extraordinary personal, heroic, or divine traits that justify
his leadership. Recognition of the authority of the charismatic
leader is treated as a "duty." But this charismatic rule, suggests
Weber, may be affected by broader political, economic, and
social changes. We have seen how eighth-century developments
likely placed pressures on the political organization to make
issues of leadership increasingly public. These pressures create
a seemingly subtle transformation in which recognition of charismatic authority is not "treated as a consequence of legitimacy"
but "as the basis of legitimacy."[32] The leader, though he may
retain charismatic elements, comes to have authority that is
premised on the recognition by the ruled.

Plebiscitary leadership is not distinct from the chiefdom form
of organization discussed by Donlan. Nor does plebiscitary
leadership lack claims by individuals to extraordinary, even divine,
associations. What I want to emphasize is the strange mixture in
which personal authority is connected to public acclaim. We do
not see a democratic principle of voting, or even formalized
procedures. We do see some formalization of public assemblies,
since there is both a role for the heralds who summon the people
(2.99) and a notion of a proper position and seating of the
people in assembly (2.96–97, 99).[33] And within this space, leaders
play to the crowd, seeking to persuade, cajole, or elicit support.
But this alters the nature of the political dynamic, and the
nature of political legitimacy, since leaders draft their appeals

in anticipation of a response. Within the broader political field composed of the *dêmos*, *laos*, or *plêthos*, the decisions, and the authority of leaders in proposing these decisions, derive at least part of their legitimacy from the acclaim, or perceived acclaim, of the people.

The peculiar combination of a charismatic and public basis of legitimacy is suggested in the opening of the *Iliad* when Achilles calls the people to assembly (*agorênde kalessato laon*) to address the plague that threatens to kill the entire army (1.54). The charismatic basis of Achilles' authority is indicated not just by his heroic stature within the community, but by the role of Hera in prompting Achilles to call the people to assembly (1.54–55).[34] Achilles' personal authority operates in a public setting in which the people seem to play some role in expressing their opinion. When Kalchas, a seer, tells the people why Apollo has sent a plague to the people, they "cried out in favour" (*epeuphêmêsan*) that Chryseis be returned to her father (1.22). The people are not successful, but what is striking is that even Achilles, in recounting the events to his mother, should mention their outcry as support for his position (1.376).

In a later assembly, Diomedes advises that the people should refuse the offer of gifts, rather than the return of Helen, by the Trojans. In responding to him, all of the Achaians "shouted" (*epiachon*), "admiring" (*agassamenoi*) the words of Diomedes (7.403–404). Two aspects of the verse are worth mentioning. First, the public acclamation has elements of personal admiration, since *agamai* is used frequently to express a wonderment toward an exceptional individual.[35] Second, Homer uses the language of the heroic war-cry to depict the voice of the people in assembly. Elsewhere, *iachô* is compared in noise to the roaring sea, blazing forest fire, wind in the oaks, and the tempering of an ax blade, and is associated with great feats of personal prowess, communal strength, and divine terror.[36] In the competitive world of the warrior, the cry corresponds to strength, courage, and individual distinction.[37] By depicting the people as shouting their approval, Homer not only reveals the force of the people, but also lends their voice some legitimacy by associating it with the agonistic, heroic world.

In a purely charismatic form of association, the acclaim of the people is treated as a duty that is directed toward one recognizably charismatic leader. In plebiscitary politics, however, acclaim is up for grabs. This makes the Homeric political field volatile. The leaders, in seeking acclaim, can go in two directions. They can use whatever personal authority they have to seek public acclaim for a community good, as does Achilles in Book 1. Or they can play upon the more autocratic elements of charisma by "hid[ing] behind" a legitimacy that appears to be derived from "the will of the governed."[38] Unlike democratic forms of politics in which the office, and not the individual, has authority, under a plebiscitarian form of politics the choices of the people can be used as "unconditional acclamations of the leader's authority."[39]

We get our first hint of this volatility in Book 2 when Agamemnon summons the people to assembly to test their desire to continue fighting. Achilles, to recall, not only assailed Agamemnon's courage and leadership the day before, but had suggested that no one would readily obey him. Agamemnon, in calling the assembly, attempts to shore up his personal legitimacy by looking to the acclaim of the people. In stirring up the "passion" (*thumon*) of the multitude (2.142), though, Agamemnon misjudges badly the reaction of the people. The assembly resounds with a "thundering shout" (*alalêtôi*, trans. modified), a term used also to describe the cries of war (2.149). Powerful in their numbers, the people almost create "a homecoming beyond fate" (2.155). Ironically enough, the political field fragments through the acclaim of the people, and is restored only through the actions of Odysseus, as he is instructed by Athene (2.166–210).

The danger that the people, powerful in their voice, will seize upon ill-advised words is also expressed later by Odysseus, who rebukes Agamemnon for his potentially "ruinous" advice to leave battle (14.84). Odysseus's concern is that the people will follow words that are not spoken soundly, and rise, in a unison born of passion, to unthinkingly obey the leader. And Nestor points to the general volatility of plebiscitary politics when he speaks of how the Achaians act "like children" when they hold assembly (2.337) because they too easily forget the work of war as they swing quickly from fear to enthusiasm.

Not only may a leader endanger the stability of the public space by speaking unwittingly to the people, but the instability of the crowd may undermine the recognition of good counsel. When Agamemnon speaks at the assembly upon Achilles' return, Agamemnon says that "it is well to listen to the speaker, it is not becoming / to break in [*hubballein*] on him. This will be hard for him, though he be able [*epistamenôi*]. / How among the great murmur of people shall anyone listen / or speak either? A man, though he speak very clearly, is baffled [*blabetai de ligus per eôn agorêtês*]" (19.79–82). Even the best counsel risks being lost in the noise of a disorderly crowd.

In two encounters between Hektor and Poulydamas, the volatility—and warnings—about plebiscitary leadership are most clear. At a critical juncture in battle, when deciding whether to continue to attack the Achaians or to retreat for the moment, Poulydamas says to Hektor, "Hektor, somehow in assembly you move ever against me / though I speak excellently [*phrazomenôi*], since indeed there is no good reason / for you, in your skill, to argue wrong [*parex*], neither in the councils / nor in the fighting, and ever to be upholding your own cause" (12.211–14). According to Poulydamas, Hektor continually uses the acclaim of the people to confirm his personal authority. To counter Hektor's sway over the people, Poulydamas calls for an "interpreter of the gods" who would be able to explain "the truth of portents, and whom the people believed in" (12.228–29). Hektor rejects Poulydamas's argument. The problem, as Poulydamas suggests later, is that Hektor is "too intractable to listen to reason" (13.726) because he believes that he possesses both prowess in battle and wisdom in counsel.

Hektor's willingness to play to the people has disastrous consequences for the later debate about how to respond to the reentrance of Achilles in battle. The decision is so important, and the fear so great, that the people cannot even sit (18.245–314). Poulydamas suggests that the army take a defensive posture behind the walls of the city rather than risking the onslaught of Achilles. Hektor speaks for the glory of victory over the Achaians rather than being "fenced in our outworks" (18.287). Homer, in this case, brings in his own perspective on the debate. Rather than listening to counsel and being open to possible arguments against attack, Hektor wins the debate through the "applause" (*epêinêsan*) of the people. It is an acclaim that comes because Athene has "taken away the wits" from the people" (18.311–12). Poulydamas, "who had spoken good sense [*esthlên boulên*] before them," received no applause (18.313). Like Agamemnon in the beginning of the *Iliad*, Hektor attempts to use the public space to affirm his personal authority. The results are as unpredictable as they are severe. In their unwitting endorsement of Agamemnon's suggestion in Book 2, the thundering acclaim of the people fragments the political field. And in playing upon the impulses of the assembly, Hektor imperils the survival of the community.

In this volatile political space, we can see the operation, however rudimentary, of a public ethic that attempts to balance the charismatic and public aspects of authority. Combining these two aspects, elites can gain glory through a "political heroism," not just by performing great deeds in battle but also by speaking great words in assembly. When Achilles withdraws from battle, he is portrayed as never again going either to battle or "to

assemblies [*agorên*] where men win glory [*kudianeiran*]" (1.490).
Similarly, Phoenix reminds Achilles that it is in "debate" (*agoreôn*)
that "men are made pre-eminent" (*ariprepees*) (9.441). As Schofield comments, in discussing the advice that Diomedes offers
in Book 9, "the crucial point for the present is that Diomedes'
speech is in its own way as much a feat of prowess as one of his
exploits on the battlefield."[40] We see a notion of distinction and
acclaim that corresponds to the words of the elite in the assembly of the people.

This political excellence rests, in part, upon the favor of the
divine (which is why Hera is associated with Achilles' calling of
the assembly in Book 1). But such excellence also rests upon an
ability to articulate a position in a public space. This political
language, as Martin's helpful analysis indicates, consists of public
speech acts (or *muthoi*) that involve a "performance" and a claim
to authority "before an audience."[41] Such political excellence
seems to rest on a number of factors. In part, there are rhetorical
abilities, including an ability to order words properly (the opposite of Thersites' disorderly, or *akosmos*, speech) (2.213),[42] and
the ability to speak concisely (*pauros*) (3.213, also 3.215) and
lucidly (*ligus*) (3.214). Physical gestures as well (3.216–19)
impart authority on the message. Antenor describes Odysseus,
for example, in a debate with Menelaos. When it was his time
to speak, Odysseus "would just stand and stare down, eyes fixed
on the ground beneath him, / nor would he gesture with the
staff backward and forward, but hold it / clutched hard in front
of him, like any man who knows nothing [*aidrei*]" (3.217–19).
Yet, his "voice" and "words" were second to no other mortal
(3.221). And political excellence requires virtues of the mind,
such as soundness (*artia*) (14.92) and "good sense" (*esthlên
boulên*) (18.313).[43]

An important part of this new political language is, as Nestor
explains to Agamemnon, an ability to speak for the good (*agathon*,
9.102). This is important because it both restricts the use of

public acclaim for one's personal power, and identifies a
responsibility by the leader to maintain the public, participatory
space. As Nestor advises Agamemnon, "When many assemble
together follow him who advises / the best counsel, for in truth
there is need for all the Achaians / of good counsel, since now
close to our ships the enemy / burn their numerous fires"
(9.74–77). On a number of occasions, the community good
assumes prominence in arguments or concerns of the leaders.[44]
Agamemnon, for example, says in the debate in assembly that
he will agree to give up his war prize because he "desire[s] that
my people be safe, not perish" (1.117). Later, Agamemnon will
lament that he will be dishonored because he has lost so many
of his people (2.115). Outside the assembly, the leaders appeal
to Paris to return Helen because the Trojan people are dying
(6.327). Ajax appeals to Achilles to return on behalf of the
"multitude [*plêthous*] of the Danaans" (9.641). And Hektor fears
that he will be shamed because he brought ruin to his people
by not listening to good counsel (22.104–107). We do not need
to view these moments as selfless gestures. Rather, these shows
of concern suggest a connection, often fragile, between individual excellence in words and deeds and the well-being of the
community. In this volatile political space, in which there is little
institutional mediation, the maintenance of community stability
requires a sobriety (2.99) on the part of the people, and soundness (14.92) and "good sense" (18.313) on the part of leaders.

When scholars dismiss the public role of the assembly, they
often do so by noting that the leaders make the ultimate decision, often in disregard of the opinion of the public. As Finley
states at one point, the "assembly was normally summoned by the
king at his pleasure" and the people "neither voted nor decided"
but simply expressed their "acclamation," which the "king was
free to ignore."[45] Andreyev, too, argues that the "people's assembly" is either a "docile tool in the hands of a small group of kings"
or ineffective on occasions when it does express an opinion

because it lacks any "legal force."[46] But this shows a misunderstanding of the nature of plebiscitary politics. As Weber indicates, the assent or dissent of the public in a plebiscitary form of government may at times be "only formal or fictitious."[47] Indeed, as we see with the intimidation of Kalchas and Thersites, as well as the disregard that Paris has for the request of the Trojan assembly (7.362), this is not a democracy. But that does not render these changes unimportant. A plebiscitary form of politics rests upon a system of values in which decisions are enacted in a public space and subject to community acclaim and sanction. This is a space constituted by both the elite and the *dêmos*.

PLEBISCITARY POLITICS, TYRANNY, AND DEMOCRACY

A plebiscitary form of politics is useful not only for making sense of authority relations portrayed in the Homeric world, but also for situating Homeric politics in later political developments, particularly the appearance of tyranny and the rise of more participatory forms of politics. Understanding the relationship between the eighth-century world of Homer, the rise of tyrannies starting in the seventh century, and the emergence of more participatory forms of government in the succeeding centuries has often been complicated by attempts to place these developments in an evolutionary trajectory from the coercive rule of monarchy or oligarchy to the popular rule of democracies. We have already seen that Homeric authority relations are more complex than this. The appearance of tyranny does not fit easily into this scheme, either. Tyrannies are often established at a point in which the public space and public protections are expanding, as with the rise of Peisistratus after the Solonian reforms. To account for this, some scholars have viewed tyrannies as either a monarchical "counterrevolution"[48] or the outcome of elite rivalry that is asserted on a quiescent public.[49] But viewing tyranny as a reassertion of monarchy makes it difficult to understand ancient testimony about the participation of the people in this form of rule. We are no better served, however, by reading tyranny as an "expedient"[50] to break down a closed system of "hereditary aristocratic dominance" and create "a much more 'open' society."[51] Tyrannies certainly altered the political landscape, breaking the political hold of traditional aristocratic families, reorganizing the citizenry, and increasing both the material and symbolic importance of the polis through public works projects, monumental architecture, civic and religious festivals, and the cultivation of art.[52] This argument becomes murky, though, when used to explain the political context from which tyrannies arose in the first place. Seeing tyranny as an expedient, and thus assigning democratic purposefulness to the public in looking to tyrants, faces several problems. First, we cannot explain why the very group that was interested purportedly in economic and political reform would rest content with tyranny for over thirty years in Athens, over seventy years in Corinth, and one hundred years in Sicyon.[53] Second, we cannot explain why the end of tyranny is sometimes resisted by the populace, as in Samos.[54] Finally, we cannot explain why popular rule sometimes precedes tyrannies, as in Heraclea Pontica and Mesopotamia,[55] and why, in these cases, a form of popular rule is sometimes restored (as in Heraclea Pontica) and sometimes not (as in Mesopotamia).

The notion of plebiscitary politics provides us with a way to understand both ancient testimony about the public's role in the establishment of tyrannies, and how democracies (or more participatory forms of rule) would emerge from tyranny. I am suggesting a relationship in which both tyranny and democracy emerged from the volatile plebiscitary political space that developed in the previous two centuries. In fact, this plebiscitary realm served as a laboratory for democracy, giving to the elite and the *dêmos* the practice, and, in turn, an evolving vocabulary, of public enactment. Plebiscitary politics was not a sufficient condition for democracy. But the existence of a plebiscitary space before tyranny, and the maintenance (and sometimes elaboration) of this space by the tyrants, provided the context for the discussion, expansion, and institutionalization of more democratic forms after the fall of tyranny.[56]

Aristotle lends important insight into this role of the people when he draws a distinction between an older form of tyranny, in which kings went beyond their hereditary power to establish a "more despotic rule" (*despotikôteras archês*), and a newer form, in which tyrants rise to power by gaining the trust or belief (*pisteuthentes*) of the people (*dêmou*) and the multitude (*plêthous*). This trust may be created by the tyrant portraying himself as one of the people, by speaking against the nobles, or by claiming to defend the people against injustice.[57] Aristotle calls this new type of tyrant a demagogue (*dêmagôgos*). In this context, the term does not refer to a politically conscious movement on the part of the people, but to a different form of tyranny that acquires legitimacy from a public space of the people.[58]

Oost, in downplaying the role of the people in the establishment of tyranny, suggests that *plêthos* and *dêmos* are used anachronistically by Aristotle. The mass of people "are not politically conscious yet." Rather, Oost argues, these terms more likely refer to support from a smaller group of the "hoplite middle class."[59] Though Oost is certainly correct that "demagogue" is a term developed later, and that the hoplites may have played a critical role in the formation of tyranny, he is incorrect in his characterization of the eighth- and seventh-century meaning of the *plêthos* and *dêmos*. We have seen from the Homeric epics that *plêthos* and *dêmos* refer to the common people, who are, indeed, capable of acting in concert. Such action has consequences for the leadership and the community even though the people may not act according to a coherent set of political principles. The *plêthos* of the sixth and seventh century, like the multitudes portrayed in the Homeric epics, did not initiate a political program, but they were not passive, either. And the leaders of the sixth and seventh centuries, like the Homeric elite, did not simply command, but enacted their decisions publicly to gain the acclaim of the people.

Aristotle's and Herodotus's conflicting stories of the rule of Peisistratus reveal this paradox of the public nature of tyranny. Though they differ in the conclusions they draw, both tell of Peisistratus's return from exile in which he enters on a chariot, led by a woman dressed as Athene. Whereas for Herodotus, Peisistratus dupes the people,[60] for Aristotle, Peisistratus gains power through the acclaim of the people. In his description of Peisistratus's first return from exile, for example, Aristotle points out that the people "fell to the ground and accepted him with awe." With his second return, Peisistratus had the crowd disarmed while he spoke. After the arms were locked away, Peisistratus "concluded his speech" and "told the crowd not to be surprised or alarmed by what had happened to their weapons; they should go home and look after their private affairs—he would take care of the state."[61]

We can make sense of the seeming paradox of a tyrant coming to rule through an appeal to the people by placing these activities in the context of plebiscitary politics. The notion of a plebiscitary space allows us to understand the role of the people in participating in the illusion of Peisistratus's "divine presence."[62] As Connor has pointed out, "The ceremony thus served as an expression of popular consent—two-way communication, not, as so often assumed, mere manipulation."[63] It is within this plebiscitary space that Peisistratus is able to gain legitimacy. But once in power, Peisistratus disperses the people from any public role even though, by Aristotle's account, he rules moderately. The collapse of the political field, as this case illustrates, need not rest on force but may result from the acclaim (whether sensible or not) of the public.

What stands out, not only in the accounts of Peisistratus, but in the accounts of other tyrants,[64] is the continual appeal made by the tyrant to the people, even if that appeal is duplicitous. This appeal is made not only in the rise to power but in the maintenance of power. Salmon suggests, for example, that a small council, a *probouloi* consisting of representatives from each of the eight tribes, and an assembly may have been established under the tyranny at Corinth. The assembly clearly did not decide policy. But suggestive of a plebiscitary form of politics, the *probouloi* may have served to convey the attitudes of the people to the leadership and, in turn, to guide the assembly to "take decisions which conformed with the views" of the council.[65] With the death of Polycrates in Samos, Maeandrius called an assembly (*sunageiras*) to set out the terms of his reign, though the assembly refused his conditions.[66] And Peisistratus is said to have kept both the political and legal institutions intact during his rule.[67] Though it is not clear what role the people played in the rule, it is likely that a council and some form of a people's assembly were established and consulted.[68] In his conclusion to his book on Greek tyranny, McGlew observes, "If tyrants presented themselves as liberators or founders, they must have understood the polis's power to judge them, for they were determined to finesse that judgment by appearing to act in the polis's interest, to deserve its honor, and to have passed its scrutiny." In comparison to earlier despotism, "the tyrant's relationship to his subjects was changing."[69] We can understand this changing relationship as one in which leaders—even tyrants— were expected to enact their decisions and their claims to authority in a public space.

This notion of a plebiscitary realm may be helpful, as well, in thinking about the relationship between the aristocracy and people in the development of democracy. There is a tendency in this debate to see the emergence of democracy as led either by an elite or a mass. Thus, Ober, in discussing the development of democracy in Athens, argues against the "view of history that supposes that all advances in human affairs come through the consciously willed actions of individual members of an elite." He suggests, instead, that the democracy in Athens "was the product of collective decision, action, and self-definition on the part of the demos itself."[70] In fact, Ober argues that in 508–507, when Isagoras and Cleomenes attempted to seize control of Athens, the *dêmos* initiated and carried through a democratic "revolution without leadership" that created a "rupture" between one "understanding of the world and another."[71] Raaflaub, on the other hand, points to the central role of the aristocracy in formulating notions of political equality as a response to tyranny.[72] The aristocratic notion of equality would, in turn, be expanded slowly to encompass a broader segment of the population, including the *thetes*. To make their incorporation acceptable to the elite, the "full political integration of the thetes" would require a "*massive and lasting* change in their economic or social status and/or communal function." Raaflaub traces this change to the role of the *thetes* as "decisive contributors to their city's security and power" as rowers for the naval fleet.[73]

Our notion of plebiscitary politics allows us to identify a much more paradoxical relationship between the elite and people. Not only may it have been the people who took part in the establishment of tyranny, as I suggested earlier, but it may have been the aristocracy who would draw on these plebiscitary relationships with the people to establish democracy.[74] The model suggested here does not require either individual moments of elite volition or revolutionary moments of mass consciousness, but is more interactive in creating the conditions for democracy.

The elite play an important role. As Raaflaub points out, "Tyranny deprived the aristocrats of such shared control of power, which now became a value that needed to be formulated, claimed, and fought for." It is in this context, according to Raaflaub, that "*isonomia* [equality before the law] and *isêgoria* [equality of speech] were created and became prominent." Elite articulation of these principles may well have underlain the resistance to attempts by Isagoras and Cleomenes to abolish the *boulê* in Athens.[75] In formulating these concepts, though, the aristocracy had to draw on an already developing *dêmos*-consciousness. The *dêmos*, who were of one mind (*ta auta phronesantes*) by Herodotus's account, played an important role, by acting to expel Isagoras and Cleomenes (Herod 5.73). But we do not have to posit, as does Ober, that this action marks the birth of a sustained, leaderless, and revolutionary program by the *dêmos*.[76] In fact, the textual evidence cannot bear the weight of Ober's interpretation. First, the elite are not irrelevant in this story but initiate resistance that is then continued at a larger scale by "the rest of the Athenians." Second, the *dêmos* does not create a program but are acting in the context of promised reforms by Cleisthenes.[77] And third, the description of the people as *ta auta phronesantes* certainly describes a civic consciousness, though there is nothing to suggest that it means an exclusive, revolutionary consciousness. As we saw in Homer, the *dêmos* is often depicted as acting in concert, sometimes in agreement and sometimes in disagreement with the elite. When Homer uses forms of *phroneô*, such as when Nestor recounts his agreement with Odysseus (*Od.* 3.128–29), the language often describes a common sense of purpose oriented to the community good.[78] Herodotus, too, seems to suggest a shared sense of purpose among the mass and elite when he links the actions. The elite resist, and then "the rest of the Athenians," who shared in this purpose, also resist (Herod 5.72).[79]

Herodotus, in fact, seems to depict the operation of plebiscitary politics in which mass and elite act, react, and, impor-

tantly, interact in a public space. After the fall of the Peisis-
tratids, Cleisthenes initially loses to Isagoras in the struggle
for power among the elite (Herod 5.69). So, Cleisthenes wins
over the people (*dêmon*) by promising them some political share
(*moiran*) (Herod 5.69). Having attracted the people, Cleisthenes
now emerges as stronger than Isagoras's faction (Herod. 5.69).
Herodotus is describing a plebiscitary realm in which Cleisthenes vies for power through an appeal to the people. This
account is supported by Aristotle, as well, who states that Cleisthenes wins the support of the people (*dêmon*), offering a share
(*apodidous*) of government to the multitude (*plêthei*) (*Ath. Pol.*
20.1–2).[80]

Herodotus continues, describing how Isagoras enlisted the
help of Cleomenes, from Sparta, to banish Cleisthenes and other
prominent Athenians, and attempted to dissolve the Council
(Herod 5.72). At this point, the Council resisted (*antistatheisês*),
Isagoras and his followers seized the Acropolis, and then "the
rest of the Athenians who were of one mind" (*Athênaiôn de hoi
loipoi ta auta phronêsantes*) joined together and besieged the
Acropolis (Herod. 5.72). By the third day, an arrangement was
made whereby the Spartans on the Acropolis were sent back
and the rest were sentenced to death (Herod 5.72). In Aristotle's account, the Athenians bring back Cleisthenes, who
becomes the leader of the people (*Ath. Pol.* 20.3). Herodotus
even says that Cleisthenes gave the Athenians their democratic
state (Herod. 6.131). In assigning an important role to both
Cleisthenes and the *dêmos*, Herodotus is not contradicting himself,[81] but describing a complex and volatile interaction between
the *dêmos* and the elite in which claims to authority must be
enacted among the people. Ober, in fact, seems to point to this
operation of plebiscitary politics in his own analysis. In his
earlier writing, Ober identifies a growing community consciousness of the people under the tyranny of Peisistratus.[82] And in

his discussion of the "Revolution" of 508–507, Ober notes how Cleisthenes, in his struggle against the Spartan tyranny, allies with the *dêmos*. As Ober points out, "Kleisthenes' leadership was not dependent on constitutional authority, but rather on his ability to persuade the Athenian people to adopt and to act on the proposals he advocated."[83]

For Ober, the "Athenian Revolution" of 508–507 B.C. is a revolutionary act of collective self-definition by the *dêmos*. But, as I have suggested here, we see this development of a shared space, both among the elite and with the *dêmos*, established much earlier in the creation of plebiscitary politics. Rather than being a "revolution in the demos' perception of itself and of an aristocrat's perception regarding his own relationship, and that of all men of his class, to the demos,"[84] this period marked a response by both the elite and the *dêmos* to the volatility of the plebiscitary space. The "Revolution" did not mark the creation of new relationships but a transformation of this plebiscitary space into a more stable, rational-legal configuration of office and law.

We have come far from our discussion of the Homeric world. The point is not that Homeric politics is important only as it contains the evolutionary seeds of later polis development; rather I want to suggest some of the complexity and implications of the notion of politics that we see articulated in the *Iliad*. The *Iliad*, I have suggested, does not fit easily into a pattern in which traditional values are restored after a crisis. Rather, the social drama of the *Iliad* invites a rethinking of the nature of relationships among the elite and between leaders and led. We see, most importantly, the constituting of a public space that is conditioned both by collegial relationships among the elite (marked most significantly by a claim to *themis* as a shared right) and by plebiscitary relationships with the emergent *dêmos*. This space is endangered (as is the community) as elites either fail to recognize the public claims of other elites or improperly use the plebiscitary space to stir the passions of the people. It is through human enactment that the contours of Homeric political thought emerge. And it is through such enactment, I will suggest in the final chapter, that we arrive at a Homeric reflection on our ethical relationship to others.

7

Toward a Political Ethic

νῦν δὴ καὶ σίτου πασάμην καὶ αἴθοπα οἶνον
λαυκανίης καθέηκα. πάρος γε μὲν οὔ τι πεπάσμην.

Now I have tasted food again and have let the gleaming
wine go down my throat. Before, I had tasted nothing.

24.641-42

I began this book by looking at the philosophic
rejection, beginning with Plato, of the epistemological status of
epic poetry. The problem with the Homeric epic for Plato is
that it imitates phenomenal appearance (*phainomena*) since it
depicts the shadowy world of human action. Unlike Homer,
whose art can tell us nothing about how to live because it merely
imitates what we already do, the philosophic craft, as it draws
its inspiration from the contemplation of truth, is capable of
producing political judgments of what conduct makes individuals better or worse (*Rep.* 599d). Overlaying this Platonic
argument in modern times is a Kantian distinction between
"pure moral philosophy" and other precepts that "may be only
empirical and thus belong to anthropology."[1] Moral philosophy
is seen as derived from abstract and universal principles that
impose a categorical duty on humans. Empirical precepts, such

as norms of behavior or even ethics,[2] are seen as culturally grounded and so not critically reflective.

Applied to the Homeric world, this distinction between moral philosophy and empirical concepts underlies a view of Homeric individuals as conforming to external cultural norms rather than acting and reflecting upon internal motivations of what is morally right and wrong. In Snell's influential formulation, Homeric man lacks consciousness of himself as making moral choices and an ability to reflect on those choices.[3] For Fränkel, no encounter occurs between an outside world and an "inner selfhood."[4] Homeric individuals possess only an "elemental vitality" in which they live in the joys and sorrows of the moment and act according to the "forms" of society.[5] Dodds would employ a now-famous anthropological distinction between "shame" and "guilt" cultures to describe the operation of the Homeric value system in which an individual's sense of right and wrong is governed by what the community will think of him or her, rather than by an internal sense of moral guilt.[6] And Redfield, in his anthropological reading, suggests that Homeric man "has no innerness" and is "incapable of development" because he "responds fully and uncritically to each situation."[7] From these perspectives, neither personal decision nor judgment is possible because no image exists of oneself apart from the norms of society.[8] Homeric man functions unreflectively as an expression of the external standards of society.

Yet, these formulations make it impossible to understand who or what is doing the conforming, and how the conforming even takes place. Even Redfield, who rejects any innerness to Homeric individuals, notes that in the shame culture of Homeric society, the "expressed ideal norm of the society" is "experienced with the self, as a man internalizes the anticipated judgments of others on himself."[9] Honor is not just the value of a person "in the eyes of his society," but, as Pitt-Rivers notes, it "is the value of a person in his own eyes." Honor, and its sanction of shame,

provides "a nexus between the ideals of a society and their repro-
duction in the individual through his aspiration to personify
them."[10] The recognition of how one's actions might damage or
enhance one's status, suggests Cairns, requires "a subjective
idea of one's own worth, an ideal self-image which is placed
under threat, and an awareness of the standards under which
one is liable to be criticized" or praised.[11] The claim by an individual that he or she was inappropriately dishonored, for
example, rests upon a particular image and valuation of oneself
as deserving honor. I follow Cairns in his characterization of
this valuation of oneself as "self-esteem."[12] Esteem, in the sense
used here, does not denote some authentic inner self but is *an
image of oneself in relationship to others* that necessarily involves
questions of how this self relates to "the demands, needs, claims,
desires, and, generally, the lives of other people."[13]

   Like politics, ethics is both cultural as it is tied to the expectations of society, and critical as it is shaped and reshaped in its
performance. The ethical self is an enacted self that must interpret and apply the standards of a community, as well as encounter
occasions in which community expectations are ambiguous, contradictory, or unsatisfactory. At the core of these enactments is
the notion of esteem. I identified in chapter 2 the cultural basis
of esteem, in that the warrior's sense of worth is tied to the
receipt of honor and glory for the performance of great words
and deeds in battle and assembly. I argued in chapter 4 that
Achilles interprets the loss of Briseis as a violation of his esteem
and responds by rejecting a notion of worth that is tied to recognition by others. In this chapter, I explore the critical aspect of
the notion of esteem by examining how Achilles comes to revise
his sense of worth through recognizing how his choices affect
him, as his choices affect others.

   The focus on esteem will serve as a complement in some ways,
a corrective in others, to recent discussions of the ethical transformation of Achilles. For Crotty, Achilles has initially only "the

most rudimentary sense of self" that is simply reactive to challenges to his superiority. Achilles' grief over the death of Patroklos, though, allows him later to "sense vividly" the suffering of Priam. In generalizing from his experience to Priam's, Achilles "reforms or restructures his sense of himself" to appreciate "the similarity of another's experience to his own." Crotty writes, "In appreciating his resemblance to another, Achilles no longer confines his reactions to the immediate stimulus but can see in another's distress the kind of danger to which he is *in general*, or *as a kind of being*, exposed." What becomes difficult to reconcile is the two people that Crotty portrays as Achilles. Up through Book 23, Achilles appears as Fränkel's "Homeric man" who, because he lacks innerness, can react only to "external stimuli." In Book 24, Achilles appears as a "more complex self" in which he is able to reflect on the experiences of others and establish new bonds outside the conventions of warrior society.[14] Rather than positing a reactive and reflective Achilles, we can better trace in Achilles a clarified sense of his own esteem in response to different experiences of suffering: the suffering of battle, the loss of Patroklos, and the pain excited by the sight of Priam.

Zanker, too, sees a "change of heart" in which the "affective drives" of pity, respect, and affection are emphasized in Achilles' actions toward Priam. This heroic magnanimity, as Zanker describes it, is made possible by Achilles' "unique experience and knowledge of death." Through his "deepened sense of mortality" and his "personal realization of the reality of death," Achilles acquires a "totality" of "vision" that is alone among other mortals and "outstrips even that of the gods." With this vision, Achilles is able to "attain to the companionship in suffering that he shares with Priam and the sublime generosity that he shows toward him."[15]

Zanker is not alone in emphasizing the importance of death in affecting the transformation or reintegration of Achilles.[16] These formulations are ambiguous, though, for it remains unclear what, precisely, it means to "accept" or "face" or have a "deeper" sense of one's death and how this is related to a changed comprehension of human relationships. Tying Achilles' development to his distinctive knowledge of death is particularly tricky because Achilles already has knowledge of his death that surpasses in certainty and clarity the knowledge of every other warrior. Yet, with this depth of knowledge, Achilles chooses variously not to fight, to fight savagely, and then to postpone fighting. In understanding Achilles' development, we may wish to avoid a language of comparatives (greater, lesser, deeper, fuller) in talking about death. This language creates ambiguities precisely because it implies a scale of measure that does not exist. We can better speak of how Achilles comes to understand death differently, and how that difference is related to a changing notion of esteem (as an image of himself in relationship to others).

Whatever his faults, the Achilles of Books 1 and 9 is neither reactive nor unwilling to face his death. As we saw in chapter 4, Achilles' response to the loss of his war-prize arises from a sense of esteem that he shares with the rest of the Achaians: worth is tied to the receipt of honor and glory by the community. When the community fails to show gratitude for his fighting, the struggle of battle appears not as a heroic pursuit of glory, but as a rather humiliating submission to suffering. More than that, though, this violation of esteem recasts Achilles' understanding of fate and death, since his willingness to risk his life for others no longer enhances his worth but appears downright foolish. Angered by Agamemnon's slight, Achilles seeks to restore his worth by humiliating those who brought him pain. The death of Patroklos, though, recasts Achilles' experience of pain since he becomes implicated in the suffering of another. The awareness of how he is implicated in the suffering of another provides the foundation for a more generalized expression of pity toward Priam. This awareness has political significance since it answers to the fundamental political problem that is raised in the *Iliad*:

how can communities, as political fields, endure since they are formed by human relations and consequently endangered by human collisions that can be neither foreseen nor controlled?

ESTEEM FOR ONESELF AND VULNERABILITY TO ANOTHER

The ethical problem in the *Iliad* is created, as Gregory Nagy notes, when Achilles refuses to fight.[17] We saw in this refusal a claim to self-sufficiency, in which Achilles will not be bound by others. He needs neither the honor nor the glory that others can provide. Nor does he feel a sense of obligation or pity to others born of any corporate bond. He derives his sense of worth, instead, from an ability to impose suffering without suffering himself.

In contrast to Achilles, Patroklos is moved by the suffering that has befallen the Achaians (16.22). Patroklos exclaims that Achilles is pitiless in his unwillingness to help (16.33) and dons Achilles' armor to fight in his absence.[18] Patroklos's death has the narrative importance of bringing Achilles back into battle.[19] As Nagy argues, for the "uninvolved audience of epic," the death of Patroklos and the pain Achilles feels is the "subject for *kléos*," or immortal glory. By avenging Patroklos's death, Achilles will achieve glory in "the epic tradition itself" since his story will be worthy of being told.[20] But, as Nagy notes, pain and glory operate at two levels in the epic. The glory of Achilles is heard and celebrated by the audience of the epic, but the pain is experienced as unforgettable by the characters involved.[21]

Pain points to the inextricable, and often immediate, connection between an image of oneself and one's relationship with others. In Achilles' earlier experience of pain, he saw himself as *suffering-from* the dishonor brought about by Agamemnon. Achilles' response is one of anger in which he seeks to restore his esteem by reversing this suffering, inflicting pain upon others while staying removed from the infliction of pain by others. With the death of Patroklos, though, Achilles experiences a *suffering-with*, in which his own pain is connected to the suffering of another.[22] Achilles does not feel the other person's pain. Nor does his sense of suffering from the afflictions of war end, as suggested by his anger toward Hektor (see 15.68). What is different is that Achilles is unable to dissociate himself, and his own sense of esteem, from the loss of another. This sense of suffering-with has cognitive significance since it alters Achilles' image of himself in relationship with others. As his suffering-with reveals his fundamental connectedness to Patroklos, Achilles begins to see himself as the occasion for (if not the cause of) Patroklos's death. Achilles begins to articulate a sense of being responsible for the death of Patroklos.[23] This responsibility is not so much the attribution of himself as a cause as a statement of Achilles' own failure to stand by (or be responsible for) Patroklos. What follows is an elaboration of how Patroklos's death revises Achilles' notion of esteem by making his sense of worth *vulnerable* to another who is *distinctive.*

ESTEEM FOR ONESELF AND VULNERABILITY TO ANOTHER

Upon hearing of Patroklos's death, Achilles pours dust on his head and face as he "fouled [*êischune*] his handsome countenance" (18.24) and "defiled" (*êischune*) his hair (18.27). Removed from the disgrace others can bring to him, Achilles now debases himself. The verb *aischunô* is used most frequently in the *Iliad* to describe the shame brought about to another through the mutilation and defilement of a corpse (see 18.180, 22.75, 24.418).[24] As Vernant notes in describing the relationship between the "heroic ideal and the mutilation of the corpse," the "hero's beautiful death, which grants him eternal glory," has as its corollary "the disfigurement and debasement of the dead opponent's body, so as to deny him access to the memory of men to come."[25] In this case, though, Achilles defiles himself and, in fact, remains covered in filth after he kills Hektor and even after the Achaians implore him to wash himself (23.40–42).[26]

In characterizing this mourning for Patroklos, Crotty suggests that it bears a similarity to the expression of pity (*eleos*), an expression that Crotty will suggest is later extended to Priam. For Crotty, "the appeal of pity is seen at its clearest in the context of intimate relations" where "the plight of one" becomes another's "own plight."[27] Though Achilles weeps, defiles himself, suffers, and wishes he were never born, he is never described after the death of Patroklos as pitying either Patroklos or himself.[28] The reason the language of pity is not used lies in Achilles' closeness to Patroklos. There are three occasions in which intimates are associated with pity: Andromache's appeal to Hektor (6.407, 431);[29] Achilles' response to Patroklos's crying (16.50); and Priam's appeal to Hektor (22.59, 82). Not only do these appeals fail, suggesting that pity is not most powerfully felt among intimates, but they are a vast minority of usages in the *Iliad.* More often, some distance exists between the pitier and the pitied, such as the pity of a god or the pity for one's comrades. To see an intimate (*oikeiotata*) suffer, as Aristotle suggests, is not to feel pity, but to feel oneself suffer as the other person.[30]

It is just this suffering, as a loss of a part of himself, that Achilles feels with the death of Patroklos. This loss is significant in altering Achilles' claim to happiness.[31] When Thetis reminds Achilles that everything he has asked for has been "brought to accomplishment [*tetelestai*] / through Zeus" (18.74–75), she recalls Achilles' own words to the embassy that he does not need the honor of others because he is already honored by Zeus (9.607–608). Yet, even with Zeus's honor, Achilles declares, "But what pleasure [*êdos*] is this to me, since my dear [*philos*] companion has perished" (18.80). Where Achilles' sense of suffering

led him previously to assert his esteem through a claim of self-
sufficiency, he now places his life in a relational context, suggesting that he loved Patroklos "equal to [*ison*] my own life"
(18.82, trans. modified). This equality makes it impossible for
Achilles to see his life as simply his own because he now shares
it with another.

Achilles articulates now a close connection between his own
sense of worth and his failure to take care of another. His failure
to act stands out in his mind because of his strength, "as no
other of the bronze-armoured Achaians / in battle" (18.105–
106). In describing himself as a "useless weight on the good
land" (*etôsion achthos arourês,* 18.104), an image that certainly
strikes at the heart of self-esteem, he connects this esteem to a
failure to take care of another. In Achilles' words, "I was not to
stand by my companion / when he was killed" (18.98–99).
Patroklos perished, laments Achilles, because he "lacked my
fighting strength to defend him" (18.99–100). Not only was
Achilles "no light of safety to Patroklos," but he was no help to
"my other / companions, who in their numbers went down
before glorious Hektor" (18.103–104). Achilles portrays himself
as an individual who failed to care for his comrades.[32]

Achilles' response to the death of Patroklos seems to point
toward a recognition of a more complex operation of fate than
he had suggested earlier, a recognition that underlies this
changing notion of esteem. In Book 9, Achilles declares that
there is an equality (*isê*) of fate in which death comes to both
the brave and the coward (9.318). Equality appears as the
finality of death that all mortals face alike (*homôs*) (9.320). As I
suggested in chapter 4, this equality is one which individuals
are alike, but not necessarily connected. After the death of Patroklos, though, Achilles comes to express a different relationship
between equality and fate. Achilles points to an equality in
which fates, such as the relationship between Patroklos and
Achilles, become shared through an inextricable connectedness

of one life to another. Fate is no longer an individual possession but a collision that occurs through the intertwining of choices and actions. When Achilles says that he will avenge Patroklos's death by killing Hektor, Thetis reminds him that his fated death (*potmos*) will follow (18.96). In Achilles' answer, he seems to recognize the necessary consequences of his choice: "Then I shall die [*autika tethnaiên*], since [*epei*] I was not to stand by my companion / when he was killed" (18.98–99, trans. modified).

This notion of fatefulness, in which destinies are fulfilled through their intersection and collision with each other, is integral to the narrative construction of Achilles' situation. In the opening verse of the *Iliad*, Homer portends this collision, since men are "set . . . together" (*xuneêke*) (1.8). The audience, like the gods, witness these collisions throughout the *Iliad*, while Achilles sees himself not as a part of, but as willing, these collisions. The death of Patroklos changes that, since it demonstrates the impossibility of a withdrawal from a world of collision. The knowledge of destiny that Achilles possesses is not wrong as much as incomplete because it does not, and cannot, account for the connectedness of humans to each other. As Achilles observes in his lament of Patroklos, "It was an empty word [*halion epos*] I cast forth on that day / when in his halls I tried to comfort the hero Menoitios. / I told him I would bring back his son in glory to Opous / with Ilion sacked, and bringing his share of war spoils allotted. / But Zeus does not bring to accomplishment [*teleutai*] all thoughts in men's minds [*andressi noêmata panta*]. / Thus it is destiny for us both to stain the same soil / here in Troy" (*amphô gar peprôtai homoiên gaian ereusai autou eni Troiêi*, 18.324–28). Hera confirms the incompleteness of Achilles' knowledge when she responds to Zeus that "Even one who is mortal will try to accomplish his purpose / for another, though he be a man and knows [*oide*] not such wisdom [*mêdea*] as we do" (18.362–63). What Achilles cannot know is how to confine the consequences of his actions to punishing Agamemnon.

Instead, Achilles' decisions affect, in unintended and unanticipated ways, both Patroklos and himself. We see the beginning
of an enlarged sense of Achilles' connectedness to others, not
simply as a cause of troubles for others, but as vulnerable to
their suffering.[33]

ESTEEM AND THE DISTINCTIVENESS OF ANOTHER

Through the death of Patroklos, Achilles experiences not only
a vulnerability to the suffering of another, but also a longing
that, ironically, he had promised the Achaians would feel for
him (1.240–44). Something has changed in the nature of this
longing, though. Whereas the longing of the Achaians would
be based on Achilles' value to them in war, the longing that
Achilles now experiences is for the loss of someone irreplaceable.
Even after Achilles has avenged Patroklos's death and honored
him through a funeral, Achilles' "longing [*potheôn*] for Patroklos"
continues, as he misses "his manhood and his great strength /
and all the actions he had seen to the end with him, and the
hardships / he had suffered" (24.6–8).

Suggestive here is Aristotle's discussion of the motivations
for friendship as those based on pleasure, utility, or a love of
another's character.[34] We do not have to read Aristotle's categories back into the *Iliad* to see how Achilles' regard for his
comrades is expressed earlier almost solely in terms of how they
can serve the ends of his desire for vengeance. Even when
Patroklos comes weeping to Achilles because of the pain (*achos*)
that has befallen the Achaians (16.22), Achilles' response is carefully cloaked in an instrumental language. Achilles allows
Patroklos (at Patroklos's urging) to defend the ships so that the
Trojans will not "take away our desired homecoming" (16.82).
Moreover, he tells Patroklos to "obey to the end this word I put
upon your attention / so that [*hôs*] you can win, for me, great
honour and glory / in the sight of all the Danaans, so they will

bring back to me / the lovely girl, and give me shining gifts in addition" (16.83–86). Achilles, to be sure, does not want Patroklos to die. But Achilles defines Patroklos's reentrance into battle almost solely in terms of how Patroklos (without dying) can serve Achilles' desire for vengeance.

Achilles never strays very far from an esteem for Patroklos. With his death, though, Achilles recognizes and articulates more fully his relationship to Patroklos as the esteem of another who is distinctive.[35] In the midst of desecrating Hektor's corpse, Achilles presents himself to the memory of Patroklos, saying: "I will not forget him [*ouk epilêsomai*], never so long as / I remain among the living and my knees have their spring beneath me. / And though the dead forget [*katalêthont'*] the dead in the house of Hades, / even there I shall still remember [*memnêsomai*] my beloved [*philou*] companion" (22.387–90). The poignancy of this statement is suggestive of the depth of the friendship. Nothing is to be gained, even potentially, from Achilles' promise of a continued enactment of his relationship to his slain friend. But this invocation is still more suggestive. Whereas relationships based on pleasure or usefulness are necessarily temporary, dissolving once the motives disappear, true friendships endure because they are based on an attitude of esteem.[36] As Aristotle notes, "When friends live together, they enjoy each other's presence, and provide each other's good. When, however, they are asleep or separated geographically, they do not actively engage in their friendship, but they are still characterized by an attitude which could express itself in active friendship. For it is not friendship in the unqualified sense but only its activity that is interrupted by distance."[37] In this case, Achilles' esteem for Patroklos will endure the distance of death and memory.

Achilles comes to express, as well, that which is distinctive in his comrades. Most notably, he rewards an extra fifth prize to Nestor in the funeral games, even though Nestor does not compete. As Achilles explain, "I give you this prize / for the giving

[*autôs*]; since never again will you fight with your fists nor
wrestle, / nor enter again the field for the spear-throwing, nor
race / on your feet; since now the hardship of old age is upon
you" (23.620–23). Achilles' esteem for Nestor is decoupled
explicitly from any further military contribution the old man can
make. And Nestor, in fact, seems to recognize this as he expresses
gratitude "that you have remembered [*memnêsai*] me and my
kindness [*enêeos*], that I am not forgotten [*lêthô*]" (23.648).

I have suggested, thus far, that Achilles' feelings of loss and
pain with the death of Patroklos have cognitive significance. In
particular, these feelings alter Achilles' earlier understanding
of himself as suffering-from the inflictions of others. With the
death of Patroklos, Achilles suffers-with Patroklos, unable to
separate his own suffering from the loss of another. This experience exposes the untenability of Achilles' earlier stance of self-
sufficiency. His sense of esteem, as an image of his worth in
relation to others, is modified in two ways. First, as his sense of
esteem is now made vulnerable to the loss of another, he comes
to define his own worth as premised on a sense of responsibility
or care for his intimate friends and comrades.[38] Second, and
related, this care rests upon an esteem for others as distinctive,
rather than as instruments of his revenge. What begins to
emerge in the context of intimacy and friendship is an esteem
for himself as connected to, and bearing some responsibility
for, the care and suffering of distinctive others. This altered
sense of his esteem for himself and esteem for another will
provide the basis for Achilles' response to Priam in Book 24.

ESTEEM AND THE EXPRESSION OF PITY

The pain of Patroklos's death does not immediately unite Achilles
with others. The incommunicability of the pain leads him to
stand apart from the other Achaians. The boundlessness of the

pain causes him to slaughter endlessly. And the inconsolability
of the pain drives Achilles not just to kill Hektor, but to attempt
to desecrate the corpse beyond recognition. This suffering, as
we have seen, underlies Achilles' sense of being responsible for
the loss of Patroklos. But it also leads to an inconsolability that
threatens to consign Achilles to a reactive cycle of anger and
vengeance that can know no end.

Against this backdrop of suffering, the poet creates a space
in which Achilles and Priam meet. There is both a literal and
figurative aspect to this space. Homer describes the contours of
this bounded space as a "towering / shelter" (*klisiên*) that is sur-
rounded by a "courtyard" with "hedgepoles / set close together"
(*pukinoisi*) (24.448–49, 452–53). As Lynn-George notes, the
association of *pukinos* with architecture describes structures that
are "closely constructed" or "well fitted together."[39] It is an image,
as it appears in Book 24, that suggests a return to "closure and
order" (a return that, as Lynn-George suggests, is also resisted).[40]
This architectural image is important for conveying in physical
terms the existence of a bounded space in which Priam and
Achilles meet. Within this space, Priam and Achilles encounter
each other's pain.[41] Achilles' and Priam's pains cannot be com-
pensated and their grievances with each other cannot be resolved.
But the pain that separates them initially—the grief that Priam
and Achilles have brought to each other—is now brought into
a common outline. The space of meeting, established in conflict,
now brings into the open "the intimacy with which opponents
belong to each other."[42] They appear to each other with the physical marks of their suffering-with another. Achilles, in his longing
for Patroklos, and Priam, as he mourns the loss of Hektor, have
both defiled themselves (18.22–27, 22.414, 24.162–65), suffered
sleepless nights (24.3–13, 24.637–39), and gone without food
(19.209–14, 19.303–308, 24.641–42).[43]

Whereas the funeral games appear as a ritual enacted by
the community to redress the schism between Achilles and

Agamemnon over the issue of authority, the meeting between Priam and Achilles addresses what Lord describes as the "feud" that erupts between Achilles and Hektor with the death of Patroklos.[44] Crotty and Seaford both have shown how this scene draws upon rituals of supplication: to invoke recognizable patterns of interaction "between individuals from different social units," to bring an end to Achilles' lamentation, and to establish some solidarity between Priam˙and Achilles.[45] I would suggest, as well, that this gathering is made possible by an ethical stance that, in its most fundamental sense, allows another to appear. This ethic is premised on the sense of esteem for oneself and another that is now generalized by Achilles from the intimacy of friendship to a pity for an enemy. Far from taking "place on the level of nature, outside the human world,"[46] as Redfield suggests, the meeting of Priam and Achilles has political significance since it points to the possibility of lending durability to this world.

Priam begins his appeal to Achilles by invoking him to "remember your father, one who / is of years like mine, and on the door-sill of sorrowful age" (24.486–87). As Crotty suggests, Priam summons a "memory of grief" in which Achilles is asked to "generalize from his own experience" of the death of Patroklos and the absence of Peleus "to another's similar experience of loss."[47] Priam attempts to establish a resemblance with Peleus, by evoking those "who dwell nearby encompass him [Peleus] and afflict him, / nor is there any to defend him against the wrath, the destruction" (24.488–89). But Priam as carefully distinguishes between his plight and Peleus's. Priam emphasizes in his next line that this harm has not yet befallen Peleus: "Yet surely he [Peleus], when he hears of you and that you are still living, / is gladdened within his heart and all his days he is hopeful / that he will see his beloved son come home from the Troad" (24.490–92). Peleus's hopes are, of course, in vain. But this qualification by Priam, which is seldom discussed, makes sense in the context of an appeal for pity.[48] Priam establishes a resemblance to Achilles' father, but does not establish an identity. In this way, Priam attempts to arouse in Achilles the impulse of pity that comes not from the sight of pain befalling an intimate, but the sight of pain that one fears may, *in the future*, come upon oneself or one who is close. A distance is maintained between the pitier and pitied that befits the relationship between the supplicated and suppliant.[49] Priam does not say, "Remember the suffering of your father and, from there, you can understand my suffering." He says, "Remember your father who may soon suffer as I do now."

Achilles' initial response to Priam's supplication is not pity, but mourning. Priam's words, as they recall images of suffering, "stirred" (*ôrse*) in Achilles "a passion of grieving [*gooio*] / for his own father" (24.507–508). Achilles pushes away Priam's hand gently, transforming their relationship into one of mourning (*stonachê*) (24.512). The "two remembered, as Priam sat huddled / at the feet of Achilleus and wept close for manslaughtering Hektor / and Achilleus wept now for his own father, now again / for Patroklos" (24.509–12). Depicted here is the expression of loss by both Priam and Hektor.

Only after Achilles "had taken full satisfaction in sorrow [*gooio*] / and the passion [*himeros*] for it had gone from his mind and body" (24.513–14) does he look to Priam "in pity" (*oikteirôn*) (24.516). But how can we explain this transformation from mourning to pity? And why would Priam's appeal for pity work now, and not for the embassy in Book 9? The answer lies in Achilles' ability to imagine himself in the position of another, an imagination that grows out of his experience of suffering-with another. Achilles first experiences this vulnerability when the death of Patroklos precipitates a corresponding loss of himself. The appearance of Priam now calls to mind Achilles' own vulnerability to the suffering of Peleus, as well. Whereas the vulnerability experienced through the death of Patroklos is immediate, the vulnerability to Peleus's suffering is both immediate, as Achilles experiences Peleus's absence, and more distant, as Achilles imagines the experience of Peleus. As Priam pleads for the return of his slaughtered son, Achilles sees himself through the eyes of Peleus as "a single all-untimely child" who gives his father "no care as he grows old" (24.540–41). The pain of Achilles' wandering is experienced as a loss of esteem, not as he is denied the recognition of others, but as he fails to care for his father (like he failed to care for Patroklos). In this projection, Achilles is able to imagine himself similarly through the eyes of Priam. Achilles appears to Priam as he does to Peleus: as the occasion for their suffering. After describing the suffering he has brought to his father, Achilles laments, "I sit here in Troy, and bring nothing but sorrow to you and your children" (24.542). Achilles is able to sense not just the suffering, but his own responsibility for the suffering that he now brings to Priam and has brought to Peleus.

Suffering, which once appeared as the fulfillment by Zeus of Achilles' wishes, now appears as a necessary consequence of the intertwining and colliding of fates. Whereas the "gods themselves have no sorrows" (*akêdees*) (24.526), states Achilles, mortals encounter both good fortune and evil. For those who receive from the "urn of evils," Zeus "makes a failure / of man, and the evil hunger drives [*elaunei*] him over the shining / earth, and he wanders [*phoitai*] respected neither of gods nor mortals" (24.531–33, trans. modified).[50] Achilles no longer sees himself as removed from mortal suffering, but as inextricably linked to the movement of fate in the mortal realm. Zeus's fulfillment of Achilles' oath, as he comes to see, brings about the death of Patroklos. Peleus, too, is stricken by Zeus: his father once "outshone all men beside for his riches / and pride of possession, and was lord over the Myrmidons" but now suffers from the evils of Zeus as his son sits "far from the land of [his] fathers" (24.535–36, 541–42). A similarly undeserved plight has befallen

Priam. As Achilles states to Priam, "And you, old sir, we are told you prospered once" and "you were lord once in your wealth and your children" (24.543, 546). But the "Uranian gods," continues Achilles, brought the Achaians, who are "an affliction [*pêma*] upon you" (24.547). Priam has been transformed from a lord to a suppliant, covered in dung, and soon to lose his city. What unites the suffering of Achilles, Priam, and Peleus is the collision of their fates: Priam is about to lose his home, Achilles will not return home, and Peleus will die alone.

The undeserved nature of Priam's suffering is heightened by Achilles' developing esteem for the king.[51] Achilles recognizes immediately a certain nobility in Priam's heart. Achilles asks, "How could you dare to come alone to the ships of the Achaians / and before my eyes, when I am one who have killed in such numbers / such brave sons of yours? The heart in you is iron" (24.519–21). This esteem will be expressed later, as well, when Achilles is described as seeing Priam's "brave looks" and listening "to him talking" (24.632). In this awareness is a comprehension of a "who" as a distinctive life story. Created in this encounter is a space, born of esteem for another, in which human life appears, not as an instrument of Achilles' revenge, but through its unique story.

TOWARD A POLITICAL ETHIC

With the death of Patroklos, Achilles enters a grief that is beyond endurance (*atlêton*) (19.367). When Achilles meets Priam, he tells the Trojan king to "bear up" (*anscheo*) (24.549).[52] They risk becoming frozen in grief, like Niobe who, "stone still, . . . broods on the sorrows that the gods gave her" (24.617), unable to reconcile themselves to a past for which they must suffer but could neither foresee nor control. But what can make such endurance possible, particularly given Achilles' description of a world of coming and going in which fortunes shift and lords become wanderers?

In addressing this question, scholars have often found recourse in the aesthetic of the meeting between Priam and Achilles. For Griffin, "From suffering comes song, and song gives pleasure." The hero endures, "not so much for his own glory, not even so much for his friends, as for the glory of song."[53] Redfield suggests, as mentioned earlier, that this reconciliation takes place at the level of nature, outside community. Whitman identifies an aesthetic awareness in their meeting: "Priam and Achilles see life whole, and with the freedom of men on the last verge of time, they forget the present circumstances, and admire each other's beauty."[54] For Rabel, pleasure is found "by a mortal hero's enjoyment in the reflection of his own ironhearted endurance in suffering."[55] And for Crotty, Achilles comes to recognize the "poetics" of the epic as he enters into a new kind of fellowship with Priam. This fellowship does not provide any "common project" or "cooperative effort" but serves only to enable Priam and Achilles to "better understand what each has experienced."[56] Out of this experience comes a vision of an "elemental human solidarity" in which Priam and Achilles are bound to each other through their common experience of suffering.[57]

What is striking in these formulations, but for a few exceptions,[58] is how this vision of human solidarity is elevated above or placed outside of politics and political community. This runs contrary to a continual linkage in the *Iliad* between private acts and public consequences, whether the lust of Paris, the greed of Agamemnon, the wrath of Achilles, or the pride of Hektor. The epic continually places these individual volitions in a public context, showing how communities suffer and, in fact, are endangered through the collisions of human action and reaction. The meeting of Priam and Achilles arises from these collisions and speaks to the fundamental political problem that is raised in the *Iliad*: how does one give endurance to communities made fragile by the very nature of human connectedness?

The *Iliad* answers that question by showing how pity provides the foundation for a political ethic that makes possible community life in the context of community suffering. Pity rests upon an awareness of the frailty of human affairs in which our connectedness to each other makes our deeds, in Arendt's words, both "irretrievable" and "unpredictable."[59] And pity is guided by a sense of care for others that makes possible the restoration of the bonds of community. No longer able to count on the gods, who "have no sorrows" (*akêdees*) (24.526) and who bestow good and bad fortune upon mortals, and no longer able to control the path to his future because of the interconnectedness of himself to others, Achilles now acts toward Priam in such a way as to make it possible to project themselves into a future.[60] Two actions, in particular, allow for this restoration: releasing and promising.[61]

The first of these actions, releasing, allows for the possibility of projecting the world into the future by answering to the irretrievability of action. The meeting between Priam and Achilles in Book 24 is premised, most obviously, on the release of Hektor's corpse. Thetis tells Achilles that the gods are concerned that he has not released (*apelusas*) Hektor's body (24.136; see also 24.113–16). The corpse, though, is the material manifestation of a deeper predicament. Achilles and Priam are "confined" to the consequences of their actions, which, by the nature of acting among others, they cannot now retrieve.[62] Releasing, thus, is not just a return of a body, but a freeing from an inner confinement to the past.

This confinement to the past is suggested both by the desire for vengeance and by the feelings of sorrow that cannot end. Vengeance, as a reaction to Hektor's deed, can neither end, because it is always a re-action, nor satisfy, because it cannot

reverse the original deed. Thus, Achilles seeks his vengeance not
only by killing Hektor and sacrificing twelve innocent Trojan
children, but also by attempting tirelessly, and without satisfaction, to desecrate Hektor's corpse. The unfortunate truth is that
Patroklos will not come back, no matter what form of vengeance
is taken. Without release, Achilles is caught in a reactive cycle that
knows no future. After dragging Hektor's body around the city,
he then drags Hektor's body three times around the tomb of
Patroklos (24.16), ending where he began.

The inability to release himself from the sorrow of loss is
suggested by Achilles' unwillingness to eat and drink. While
mourning, Achilles recalls how Patroklos used to prepare fine
meals for them (19.315–18). But now, sighs Achilles, "my heart
goes starved / for meat and drink, though they are here beside
me, by reason / of longing [*pothêi*] for you" (19.319–21). Thetis
asks Achilles, "My child, how long will you go on eating your
heart out in sorrow / and lamentation, and remember neither
your food nor going / to bed" (24.128–30)? Food and drink
will not pass Achilles' "dear (*philon*) throat" now that Patroklos
has fallen (19.210, trans. modified). As Benveniste notes, *philos*,
in modifying "throat," suggests the intimacy of association
between Achilles and Patroklos. Food and drink will not pass
his *philon* throat because "the sorrow of Achilles is that of a
phílos, and the feeling of having lost his *hetaîros* [companion]
makes him put aside all desire for food."[63] Food and drink are
not just necessary for human survival, but are aspects of associations of *philotês*, whether the friendship of intimacy, community,
or toward guests. The loss of a *philos* who is so dear renders
Achilles unwilling to participate in these activities of community.
The image of digestion appears, as well, in the use of *pessô* to
describe the confinement to one's sorrows. *Pessô*, which is associated with swallowing or digesting, also means "brood," suggesting a sorrow that does not go away but remains within the
person (as though indigestible). Niobe is unable to eat or drink,

but instead forever "broods" (*pessei*) about her sorrows (24.617). And Priam neither tastes food nor sleeps because he "broods" (*pessei*) over his suffering (24.639).

The meeting between Priam and Achilles allows for a release from the suffering each has brought. In telling Priam that he is "minded / to give [*lusai*] Hektor back" (24.560–61), Achilles experiences a release of the grief that had bound his heart in this reactive cycle of vengeance and sorrow. Before, Achilles' love of Patroklos had excluded any pity or care for the return of Hektor's corpse. Achilles dismissed Hektor's entreaty to ransom the corpse back to his family (22.338–43). Patroklos will be buried properly, proclaimed Achilles, but Hektor shall lie on the plain to be "foully" ripped by dogs and vultures (22.335–36).

In the expression of pity toward Priam, though, Achilles calls for the servants to wash, anoint, and clothe Hektor's corpse and then "Achilleus himself lifted him and laid him / on a litter" (24.581–90). The cleaning of Hektor, which parallels Achilles' treatment of Patroklos's corpse, does not signal a love of Achilles for Hektor. It does, however, correspond to the extension of the language of *philos* by Achilles. He is able to imagine his love for Patroklos as having a parallel in Priam's love for Hektor. This so clearly challenges the exclusive love that he had for Patroklos that Achilles even calls to his "beloved [*philon*] companion" not to be angry since he has given back Priam's "beloved [*philon*] son" to his "loved [*philôi*] father" (24.591, 619, 594).

This more inclusive language of *philos* is played out symbolically, since both Achilles and Priam can "remember" their dinner (24.601) and sleep.[64] While they were confined to the sorrow for one who is beloved (*philotês*), neither food nor drink could pass their dear (*philous*) throats. Like Achilles, Priam only broods (*pessei*) over his sorrow. Now, with the release of Hektor, both can taste food and drink again. As Priam exclaims to Achilles, "Now I have tasted [*pasamên*] food again and have let the gleaming / wine go down my throat. Before, I had tasted [*pepasmên*] nothing" (24.641–42). Through this release, the eternal brooding of Niobe, frozen in time by the impossibility of release, is replaced by images of eating, drinking, and sleeping.

While releasing answers to the irretrievability of the past, the second action, promising, answers to the unpredictability of the future. This unpredictability arises, as Arendt suggests, from "the impossibility of remaining unique masters" of what we do, "of knowing its consequences and relying upon the future."[65] The promise does not guarantee the future any more than it provides mastery over the present. What promising does is give some durability to human community by projecting it into the future. That is, the promise suggests a stance of responsibility for the future in which individuals, recognizing their connectedness, bind themselves to one another.

Promises, more than any other act, establish relationships that constitute Homeric political fields. Oaths, guest friendships, ties of reciprocity, and the distribution of material rewards all rest on promises that are essential to the maintenance of a community space. In fact, the Achaian community is jeopardized by its broken promise to Achilles when it retrieves the gifts that had been given. This broken promise prompts Achilles not only to refuse to fight, but to withdraw to a realm in which he will not be bound to others through promises or obligations. Achilles will be bound only by his promise to himself: that he will bring unendurable suffering and loss to the Achaian community.

Even in his reentrance into battle, Achilles promises only to Patroklos. He ignores Agamemnon's offer of his oath that he did not sleep with Briseis. And he rejects Hektor's offer of an agreement (*harmoniê*) that whoever wins should return the corpse to the community. Achilles' answer is telling, as he responds that he cannot make agreements (*sunêmasunê*) with someone whose deeds he will not forget (22.261). Caught in a reactive cycle of vengeance, Achilles is unable to make any such promise. "As there are no trustworthy oaths [*horkia pista*] between men and lions, / nor wolves and lambs have spirit that can be brought to agreement [*homophrona*] / but forever these hold feelings of hate for each other, / so there can be no love between you and me, nor shall there be / oaths [*horkia*] between us" (22.262–66). There is something distinctively human about this ability to promise, as it rests upon a like-mindedness (*homophrôn*) that only humans share.

Now, though, Achilles binds himself to Priam. When Achilles addresses Priam as "good friend" (*phile*) (24.650), he fulfills Priam's wish "for love [*philon*] and pity [*eleeinon*]" (24.309). This language not only signals the end of the feud, but is restorative by establishing a relationship in which they have become bound together through a promise.[66] Achilles asks Priam to tell him how many days will be needed for the burial of Hektor so "I myself shall stay still and hold back the people" (24.658). Priam responds, saying this "is what you could do and give / me pleasure" (*kecharismena*) (24.661). As Richardson notes, in other situations *charizesthai* means "to oblige someone."[67] Achilles seems to recognize his assumption of an obligation when he answers that this "shall be done as you ask it. / I will hold off our attack for as much time as you bid me" (24.669–70). Coming from Achilles, who has "destroyed pity" (24.44), such a promise that he will be this self in the future and honor the agreement would be met rightly with some hesitancy. And Achilles seems to recognize this as he grasps Priam's wrist "so that his heart might have no fear" (24.672). This act, following on his words, allows Priam and Achilles to move from eternal mourning to an anticipation of a future. Though Achilles will die in battle, he cares for himself now for the first time. Whereas before he remembered "neither . . . food nor going / to bed" (24.129–30), indifferent to his own future, Achilles now eats with Priam (24.601) and sleeps with Briseis (24.676). In contrast to Foucault's claim that "the care of the self is ethically prior" to a "care for others,"[68]

Achilles discovers that the care of the self, as a matter of self-esteem, is inextricably bound up with others.

Achilles' promise is unlike earlier promises in the *Iliad* because it does not rest on even the possibility of getting something in return.[69] Achilles knows he will die, and Priam knows his city will fall. Yet, this promise is significant because it allows the *Iliad* to close on the poignant image of a Trojan community space. In contrast to the scene in Achilles' shield in which the city's people await an ambush, now, in Priam's words, "Achilleus / promised [*epetelle*] me, as he sent me on my way from the black ships, / that none should do us injury until the twelfth dawn comes" (24.780–81). In promising to another, Achilles binds the Achaians to the Trojans. The promise is restorative of the public life of human community, as the Trojan people (*laos*) "all were gathered to one place and assembled together" (*êgerthen homêgerees t' egenonto*) to mourn and remember Hektor, to build a grave with stones "laid close together" (*puknoisin*), and then gather for a feast in Priam's house (24.789–90, 798, 802). The space itself is indeterminate since the fall of Troy is near. But the activity of human dwelling is preserved, as the *Iliad* ends with a moment of care that is set against the frailty of a world of coming and going.

POIESIS AND THE CALLING FORTH OF THE HUMAN WORLD

Throughout this book I have been asking, "What is it that the poet makes?" For it is around this question, though often unstated in scholarship, that so much of our understanding of the *Iliad* is built. For Plato, the craft of the poet is to imitate appearance and, so, the poet has little to say about how one should act. For Parry, a focus on the mechanical demands of oral composition overshadows any discussion of the meaning of the poem. Combining Plato's philosophic concerns with Parry and Lord's insights into the structural demands of oral composition, Eric Havelock contends that an oral consciousness places conceptual limits on the Homeric epic. The conscious task of the pre-Socratic, suggests Havelock, was to critique not just the content of Homer and Hesiod, but the error of thought that arises out of orality.[70] The claim of the pre-Socratic, argues Havelock, was that "the resources of poetry as commonly exploited in performances are unsuitable for the expression of philosophy" because of "the idiom of common speech and thought, which narrativizes our experiences, recounting it as a series of events, of becoming and perishing."[71] This error of thought extends to the "moral dimension" of the epic since morality appears simply as a "pragmatic response" to particular situations.[72]

There is a fundamental similarity in the activity of both an oral and philosophic language, though, that belies the distinction that Havelock draws. The activity of language, as Arendt notes, is "the human way of *appropriating* and, as it were, disalienating the world into which, after all, each of us is born as a newcomer and a stranger." Language is a way of making sense of and giving meaning to the world. Language does this in two ways: through the "naming of things," and through metaphors by which we relate things that are otherwise unrelated. Philosophy shares in this activity through the only way it can appear: namely, as it is manifested in language. The philosopher names the world, giving linguistic substance to the phenomena of "truth," "mind," "reason," and "soul." And philosophers relate the world through metaphor, creating analogies to bridge "the abyss between inward and invisible mental activities and the world of appearance."[73]

Plato certainly understood the importance of metaphor since he sought to appropriate the poetic task of "making" for philosophy. His philosophic language is replete with images from this world: of metals that constitute our capabilities, of the journey of the soul, of the philosopher as navigator, and of philosophic truth as the light of the sun. The objective system of thought that Havelock sees as characteristic of logos does not stand apart from the phenomena of appearance but appears more as "frozen analogies": metaphors used to describe relations of permanence. The pre-Socratics may have sought to create a conceptual vocabulary, but they did so, as Arendt suggests at one point, by going "to Homer's school in order to emulate his example."[74]

The point is not to downplay the importance of philosophic thinking. Rather, it is to suggest the close connection between poetry, philosophy, and thinking as an activity of language. Language appears not as a ready-made tool that the poet uses to make a poem, nor does language appear unconceptual since it is grounded in the particulars of experience. Rather, through language the poet calls forth a world. The poem becomes a world that is made familiar as the things of the poem are named and brought into relationship with each other. But it is a world that is neither purely fictive nor representative, since both terms suggest an unacceptable instrumentality and transparency to language. The poet, to be sure, uses the language, but the language, through the cumulating of tradition that describes the world, also uses the poet. In constructing a poem, the poet calls forth a world that the poet and audience know through language.

What is it that the poet makes? Even Havelock recognizes that the product of the poet, the poem, cannot be reduced to a purely instrumental expression of "how to." Such a reduction is impossible because the language that builds the poem is, itself, not reducible to a tool of the poet. Language resides in the world, and through language we reside in the world. It is a similar residing that the poet creates through the poem. The poem "gathers around itself" the relations of beings that make up the world: "birth and death, disaster and blessing, victory

and disgrace, endurance and decline" that "acquire the shape
of destiny for human being." In calling for, and allowing to
appear, the particulars of the experience of the world, the poem
"brings man onto the earth."[75] That is, the poem does not tran-
scend the human condition but presents us with, perhaps even
reminds us of, our condition as dwellers in the world: "To say
that mortals *are* is to say that *in dwelling* they persist through
spaces by virtue of their stay among things and locations."[76]

We are not talking here about the particular intentions of a
poet, whoever that poet may be, but about the attitude that the
poem evinces toward the world. The poet constructs a vision of
the world, rendering visible through metaphor the invisibility
of human yearning, desire, and pain, and bringing into relationship with one another the successive experiences that make
up the passing of life. Around this notion of fate, as the passing
of time, we see the philosophic contribution of poetic making.
For the poet does not fix time in the concept—to discern essences
that stand outside time—but understands how time conditions
our being in the world.

Plato is correct in seeing in the *Iliad* aspects of suffering,
vulnerability, remorse, and pity rather than investigations of that
which is immutable. He is incorrect in concluding that such
attention to the particulars of human experience serve only to
glut our emotions and tell us little about how to live. The importance of the epic is that it invites reflection on the exigencies of
human enactment. The epic moves us to a comprehension of a
political and ethical relationship to others, a relationship that is
grounded not in the philosophic world of autonomy, universality, invulnerability, and transcendence but in the Homeric
world of contingency, particularity, vulnerability, and imma-
nence. The story Homer tells us, like the story Achilles tells Priam,
is one in which we are moved toward a recognition of a shared
world, a recognition that arises not from outside but from within
a world constituted by experience.

Notes

INTRODUCTION

1. See Robb 1994.
2. Havelock 1983, 24, 19.
3. The view of the epic as uncritical is wide-ranging, as it is expressed by political theorists (Wolin 1960, 28), by classicists (Havelock 1963, 66; 1978, 14; 1983, 13; A. Parry 1956, 3; Adkins 1982; Adkins 1997, 713; Tandy 1997, ch. 7), by literary theorists (Bakhtin 1981, 13, 15–16, 35; Auerbach 1953, 16), in Hegelian readings of history (Snell 1982), in structuralist interpretations (Vernant 1990, 50), and in postmodernist arguments (Lyotard 1993, 18–23; 1989, 321). Textbooks, both old and new, conform to this view. Homer, in Catlin's *The Story of the Political Philosophers*, appears as the "barbaric" antecedent out of which a flourishing Greek culture emerged (1939, 40). Homer makes no appearance in Sabine's classic survey *A History of Political Theory* (1950), which educated a generation of scholars, nor is he mentioned in the three-volume textbook *Western Political Theory* (McDonald 1968), nor in Losco and Williams's *Political Theory* (1992), nor in McIlwain's *The Growth of Political Thought in the West* (1968), nor in Arnhart's *Political Questions* (1993), nor in Hallowell and Porter's *Political Philosophy* (1997). The Homeric epic makes a couple of appearances in Klosko's *History of Political Theory* (1993). But Homer appears there, as he does to Plato in *The Republic*, as either representative of uncritical thinking that preceded philosophy (1993, 1:2) or as a cultural backdrop with which philosophy had to contend (1993, 1:71–73). Homer shows up in Elliott and McDonald's *Western Political Heritage*, as

well, via the selection from Plato that banishes Homer from his politics. And no mention of Homer is made in Thiele's *Thinking Politics*, despite its interest in integrating different genres to explore "the art and craft of political theory" (1997, xv). Important exceptions exist. For discussions of the *Iliad* as containing aspects of political thought, see Raaflaub 1989, 2000; Flaig 1994, 31; Donlan 1973; Rose 1992; Osborne 1996a, 149–51, and in textbooks, see Bowle 1948, 44, and, more recently, Gagarin and Woodruff 1995.

    4. Edmunds 1989, 26.

    5. Several issues relating to the dating and composition of the *Iliad* need to be addressed here. My belief is that the *Iliad* assumed its current form in the second half of the eighth century (perhaps as late as the first half of the seventh century). I use Homer as a shorthand for the poet or poets who composed the *Iliad*. For an overview of what is known as the "Homeric question," which now appears as questions about both the authorship and dating of the epic, see Davison 1962; Schein 1984, 1–44; and F. Turner 1997. Evidence for dating the composition of the *Iliad* in the second half of the eighth century is provided by Raaflaub 1991, 1993, 1997b, 1998a; Kirk 1962, 282–87; Kirk 1985, ch. 1; Latacz 1996, 77–90; Janko 1982, 228–31; Morris 1986, 92–94; Rose 1997, 171; Tandy 1997; and Osborne 1996a, 157–58. Evidence for the composition of the epic in the first half of the seventh century is provided by West 1966, 46–47; 1971, 205; 1995; Burkert 1976; Taplin 1992; van Wees 1992, 54–58; 1994, 138–46; Crielaard 1995; and Dickie 1995 (with review by Papadopoulos 1996). My argument does not depend on this later dating. Though Homer draws extensively from an oral poetic tradition (see Nagy 1979, 1990; and Page 1959), the unity of its structure and images, as well as the creative reshaping of this tradition in the development of a unified plot, suggest (though it does not prove) the work of one poet. I tend to agree with Redfield (1994, 58) that while "stories can be borrowed, plots cannot; the invention of a plot is the essence of the invention of a (narrative) poem" (see also Whitman 1958). Finally, though the epic refers to an epic and heroic past, it is "near-contemporary" in meaning (Raaflaub 1998a, 181; see also Raaflaub 1993, 44; 1997b, 628; Morris 1986; Ulf 1990; van Wees 1992; and Redfield 1994). In creating the epic poem, the poet likely archaized, exaggerated, and drew upon memories and myths that "were still accessible by the audiences' collective memory" (Raaflaub 1998a, 181). But successful composition of the poem during performance requires that the poetry makes sense to the audience.

6. Lord 1960, 5.

7. See M. Parry 1987a, 1987b, 1987c, Lord 1960, and Ong 1982.

8. See M. Parry 1987b, 6–7, 16–17; 1987c, 276 (using the terms "length" and "thrift").

9. C. Edwards 1983, 161. See Lord 1960, 130.

10. M. Parry 1987c, 272.

11. M. Parry 1987b, 332, 195.

12. M. Parry 1987b, 195. See also Parry 1987a, 1987c, and Ong 1982, 20–27, 33–42.

13. M. Parry 1987b, 195.

14. Lord 1960, 5. See also M. Parry 1987c, 272.

15. Such concerns have been expressed by a number of scholars over the last several decades. See, for example, A. Parry 1971, Bolter 1977, Griffin 1980, and Hainsworth 1992.

16. Lynn-George 1988, 61.

17. M. Parry 1987d, 370. Parry distinguishes between formulaic and ordinary language (1987c, 304). For a critique of this distinction, see Bakker 1995, 100.

18. M. Parry 1987c, 272, 270. Russo points to the "central ambiguity" of the Parry-Lord approach as "its wish to equate poetic composition that *employs* formulas with the kind of improvised performance that *is completely dependent* on them" (1978, 40).

19. M. Parry 1987a, 156.

20. Walter Ong provides an important supplement to Havelock's discussion by formulating a more general conceptual framework for understanding the modes of thought and expression of an oral culture. Ong sets out several characteristics of oral expression, a few of which I will highlight here because of their importance in subsequent understandings of the contributions of the Homeric epic to political thought. First, Ong suggests that narration is additive rather than subordinative, much like Havelock's "tribal encyclopedia" (Ong 1982, 37–38). That is, whereas written texts can create subordinate structures that may be used to emphasize the primary themes, oral texts operate by juxtaposing elements next to each other (in what is called parataxis). The narration, thus, proceeds through an accumulation of verses and scenes. A second characteristic, which is related to the first, is that narrative discourse will make use of redundancy and repetition to recall and reemphasize particular themes (Ong 1982, 39–41). An implicit assumption built into these characteristics, and one that I will mention briefly now but develop more fully later, is that

repetitions reproduce themselves: that the appearance of similar verses, or formulaic repetitions of epithets for that matter, produces a sameness of meaning that contributes to the appearance of an inalterable and unreflective epic. As Ong suggests, since oral poetry proceeds through the memorization and repetition of conceptualized knowledge, any change appears as "formulas and themes are reshuffled rather than supplanted with new materials" (Ong 1982, 42). In contrast, written texts free the mind from memorization, allowing the mind to turn to "new speculation" (Ong 1982, 41).

Three other aspects of oral expression are noteworthy: that knowledge is presented as a story rather than through analytic categories (Ong 1982, 42–45); that oral stories are empathetic and participatory rather than creating, as with text, objectivity and distance (Ong 1982, 45–46); and that stories are situational rather than abstract (Ong 1982, 49–57). Ong is careful to point out that the oral mind is no less intelligent than the literate mind. What is different are ways in which we organize and understand experience. Oral poetry is capable of great renderings of human experience, but does not exhibit conceptual or analytic categories that allow the positing of causal sequences or the development of propositions from logical premises (Ong 1982, 57).

21. Havelock 1963, 66; 1978, 6, 13.

22. Havelock 1983, 13. See also Scholes and Kellogg, who argue that the "primary allegiance" of the oral poet is to "*mythos* itself—the story as preserved in the tradition which the epic story-teller is recreating" (1966, 12). Similarly, they view favorably Havelock's interpretation of Plato's assault on the poets to "free Greek thought, once and for all, from the tyranny of the 'grammar' of the oral tradition" (1966, 25).

23. Havelock 1983, 15, 14, 21, 19.

24. See Havelock 1983, 15–20.

25. Havelock 1983, 19–20.

26. Havelock 1963, 69.

27. Havelock 1978, 8, 9.

28. Havelock 1978, 14.

29. See Hainsworth 1992; A. Amory Parry 1971; Finnegan 1977, 1–29; Griffin 1980; and Holoka 1991.

30. See M. Edwards 1987, Martin 1989, Vivante 1970, 1982, 1985, Nagler 1974, N. Austin 1975, Fenik 1968, Russo 1968, M. Edwards 1987, and Reece 1993.

31. Ford 1992, 17, 18, 195, 170. Ford is influenced here not just by the oral culture work of Lord, Havelock, and Ong, but also by a

framework for understanding poetic creativity offered by Harold Bloom. Bloom, in an approach he describes as "Revisionism" (see Bloom 1982), attempts to get more directly into the mind of the poet, identifying in poets an anxiety about their precursors. Writes Bloom, in his introduction to *The Anxiety of Influence*, "My concern is only with strong poets, major figures with the persistence to wrestle with their strong precursors, even to the death" (1973, 5). This wrestling process, in which poets misread each other "so as to clear imaginative space for themselves," is, for Bloom, "poetic history" (1973, 5). Poetic history, which is the history of poetic influence, should be read not as a "history of ideas" nor "the patterning of images" but as the "study of the life-cycle of the poet-as-poet" (1973, 7). What the poet most rebels against, "however 'unconsciously,'" is the "consciousness of death's necessity" (1973, 10). The poet appears like "the anti-natural or anti-thetical man" who seeks an "impossible object" (1973, 10). And in the quest for this impossible realization, the poet seeks to destroy that which came before, to be free of "time's tyranny" of priority and succession (1973, 9).

32. Ford 1992, 202, 156.

33. Ford 1992, 195, 18, 202. Writes Auerbach (1953) on a similar note: "the Homeric poems conceal nothing" (11) since "the Homeric style knows only a foreground, only a uniformly illuminated, uniformly objective present" (5). The result is that Homer "cannot be interpreted" because there is nothing to interpret (11).

34. Ong 1982, 44.

35. Redfield 1994, 58, 23. See also Turner 1988, 21–22, 42. This relates to the "deictic" function of myth discussed in Jacopin 1988, 142.

36. That the *Iliad* is not simply performed for an aristocracy or on behalf of possible benefactors, but instead has a much wider appeal, is argued by Kirk 1962, 275; Scully 1990; Raaflaub 1991; Donlan 1993; Lenz 1993, 248–54; and Dalby 1995. Martin points to the agonistic dimension of the public performance of the *Iliad* when he writes that "this is poetry meant to persuade, enacted in public, created by authority, in a context where authority is always up for grabs and to be won by the speaker with the best style" (1989, 238). For a discussion of how the textualization of the *Iliad* from its oral tradition would still be "composed with a listening, critical audience very much in [the] mind" of the poet, see Robb 1995, 255–56.

37. Morris 1986, 87.

38. Raaflaub 2000, 26.

39. Stewart 1986, 43.

40. Writes James Boyd White (1994, xi): "Every speech act is a way of being and acting in the world that makes a claim for its own rightness, which we ask others to respect. Our life with language and each other involves the perpetual creation of authorities, good and bad, successful and unsuccessful." See also Butler 1995, 134, in her discussion of performitivity.

41. Arendt 1958, 187.

42. Felson-Rubin 1993, 161. Though Bakhtin, in "Epic and Novel," conceived of the epic as monological, I think we can profitably extend to the *Iliad* his approach, which "places dialogue in all its varied richness and nuances at the center of his interpretative universe, as opposed to a monologically conceived author, reader, or text" (Miller and Platter 1993, 118). See Bakhtin 1981, 1985, 1990. For an excellent discussion of Bakhtin's "anti-linguistics," see Stewart 1986. For recent applications of Bakhtin to Homeric scholarship, see Peradotto 1990, Emerson 1993, Rubino 1993, Felson-Rubin 1993, and A. Edwards 1993.

43. Morris 1986, 82–83. Morris has in mind the role of the epic as an ideological tool of the aristocratic elite (1986, 120–27). We can accept Morris's formulation of the active role of the epic without necessarily accepting his interpretation of this role. There is, as I will argue, more of a reflective dimension to the epic, one that is not simply a tool for the legitimation of the *basileis* (124) but is engaged in a critical examination of the basis of this power. Morris does recognize the possibility of critique as a part of "social formation" (124).

44. Turner 1988, 33. This notion of a "social drama" seems to give a cultural dimension to Lynn-George's notion of "epic theatre" (Lynn-George 1988, ch. 2).

45. Turner 1988, 34–35. For ritual aspects of the *Iliad,* see also Seaford 1994 and Russo 1978.

46. Turner 1988, 22. See also Turner 1981. This critical dimension of *mimesis* in the epic stands in contrast to interpretations offered both by Havelock 1963 and Auerbach 1953.

47. Turner 1988, 22; see also Turner 1981. See also Moore and Myerhoff 1977, 5.

48. Turner 1988, 27. This is consistent with scholarship that has noted elements of tension, dissonance, and even ideological conflict within the Homeric epic. So Anthony Edwards (1993, 54–55) has identified the "alien and potentially dissonant voice" of the countryside in

the *Odyssey* that "necessarily brings with it an ethics and an outlook fundamentally at odds with those dominating Homer's narrative." Others have identified, as well, the voice of dissent in the *Iliad* in the character of Thersites (see Donlan 1973, and Rose 1988, 1992). Qviller (1981) has pointed to tensions between the claim of the king who seeks to develop his position through the accumulation of wealth and the "egalitarian sentiments" (129) of his followers who demand a share of that wealth. The result is a structural conflict that points to the evolution of a *"polis-*society" (Qviller 1981, 134) in which the king's economic basis is weakened and the wealth of an aristocracy is strengthened since the king must buy, with his own wealth, aristocratic support.

49. See Donlan and Thomas 1993, 65. For discussions of how the epic portrays the world of the second half of the eighth century (or early seventh century), see Raaflaub 1998a, 1998b, 1997b, 628, 1993, 44; Morris 1986; Ulf 1990; van Wees 1992, 1994; Luce 1975; Tandy 1997; and Redfield 1994. For views of the epic as portraying an earlier time, see Finley 1979, 1981; Donlan 1997a, 1989b, 1985; Donlan and Thomas 1993; Andrewes 1967, 41–48; and Adkins 1960, 1997. For suggestions that the epic portrays a more recent time, see Stanley 1993 and Seaford 1994. Some have argued that the *Iliad* contains so many inconsistencies or inaccuracies, resulting from its composition over several centuries, that it cannot be interpreted as portraying any functioning society. Notably, see Snodgrass 1974, 1971; Kirk 1976, ch. 3; Coldstream 1977, 18; Kullmann 1995; Whitley 1991; Ruijgh 1995, 21–24; and Geddes 1984. Included in this latter group are the Analysts who sought to identify the historical layers of the poem. For an overview of the Analysts, see Dodds 1968; A. Parry 1987; Clay 1983, 1–7; and Schein 1984, 10–11. See Wolf 1985 (orig. 1795) for the seminal formulation of the "Homeric question" by the Analyst tradition and Page 1959 for a more recent approach.

50. Evidence for the existence of the polis in Homeric society is offered by Raaflaub 1997a, 1997b, 1997d, 1993, 1991, and 1988; Hölkeskamp 1997, 1994; Patzek 1992, 129–35; Morris 1986, 100–104; Murray 1980; Sale 1994; Nagy 1997; Scully 1990; Seaford 1994; Sakellarious 1989; Crielaard 1995, 239–47; Greenhalgh 1972; Thomas 1966; Luce 1975, 1978; Gschnitzer 1991; van Wees 1992; Rose 1992; Donlan 1989b; Havelock 1978; Hansen 1993; Qviller 1981; and Farenga 1998. Arguments against evidence of the polis (as a politically meaningful entity) in Homeric society are made by Finley 1979; Donlan 1980, 1985; Austin and Vidal-Naquet 1977; Runciman 1982; Starr 1961,

336; Adkins 1960; Halverson 1985; Manville 1990, 55–57; Hoffmann 1956; Strasburger 1982, 495; and Posner 1979. Hoffmann (1956) notes evidence of the polis but argues that the actions of Homeric heroes are not affected by political considerations. Corroborating evidence for the emergence of the polis in the second half of the eighth century is provided by Snodgrass 1980, 1991; Murray 1980; Finley 1981; Murray 1990; Ehrenberg 1960, 1967; Roussel 1976; and de Polignac 1995,

51. See Edmunds 1989, 27; Finley 1979, 34; Finley 1983, 9, 51–52; Scully 1990; Runciman 1982; Posner 1979; Wolin 1960, 28–29; Austin and Vidal-Naquet 1977; Calhoun 1962, 432–33; Snodgrass 1980, 44; Detienne 1996, 101; and Hoffmann 1956. There are important exceptions. See Raaflaub 1989, 1997c, Donlan 1989b, and Flaig 1994.

52. Meier 1990, 4, 5.

53. Wolin 1960, 28, 19–20, 29.

CHAPTER 1

1. Hansen 1993, 22; see also Hansen 1995. Hansen (1993, 1995) makes a persuasive argument that autonomy was neither a "defining characteristic" of the polis for Aristotle (Hansen 1995, 37) nor an empirically universal characteristic of early poleis. See also Alcock 1995, 331–34. There is the further problem that communities defined as poleis do not always have consistent institutional attributes. For example, Pausanias describes Panopeus as a polis, "even though she did not have political magistracies, a gymnasium, a theater, an agora, public buildings, a water supply modified by architecture, or regular housing of some complexity in a flat place" (Cole 1995, 295; see Pausanias 1898, 10.4.1).

2. For an example of this blending of an anthropological and Aristotelian tradition, see Manville 1990, 27–29, ch. 2.

3. For definitions of the polis as an autonomous entity, see Murray 1980, 63–64; Austin and Vidal-Naquet 1977, 40; Murray 1990, vii; Runciman 1990; Zaidman and Schmitt Pantel 1992, 7; Clemente 1991, 642–43; and Jeffery 1976, 39. Further citations are provided in Hansen 1995, n. 1.

4. Finley 1979, 34; see also Finley 1983, 51–52.

5. Finley 1983, 9.

6. Posner 1979, 27.

7. Halverson 1985, 129–30.

8. Hoffmann 1956, 155.

9. Edmunds 1989, 27.

10. Scully 1990, 109, 111, 107, 55, 112; see also 56.

11. Radcliffe-Brown 1940, xi. See also Evans-Pritchard 1952, 5.

12. Radcliffe-Brown 1940, xii.

13. Radcliffe-Brown 1940, xiv.

14. See Fortes and Evans-Pritchard 1940, 5–6.

15. See Easton 1959, 216–17.

16. Sahlins 1967, 90. See also Service 1962, 6.

17. For integration as a response to complexity, see Service 1962; Sahlins 1967, 91–92; Sahlins 1972; and Sahlins and Service 1960. For integration as a result of competition, see Fried 1967, 230. For integration as a combination of both factors, see Cohen 1978a, 15; and Cohen and Middleton 1967.

18. Donlan and Thomas 1993, 65.

19. See Donlan 1993, 155–56. It should be noted that Fried, Service, and Sahlins disagree on fundamental issues, particularly the nature of social evolution. Whereas Fried emphasizes stratification (the differential access to resources) as critical to state formation, Service argues that the impetus for state formation is integration in which early states can offer protection and coordinate activities. Stratification, for Service, is a result of state formation. What is interesting about Donlan's argument is the combination of these perspectives. Donlan focuses both on the integrative function with the emergence of the *basileus* (see Donlan and Thomas 1993, 68) and the stratification that underlies the anti-aristocratic bias in Homeric society and serves as "the basis for social change" (Donlan 1973, 154).

20. Donlan 1993, 155.

21. Donlan and Thomas 1993, 65.

22. Tandy 1997, 5. The framework that Tandy uses, which draws on Fried, Service, Donlan, and the economist Polanyi (who is, in turn, influenced by Malinowski), is fully developed in Tandy 1997, ch. 4–5.

23. The term "transformation" is purposely chosen by Tandy (1997) from Polanyi 1944.

24. Cohen 1978a, 15; Runciman 1982, 351. See also Cohen and Middleton 1967.

25. Runciman 1982, 351.

26. Runciman 1982, 351, 358, 355, 360. See also Finley 1979, 34.

27. Donlan, for example, begins his discussion of the "Pre-State Community in Greece" with an "analysis of the concepts 'household,'

'land,' and 'people,'" which established the "framework of the classical Greek community" (1989b, 16). Runciman (1982), too, begins by identifying the distinct functions performed by different institutions.

28. The genealogy of this conclusion, from a methodological orientation of structural-functionalism in anthropology, to a framework, used notably by Runciman and Donlan, to identify the nature of Homeric social organization, to an assumption about the prepolitical nature of Homeric society, can be easily traced. Finley, writing at a time in which few classical scholars were looking to anthropology, draws on Radcliffe-Brown 1952, Malinowski 1926, and Mauss 1967. Finley presents an interesting case, for in a later essay he would specifically reject structural-functional formulations of a state notion of politics (1975, 115). Finley's concern, though, was with an anthropology without history. He retains a notion of politics as tied to state structures (see 1975, 114). Runciman draws upon Cohen 1978a, 1978b, and 1978c, Sahlins 1972, Evans-Pritchard 1962, and Finley 1956 (2d edition published in 1979). Donlan looks to the work of Finley 1979, 1981, Fried 1967, Service 1962, and Sahlins 1968, 1972. Posner is influenced by the work on "primitive" societies (Posner 1979, 44) by Mair 1962, Sahlins 1967, and Finley 1979. Starr (1986, 42–46) draws primarily on Service 1975 and Hass 1982 in opting for a more integrationist approach to state development. Manville 1990 uses Cohen and Middleton 1970, Service 1975, Claessen and Skalnik 1978, and Cohen 1978a. Tandy 1997 draws on Fried, Service, and Donlan, and the economist Polanyi (1944), who was influenced by the anthropological work of Malinowski and who, in turn, influenced Finley. In other interpretations, we see a tendency to cite not the structural-functionalists but their classical interpreters. The consequence of this has been to import, often uncritically, a structural-functional set of assumptions about politics into their argument. For example, Halverson 1985 cites Finley 1979, Donlan 1981–82, and Runciman 1982. Scully draws from Runciman, Donlan, and Halverson 1985. On the role of anthropology in classical scholarship, see Roussel 1976, 99–103.

29. Donlan 1989b, 5, 12. See also Donlan and Thomas 1993, 66; and Donlan 1985, 298–305.

30. Donlan 1989b, 24.

31. I want to emphasize that Donlan seemed more aware of both the uses of structural-functional approaches in developing typologies and the limits of these approaches than those who have subsequently used his work as a point of departure.

32. Raaflaub 1989, 5. In this essay, Raaflaub (1989) makes one of the only explicit defenses of the "political thought" of the *Iliad* that I have encountered. See also Raaflaub 1997c; Holway 1989; Lenz 1993, 254; Farenga 1998; and Flaig (1994, 31), who concludes that the poet achieves political reflection in an atheoretical form ("Der Dichter leistet politische Reflexion in atheoretischer Form"). Mackie (1996) makes a distinction between the "political" language of the Achaians and the "poetic" language of the Trojans, particularly Hektor (1). I do not find this distinction particularly helpful for a number of reasons. First, the distinction rests upon a misinterpretation of Jakobson. For Jakobson (1960), the "poetic" describes a function of language. Politics is a type of message conveyed by a particular function. So, one could have a political message that was poetic, just as one could have a political message that was emotive or expressive (to name another function for Jakobson). Under Mackie's formulation, the characterization of the "political" as aggressive and the "poetic" as reflective (1–2) renders the activity of "political theory" and "political thought" as oxymorons. Second, Mackie suggests that Hektor's poetic inwardness is revealed in the tension between his desire for autonomy and his yearning for poetic recognition (117). It is precisely this tension, though, that strikes me as at the heart of politics.

33. Turner 1974, 37.

34. See Swartz, Turner, and Tuden 1966, 8; and Turner 1974.

35. Swartz, Turner, and Tuden 1966, 8.

36. Alc. fr. 112, and Thuc. 7.77. For a discussion of how the Greeks identified the state with a people more than with a territory, see Hansen 1993.

37. Swartz, Turner, and Tuden 1966, 8.

38. Writes Turner 1974, 37: "Religious and legal institutions, among others, only cease to be bundles of dead or cold rules when they are seen as phases in social processes, as dynamic patterns right from the start."

39. Turner 1974, 32; Arendt 1968c, 154, and 1958, 188. Václav Havel also uses this metaphor of the theater in talking about politics (see Havel 1997).

40. Turner 1974, 32.

41. Arendt 1968c, 154.

42. Swartz, Turner, and Tuden 1966, 8.

43. Arendt 1958, 184.

44. Arendt 1958, 187.

45. Kelly 1976, 19.

46. Raaflaub 1997b, 647. See also de Polignac 1995; Snodgrass 1982, 679; Snodgrass 1993; Raaflaub 1991, 1993. Stronger claims refer to this period as an "age of revolution" (Starr 1961), an "urban revolution" (Rose 1997, 171–77), a time of "transformation" (Snodgrass 1982, 679); and a "social revolution" (Morris 1997, 548).

47. See Powell 1991; Jeffery 1990; and Osborne 1996, 107–12.

48. On grave goods, see Popham and Sackett with Themelis 1980, 355–69; Catling and Lemos 1990; and Popham 1995a, 1995b. On the monumental tomb, see Popham, Calligas, and Sackett 1993. There is considerable debate about the function of the tomb. It is seen variously as a Heroon to honor and worship a community hero (Popham, Calligas, and Sackett 1993, 100), an "*anaktoren*" originally constructed for domestic use for a "hero and his consort" and then made into a tomb with their death (Crielaard and Driessen 1994, 264), or as a "monumental facility for ritual meals in honor of the dead," perhaps of a chieftain (Antonaccio 1995, 14). On bronze tripod molds, see Popham and Sackett with Themelis 1980, 96. For discussions of trade, see Popham and Sackett with Themelis 1980, 355–69; and Thomas and Conant 1999, 98–102.

49. See Blome 1984 and Antonaccio 1995.

50. Wathelet makes a linguistic argument that ties the Homeric epic to Euboea and suggests at the end that this would fit evidence of Euboea as a commercial center (1981, 833). West (1988, 166–72) and Powell (1991, 231–33) further develop the linguistic aspects of Wathelet and more fully draw upon archaeological evidence, including the Lefkandi finds.

51. For population trends across Greece, see Osborne 1996, 70–81; Snodgrass 1980, 1993, 31–32; Starr 1986, 38; Rose 1997. For discussions of particular sites, see Coulson, Haggis, Mook, and Tobin 1997 (Kastro at Kavousi on Crete); Coldstream 1991 (Knossos on Crete); Vlasaki 1991 (northwestern Crete); Cambitoglou, Coulton, Birmingham, and Green 1971 (Zagora); Roebuck 1972 (Corinth); Cook 1958–59 (Old Smyrna); Popham and Sackett 1980 (Lefkandi); Runnels and Van Andel 1987 (southern Argolid); Foley 1988 (the Argolid); and Fossey 1988 (Boeotia). In Boeotia, there is some resettling of old sites in the eighth century, but the largest population increases occur in the seventh century. For a cautionary note on the methodological problems of calculating the population density of settlements based on burial data, see Morris 1987, ch. 9.

52. Generally, see Coldstream 1977, 55; Tandy 1997, ch. 3; and Osborne 1996b. For evidence of increasing trade and prosperity during the eighth century for particular sites, see Popham, Sackett, and Themelis 1980 (Lefkandi); Coldstream 1991, 1994 (Knossos); Shipley 1987, 42–48 (Samos); Roebuck 1972 (Corinth); Salmon 1984 (Corinth); and Cambitoglou, Coulton, Birmingham, and Green 1971 (Zagora). In Argos, we do not see extensive imports and exports but the development, instead, of a fairly self-sufficient local manufacturing base and market in pottery and metal goods (Foley 1988, 56–57, 68, 96).

53. Evidence of social differentiation rests largely on identifying differences in the quality of grave-goods and votive offerings. For general discussions of this differentiation, see Morris 1987, 93–96, 140–55; and Coldstream 1977, 132–37. For discussions of evidence of social differentiation at particular sites, see Hägg 1983, 1974 (Argolid); Foley 1988 (Argolid); and Coldstream 1991 (Knossos). Evidence of differentiation is also inferred from the relative size of buildings. Most recently, see Thalmann 1998, 249–55 and references.

54. See Starr 1986, 38–39; Snodgrass 1980, 37–38; Rose 1997; and Tandy 1997, ch. 4.

55. This is where I would disagree with purely material explanations for politics. Tandy, for example, argues that "the polis came into existence when a newly institutionalized political and economic center undertook to exclude the peripheral members of the community from the economic mainstream" (1997, 5). Rose views the polis as emerging from an "intensified struggle over land" resulting from a shift to an agricultural mode of production and attendant population increases (1997, 180). My disagreement is not that material causes are unimportant but that they are incomplete explanations for the content of politics.

56. See Anderson 1991.

57. On hero cults, see de Polignac 1995, ch. 4; Antonaccio 1993; Nagy 1979, 115; and Qviller 1981. Such hero cults often began through increased votive offerings to Mycenaean tombs, frequently in homage to Homeric heroes (Coldstream 1977, 346–52). Examples of hero cults include cults for Academus near Athens, for Odysseus on Ithaca, and the Menelaion at Sparta. Examples of cult tombs to founder heroes include tombs for Alcathoos, the founder of Megara, and for Danaos, founder of Argos.

58. See Malkin 1998; de Polignac 1995; Sourvinou-Inwood 1993, 11; 1990; Morgan 1994 (Corinth), 1993, 19; and Snodgrass 1980, 33.

Civic deities include Athena at Athens and Sparta; Hera and Zeus at
Argos; Hera at Tiryns and Samos; Herakles at Herakleia; Artemis at
Methone, Ephosos, and probably Smyrna; Aphrodite at Knidos;
Apollo and Leto at Apollonia; and Apollo at Corinth, Delphi, Eretria
in Euboea, Thermon in Aitolia, and Dreros in Crete (Snodgrass 1980,
33; Cole 1995, 295). Snodgrass writes that it is only when dedications
are of a "marked and enduring bias that we can begin to infer any
deeper political significance (1980, 58). For difficulties in identifying
a single patron deity, see Cole 1995 and Burkert 1995. Communities,
suggests Cole (1995), would often look to a number of deities for
protection. For an excellent discussion of the civic importance of
religious life in the polis, see Sourvinou-Inwood 1990.

   59. Generally, see Snodgrass 1993, 30; Snodgrass 1980, 33, 56;
Snodgrass 1982, 680–85; de Polignac 1995, ch. 1; Coldstream 1977,
317–19, 346–47; Morgan 1993, 19; and Osborne 1996, 92–95.

   60. See Snodgrass 1980, 28–33; Crielaard 1995, 244–45; Scully
1990; and Hölkeskamp 1997, 5–7.

   61. On the development of public spaces generally, see Crielaard
1995, 243; van Wees 1992, 28–31; Scully 1990, 18, 101–102; and
Hölkeskamp 1997.

   62. Most importantly, see Morris 1987.

   63. See Snodgrass 1993, 33–34 (sanctuaries), 58–62 (monumental
temples); de Polignac 1995, 16–17; Starr 1986, 39–41; and Osborne
1996, 89–95. Coldstream 1977, 318–20, provides an index of more
than seventy sanctuary sites from the Geometric period, and de
Polignac 1995, 12, supplements this list with more recent finds. Monumental temple projects are seen by Snodgrass as evidence of "self-
assertion" and the "incipient rivalry of the new-born states" (Snodgrass
1980, 60). Such projects include the temple of Hera at Samos, the
temple to Apollo at Eretria, the temple at Gortyn in Crete, and the
temple constructed at the sanctuary of Apollo in Thermon in Aetolia
(see Snodgrass 1980, 58–59).

   64. Such infrastructures include a water collection chamber in
Corinth (Williams and Fisher 1971, 3–5) and what have been identified as granaries in Lefkandi (Fagerström 1988, 138).

   65. On the importance of town planning for understanding community formation, see Snodgrass 1993, 30. Sites that suggest evidence
of town planning include the town layout of Zagora (Cambitoglou,
Coulton, Birmingham, and Green 1971, 62; Coldstream 1977, 306);
paved road in Phaistos (Coldstream 1977, 278); roads in Vrokastro

(Hayden 1983, 374); regularization of housing structures on the Kastro of Kavousi (Coulson, Haggis, Mook, and Tobin 1997, 334) and Old Smyrna (Nicholls 1958–59, 124).

66. See Dunbabin 1948; Graham 1971; Cawkwell 1992; Osborne 1996, 119–29; Roebuck 1972 (Corinth); Salmon 1984 (Corinth); and Legon 1981 (Megara).

67. Crielaard 1995, 242. See also de Polignac 1994, 5–15; Morgan and Whitelaw 1991, 84; and Morgan 1993.

68. Thomas and Conant's recent book (1999) is a timely contribution that provides sketches of six different Dark Age communities.

69. Cambitoglou, Birchall, Coulton, and Green 1988, 237.

70. In the Argolid, for example, flourishing communities that developed in a relatively stable environment did not develop fortifications (Foley 1988, 28).

71. Generally, see Snodgrass 1980, 28–33. On the construction of the walls at Zagora, see Cambitoglou, Coulton, Birmingham, and Green (1971) and Cambitoglou, Birchall, Coulton, and Green (1988). Other city walls constructed in the ninth and eighth centuries B.C. include Old Smyrna (Cook 1958–59, 13–16; Nicholls 1958–59) and east Lokris (Dakoronia 1993).

72. Cambitoglou, Birchall, Coulton, and Green 1988, 167–68.

73. Sourvinou-Inwood 1990, 301.

74. Snodgrass notes that the earliest communities often appeared as a "community of cult" devoted to a particular patron god or gods (1980, 33).

75. Cambitoglou, Birchall, Coulton, and Green 1988, 158.

76. Cambitoglou, Birchall, Coulton, and Green 1988, 238. See also Fagerström 1988, 63–66, 138, 160.

77. Cambitoglou, Birchall, Coulton, and Green 1988, 241.

78. See Mazarakis Ainian 1997, 287–88.

79. For comparison of unit sizes, see Fagerström 1988, 65.

80. Cambitoglou, Birchall, Coulton, and Green 1988, 100.

81. Cambitoglou, Birchall, Coulton, and Green 1988, 79.

82. Mazarakis Ainian 1997, 372.

83. See Antonaccio 1993, 1995.

84. Unfortunately, graves have not been uncovered and many goods were likely taken along when the settlement was abandoned. Among the finds have been three bronze fibulae, three bronze rings that were likely part of a chain, a bronze "strainer," a lead figurine, an

iron sword tip, two seals, and a scarab that was an East Mediterranean imitation of an early Egyptian model (Cambitoglou, Birchall, Coulton, and Green 1988, 227–35). The "strainer" bears some similarity to a "grater" recently found at Lefkandi (Popham and Lemos 1995, 152). And the imitation of an earlier scarab would be consistent with elite efforts to identify themselves with prestige items.

85. Coldstream 1977, 279. See also Demargne and van Effenterre 1937, 10–11.

86. Coldstream 1977, 280.

87. See Fagerström 1988, 151–54, and Hölkeskamp 1994, 142.

88. See Demargne and van Effenterre 1937, 15–26; Miller 1978, 93–98 (who questions whether the building is a *prytaneion*); Coldstream 1977, 314; Mazarakis Ainian 1977, 389; Willetts 1977, 151; and Miller 1978.

89. Miller 1978, 4–18.

90. For dating of the inscription, see Jeffery 1990, 311. For discussion of the inscription, see Ehrenberg 1943; Willetts 1965, 68–69; Meiggs and Lewis 1969, 2–3; Coldstream 1977, 315; and Hölkeskamp 1994.

91. See Hölkeskamp 1994.

92. Ehrenberg 1943, 14–15.

93. Ehrenberg 1943, 17–18. See also Willetts 1965, 68; and Hölkeskamp 1994, 147–51.

94. See Hölkeskamp 1994, 153.

95. See Roebuck 1972, 98.

96. Reemergence of settlement: Salmon 1984, 39; population: Roebuck 1972, 103; Salmon 1994, 63.

97. Rihll and Wilson 1991, 76. This puzzle is most fully developed by Roebuck 1972.

98. Mortan 1994, 115.

99. Williams 1984, 12.

100. See Diod. 7.9; Oost 1972, 10–11; Roebuck 1972, 106; Salmon 1984, 56–57. The precise nature of the oligarchy is difficult to establish. Some have suggested that the single monarch was replaced by three elected officials: a *prytanis* (who performed royal functions), a *basileus* (who performed religious functions), and a *polemarch* (who collected fines [Nic. Dam. 90 F 57.5] and likely served as the chief military officer). See Roebuck 1972, 106; Will 1955, 298–306. Others have argued that the *prytanis* and *basileus* refer to the same official. See Oost 1972, 10–11; Salmon 1984, 56–57.

101. Roebuck 1972, 106.

102. Diod. 7.9; Oost 1972, 11; Roebuck 1972, 106; Salmon 1984, 56–57.

103. See Will 1955, 303–306. As early as the eighth century, a notion of citizenship or community membership may have been tied to land ownership. This connection is associated with Pheidon, a legendary lawgiver, who is said to have fixed land holdings so that the household with land and the citizen population would remain the same (Arist. *Pol.* 1265b12–16). Distinguishing the historical from fictional is notoriously difficult because communities quite often fashioned such a past to answer to contemporary issues (Eder 1986, 266–67). On Pheidon, see Salmon 1984, 63–64.

104. Blegan, Palmer, and Young 1964, 13. The change is not absolute. Some eighth-century graves were found in the settlement area (Young 1964, 13). See also Williams 1984, 11. The implications of changes in burial practices are discussed by Morris 1987, 1997; Osborne 1996, 82–88; Schmitt Pantel 1990, 201–202; and Morgan and Whitelaw 1991, 86, 94–95 (Argolid). The timing of this transformation varies. In Athens and Corinth, such a transformation begins around 750 B.C., whereas the transformation occurs later in Argos, Thebes, and Boeotia (Morris 1987, ch. 10; Morgan and Whitelaw 1991, 86). Identifying a point of transformation in Crete is difficult. In Knossos, one sees continuous settlement from the end of the Bronze Age and the continuation of burial in family chamber tombs from the tenth to seventh centuries B.C. But one also sees as early as the tenth century the apparent establishment and formalization of extramural cemeteries that contained both richer and "humbler" cremations (Coldstream 1994, 121).

105. Morris 1987, 8.

106. Corinthian commerce should not be understood as an early capitalist system in which community wealth derived from commodity production and exchange. But one sees the development of exchange patterns that belies the sporadic, opportunistic trade claimed by Finley (1979, 67; 1973; 1982). For discussions of Corinthian commerce, see Dunbabin 1948; Roebuck 1972, 116–18; Salmon 1984; and Morgan 1988. The earliest commercial space in Corinth is the famous Potters' Quarter, which consisted of a sixty-five-meter-long South Long Building, built in the late seventh century, and a more carefully constructed North Long Building built in the early sixth century (Stillwell 1948, 15, 20–21). Behind the buildings were "small shelters or storage places," pits for storing clay, and a network of water channels (Stillwell 1948, 17). There is the discovery of what has become known in later

scholarship, perhaps in a somewhat overstated fashion, as the "industrial sector." This area, which consists of nine shallow pits dug into bedrock, was likely devoted in the late sixth century to casting and forging iron and bronze (Williams and Fisher 1973, 14–15). Though there is literary attestation to the prevalence of Corinthian bronze, no significant archaeological evidence exists. Some of the tripods at Ithaca appear to be from Corinth (Thomas and Conant 1999, 127). Corinth is credited with the invention of the Corinthian helmet, as well (see Snodgrass 1964, 27–28). Further indicative of this differentiation of space is a "trader's complex" of the seventh and sixth centuries, which consisted of a several-roomed building with a concentration of imported wares with a similar geographical range (Williams, MacIntosh, and Fisher 1974, 23). And in the mid-sixth century there is the appearance of an installation for dyeing fabrics that would have been used for production of garments and rugs (Williams 1986, 134, and Salmon 1984, 119–20). Thomas and Conant (1999, 132) suggest that the increasing diversification of the economy likely required a "unified state with a distributed power structure."

107. Coldstream 1968, 353; Roebuck 1972, 112.

108. Roebuck 1972, 112–13; Salmon 1984, 62–63.

109. Roebuck 1972, 112–13.

110. Morgan 1994, 105.

111. Sanctuaries located in the vicinity of the agora: Apollo in Corinth, Eretria, Dreros (with Artemis), Gortyn (de Polignac 1995, 22), and Zagora (Cambitoglou, Coulton, Birmingham, and Green 1971). Sanctuaries located on an acropolis: Athena in Athens, Sparta, Argos, Mycenae, probably Tiryns, Miletus, Phocaea, and the cities of Rhodes (Lindos, Camiros, Ialysos) (de Polignac 1995, 21). Suburban sanctuaries: Apollo in Thebes, Argos, Halieis, Paros, and Naxos; those of Artemis in Sparta, Thessaly, Pheres, Delos, and Ephesus; Athena in Delphi; and a less monumental sanctuary of Demeter in Eleusis, Corinth, and Knossos (de Polignac 1995, 22). Extra-urban sanctuaries: Hera in Argos, Samos, Megara, Corinth, Pisa, and Elea (Olympia; together with Zeus); Apollo in Epidauros, Sparta, Acraiphia, Megara, Chios, Colophon, and Miletus; those dedicated to Poseidon in Athens (Sunium, with Athena), Corinth, and Calauria; Zeus in Cleonae; Aphaia in Aegina; and Artemis at Eretria on Euboea, in Mounychia and Braur (on riverbanks) or in the mountains (as in Kombothekra in Elis, Volimnos in Laconia, Lousoi in Arcadia, Kalapodi) (de Polignac 1995, 22; Cole 1995, 298; Morgan 1994).

112. Morgan 1994, 121. On the range of objects found at Isthmia, see Raubitschek 1998 and Morgan 1992.

113. Roebuck 1972, 108–109; Coldstream 1968, 353; and Mazarakis Ainian 1997, 154–55.

114. Morgan 1994, 135. For reports on deposits, see Payne 1940 and Dunbabin 1962. Different interpretations of Hera Limenia are provided by Sinn 1996 and Fagerström 1988, 157 (n. 188).

115. See Huxley 1969, ch. 5. See Pausanias 2.3.

116. See Pausanias 2.4.3 and Thuc. 2.40.2. The fullest account of the legend is provided in the scholia to Pindar (*Scho. Pi.* N. 7.155). For dating this legend to the eighth century, see Parke 1967, 130–31; Morgan 1988; and Morgan 1994, 137.

117. There are two different legends that link a cult of Medea to an earlier cult of Hera Akraia. Medea's children, according to one legend, are murdered in the temple of Hera. In another story, Medea herself murders her children and then establishes an annual sacrifice and feast to Hera in atonement. See Pausanias 2.3.11 and Broneer 1942, 158.

118. See Verdelis 1962 and Morgan 1994, 136–38.

119. The story goes that Hellotia, a daughter of the Aeolian king, threw herself and her sister into the flames of the temple of Athena during the invasion by Aletes. In supplication to the gods for this death in a sanctuary, Aletes established the festival of the Hellotia (see *Sch. Pi.* O. 13.56, and Broneer 1942, 140, 158). Little is known of the origin of the cult of Kotyto, or even when and how Kotyto died. The oils that have been associated with this public sanctuary, though, are typical of private funerary offerings (Steiner 1992, 403–406).

120. De Polignac 1995, 152. Hall, in a similar vein, discusses how "ethnic groups actively employed material culture in marking boundaries that had already been discursively constructed" (1997, 142). See also Sourvinou-Inwood 1990 and Cole 1995, 297–98.

121. 1.39, 1.440 (Achaian camp), 2.303–307, 2.549–51, 4.445–48, 6.297–310, 7.83, 8.47–48, 9.404–405, 22.169–72, 23.144–48. See van Wees 1992, 28–31.

122. 6.297, 305. Burkert notes that the Trojans as a community (rather than a particular family) made Theano priestess of Athena in Troy. He sees this action as evidence of the assumption by the polis of control over religion (1995, 203).

123. See 2.603–604, 10.414–16, 11.166–69. See Price 1973,

124. Streets: 2.12, 4.52, 5.642, 6.391, 20.254. Agora: 2.788–89, 7.345, 18.497. Washbasins: 22.153–55. Walls: 2.529 (Tiryns), 2.646

(describing Gortyn, which was not walled until the eighth century), 3.141–55, 6.373, 7.449–53, 12.28–32, 36, 121–23, 258–66, 390, 397–99, 424, 453–62 (gateway), 16.702–703, 18.274–76, 514–15, 22.4, 35–89, 455–65.

125. For a discussion of the Achaian community as a temporary polis, see Murray 1980, 64; Raaflaub 1991, 244–45; Raaflaub 1997b; Raaflaub 1997c, 23; Raaflaub 1993, 47–48; and Osborne 1996, 150. For discussions of altars within the Achaian camp, see 1.440, 448, 11.806–807. For references to assemblies within this Achaian community, see 1.53–325, 2.53–397, 7.381–412, 9.9–178, 11.806–807, 15.283, 19.34–276.

126. Raaflaub 1997c. For a discussion of the demarcation of sacred spaces in the eighth century and in the epic, see Sourvinou-Inwood 1993.

127. Achaian assemblies: 1.490 (Achilles), 4.400 (Diomedes), 9.441 (Achilles), 16.387 (general), 18.106 (Achilles), and 18.497 (shield). Military strategy: 2.53–397. Administration of "rights": 11.806–807. Witnessing of judgments: 18.497–508, 23.573–611. Resources: 23.543–54, 1.126; compare 1.161 to 23.544; see Nagy 1990, 269. Burial: 23.111–12; 23.160, 163, 23.258; see Burkert 1985, 191–92.

128. This sentiment argues against Greenhalgh's suggestion that there is "no expression of Panachaean responsibility in the *Iliad*" (1972, 533).

129. See also 9.441.

130. Qviller 1981, 144.

131. See 2.786–810, 7.345–79, 7.414–20, 11.139

132. See 8.489, 18.245, and 12.211.

133. See 11.166, 371–72 (*tumbô Ilou*), 24.349.

CHAPTER 2

1. Meier 1990, 5.

2. See Wolin 1960, 28–33.

3. For a discussion of early commentary on the role of the gods in Homer, see Feeney 1991 and Long 1992.

4. Gill 1996, 37.

5. Nussbaum 1986, 4.

6. It should be noted that the gods are not the only impediment to an understanding of Homeric agency. For some scholars, notably Snell and Vernant, what is lacking in the *Iliad* is a conception of action

as arising out of self-conscious determination. Important critiques of this argument have been made by several scholars who have identified in the Homeric characters conceptions of a self as deliberating and willing. Notably, see Williams 1993, Gill 1996, Gaskin 1990, Sharples 1983, and Nussbaum 1986. I share Gaskin's observation that the intervention of the gods does not detract from "the individual's autonomy or responsibility for the action" (1990, 6). I do not share his conclusion that this "has been conclusively demonstrated" by other scholars (1990, 6). These conclusions, as I will argue, are often premised on harmonizing the universe—that is, removing any notion of chance—by showing how divine interventions fulfill what likely would have happened anyway.

7. Nussbaum 1986, 3.

8. Dodds 1957, 15, 13, 18.

9. Snell 1982, 29, 30.

10. Snell 1982, 31; see also Snell 1930.

11. Snell 1982, 31–32.

12. Erbse 1986, 297, 299. See also Erbse 1990.

13. Vernant 1990c, 44.

14. Vernant 1990b, 50.

15. Gunnell 1987, 77–78.

16. Adkins 1960, 2, 3, 22, 23.

17. Greene 1944, 13, 14.

18. Burkert 1985, 122 (1977, 195).

19. Bremer 1987, 33–42. For the application of the concept of "focalization" to the *Iliad*, see de Jong 1987a, 1987b, and 1997.

20. M. Edwards 1987, 134. In his discussion of the role of the gods, Edwards (1987, 134) provides a list of the different functions of the gods. If there is an organizing principle to this list, it is that the frivolity of divine action contrasts with the suffering of mortals. This is true enough, but does not provide a basis for understanding why and how the characters respond to this seeming contrast. See also Adkins (1960, 15): "Evidently Apollo's presence lessens the disgrace of Patroclus' defeat; and to lessen this, as will appear, is of the utmost importance."

21. M. Edwards 1987, 136.

22. Redfield 1994, 229.

23. Havelock 1978, 50, 42. Plutarch, too, in "How the Young Man Should Study Poetry" (*Mor.* 23F–24C), notes that "those phases of causation which baffle our logic" were attributed to the gods by Homer before there was the name "Fortune."

24. Pucci 1998, 198.

25. Barnes 1974, 123.

26. Griffin 1980, 162.

27. Schein 1984, 62.

28. See Williams 1993, Gill 1996, Gaskin 1990, Sharples 1983, and Nussbaum 1986.

29. Nussbaum 1986, 20.

30. Douglas and Wildavsky 1982, 8.

31. Wildavsky 1987, 4.

32. Douglas and Wildavsky 1982, 8. Though not specifically addressing issues of chance, the work of Mary Douglas (1966, 1978, 1982) has been most useful in helping me think about this issue. See also Thompson, Ellis, and Wildavsky 1990. This cultural approach does not posit a deterministic view of human perception. Quite the opposite. Cultural theory suggests that although we enter a cultural environment of shared values and corresponding patterns of social relations, we, in some sense, are involved in "testing" these shared meanings, not against an objective, real "risk" but against whether a way of life is able to deliver "on the expectations it has generated" (Thompson, Ellis, and Wildavsky 1990, 3–4). See also Douglas 1978, 5–9.

33. Finley 1979, 75.

34. See Yamagata 1994, 203, 189, 202–207, 187, 236.

35. Nagy 1979, 184.

36. Yamagata 1994, 236.

37. Vernant 1991, 36.

38. Donlan 1993, 160, and von Reden 1995.

39. Finley 1979, 98. See also Donlan 1993, 160.

40. Muellner 1996, 34.

41. Douglas 1978, 23.

42. See Vernant 1991, 68. Further suggestion that such funeral ceremonies are consistent with a divine order occurs when Zeus ensures that the body of his fallen son, Sarpedon, is cared for so that it can receive its proper burial.

43. See Muellner 1996.

44. Writes Edmunds (1975, 191), "From the point of view of most Greek literature prior to Thucydides tyche is objective and is connected with the divine. Tyche comes from outside and is what befalls one." See also J. H. Finley 1942, 312–14, and Berry 1940, ch. 1. It is important to recognize that in the *Iliad* chance does not have the status of the divine, such as the later figure of Fortune. But *tugchanô*

does carry with it a meaning of what befalls someone (or something), most often in the *Iliad* in reference to hitting or striking (or missing) something with an arrow or spear. However, the gods, as we will see, are not unrelated to the notion of chance.

45. See M. Edwards 1987, 135. See also Lesky (1961) in his discussion of "double aspect" in Homer in which the human and divine realms provide distinct, but interdependent, perspectives on action.

46. This contrast to modern, "impersonal" notions of chance is also pointed out in Cornford (1907, 107).

47. The aorist of *thrôskô* is used at 7.182 and the aorist of *orouô* at 3.325.

48. This seems consistent with the later use of the lot by the Greeks for receiving counsel.

49. See Dodds (1957) for a discussion of the notions of the irrational in Homer.

50. I understand decision in this context to correspond more to the broader notion of desiring than the narrower, modern definition of thought out. See Vernant 1990b.

51. Yamagata 1994, 187.

52. Lattimore (1951) translates *mêdea* as "intention." I have chosen the word "plan" to avoid making assumptions at the outset about notions of agency.

53. Kullmann 1985, 8.

54. Redfield 1994, 230.

55. Willcock 1970, 6–7. Schein (1984), in his overview of Homeric thought, essentially agrees that the gods are not causal agents but means of calling attention to the greatness of the victor. Schein (58) argues that although "no rational explanation is available" for many of these "supernatural interventions," they are "explicable in terms of the poem's poetic structure, and in terms of what has been said about Athene and heroic success." However, Schein does not include in his discussion Willcock's (1970) notion of the spirituality of the experience of divine intervention. Schmitt (1982) argues that the intervention of the gods tends to match the capabilities of the humans. So, too, Gaskin argues that divine interventions "match capabilities and propensities autonomously present in the agents affected"(1990, 6).

56. See 3.439–40, 8.141–43, 15.724–25, 22.279–86, though Hektor is mistaken in this last case.

57. Lattimore (1951) translates this as follows: "and well he deserves it." I have chosen to avoid the term "deserve" because of its

contemporary moral connotations. In particular, it becomes difficult
to figure out why Eumelos would deserve a prize he did not fairly win.

58. Adkins 1960, 56.

59. Willcock 1970, 7.

60. Vernant 1991, 50–74.

61. See Douglas 1978 and Thompson, Ellis, and Wildavsky 1990.

62. Rawls 1971, 12.

63. See Douglas and Wildavsky 1982, 97.

64. While working on this piece, I came across this statement by
Bill Gates, founder and CEO of Microsoft, Corp., published in an airline
magazine: "This willingness to take risks is supported by American
culture, which admires effort when it ends in defeat. The United
States lets people rebound. The American attitude toward failure is
'try again'" (Gates 1995, 61). Strikingly, Gates both identifies and
reaffirms the construction of chance in an individualist culture.

65. Snell 1930, 150–51.

66. Vernant 1990b, 49–50.

67. Williams (1993, 142) depicts this space as a moment of choice
an individual may have that exists before the convergence of outcomes
that display "the shape of the purposive." Thus, action still takes place
outside the purposive space of the Homeric world.

68. Williams 1993, 40. See also Gaskin 1990 and Gill 1996, ch. 3.

69. This "self in dialogue," a phrase used by Gill, is discussed by
Gaskin 1990, ch. 1, and Gill 1996. Other examples of such deliberation of characters appear in 11.403–10, 17.90–105, 21.552–70, and
22.98–131.

70. Lattimore (1951) translates this phrase as "pondered doubtfully."

71. Adkins 1960, 47.

72. For a discussion of the importance of "trying" as part of a
Homeric ethic, see Long 1970, 124.

73. This helps us understand why *tugchanô* in its past perfect form
is related to having brought something to fulfillment. See, for example,
14.53 and 14.220.

74. Williams 1993, 41.

75. See Adkins 1960, 37–38, 40, 50, 52. See also Adkins 1997. This
is a problem not unique to Homeric culture but faced by all hierarchic
cultures. See Douglas and Wildavsky 1982, 90–91.

76. For a discussion of the centrifugal forces placed on Homeric
communities, see Donlan 1980, ch. 1, and Finley 1979.

77. Long 1970, 138.

CHAPTER 3

1. Finley 1979, 82–89; 1981, 81.

2. Finley 1979, 110, 82, 115. This also seems to be Sale's (1994, 9, 29, 60) understanding of Achaian politics, which he then contrasts to more developed Trojan political institutions.

3. Edmunds 1989, 27–28.

4. Luce 1978, 3.

5. Muellner (1996) places the crisis in the context of Agamemnon's violation of order in dishonoring Achilles. The result of Agamemnon's actions is to incur the "cosmic sanction" of Achilles' *mênis* (1996, 131). The argument I am offering here can be understood as looking at the political implications of this violation. Rose sees this crisis as reflecting an eighth-century "struggle *within* the ruling element over the issue of one-man rule vs. the collective exercise of power by aristocrats who view themselves as formal equals" (1997, 181). Whereas Rose sees the *Iliad* as advocating "one-man rule by the *best* man" (1997, 185), I find the very notion of "the best man" as resting on a more collective notion of leadership.

6. On reciprocity and authority relations, see Donlan 1997b and 1998. On the friction between "position and standing," see Donlan 1979.

7. Finley 1979, 115.

8. Taplin (1990) discusses this aspect of Agamemnon as unjustly cruel.

9. The comparison to the former Soviet bloc is striking at this point. The day-to-day response by Eastern Europeans to Soviet rule was one of quiet compliance in which public actions and statements were kept to an absolute minimum. Any thoughts that this compliance suggested active agreement with Soviet rule were dealt a sharp blow by the disdain with which these nations treated the Soviet legacy upon removal of fear.

10. Achilles' response to protect Kalchas points, in part, to a problem with Tandy's view of the "big man" as exercising control over the themes of the singer. Tandy specifically includes seers, including Kalchas, as subject to this same control (1997, 188). Aristocrats certainly exercised influence. But where I differ from Tandy is in his assumption that the aristocracy was itself of one voice. This assumption is necessary for Tandy to make his argument that the epics were "part of a contrived, broad effort to establish and support a self-conscious

aristocratic class" (152) and for his schematic of social control, which flows from "the big man" to the singer and then to the audience (175).

11. Pucci 1998a, 189, 183.

12. Pucci 1998a, 191.

13. Finley (1979, 111) suggests that Thersites' outburst provides an opportunity for Homer "to write a little essay on social classes and the modes of behaviour proper to each." Other scholars have not been so sanguine. To the extent that Odysseus is acting as a king, some scholars have been bothered by the violent use of the scepter by Odysseus in suppressing the "ugly truth" (Whitman 1958, 161, 261; see also Stanley 1993, 55). Others have pointed to the unsettling aspects of this episode since Thersites' questions remain even after his voice is silent. See Rose 1988, 1992, and Donlan 1973. I am inclined to agree with those who see in this episode certain unsettling aspects.

14. See Easterling 1989, 110–11; McGlew 1989; and Lenz 1993, 243–44.

15. Easterling 1989, 111.

16. Russo 1978, 48.

17. See Haubold 2000.

18. Taplin (1990) views Agamemnon as essentially a cruel, unthinking king. Agamemnon's role is seen in one recent interpretation as simply that of a "flawed king" that, as he conflicts with the hero, has become a "political irrelevancy during the archaic period" (Stanley 1993, 295). For a view of Agamemnon as a more complex character, see Griffin 1980, 70–73.

19. Arendt 1972, 143.

20. Arendt 1958, 203.

CHAPTER 4

1. See Schein 1984, 109; Beye 1993, 116; J. White 1984, 51; A. Parry 1956; Redfield 1994, 93; Nagler 1974, 157–58; and Arieti 1986, 16.

2. See Friedrich and Redfield 1978, 285; Claus 1975, 17; and Donlan 1993, 171.

3. See West 1966, 274, 276, and Gschnitzer 1981, 162.

4. Forms of this word are associated with changing dwellings, as well, in Hesiod *Theog.* 401 and Herod. 7.161.

5. Arieti 1986, 23–24. Heroes are often sons of gods. Sarpedon, for example, who is a son of Zeus, provides what is seen by many as the clearest articulation of the heroic code (12.310–28).

6. Hainsworth 1985, 144.

7. Gschnitzer 1981, 29, 162.

8. Arist. *Pol.* 1278a37.

9. Mireaux 1959, 241–42, 257. See also Starr 1982, 430; Austin and Vidal-Naquest 1977, ch. 2–3; Snodgrass 1980; and Raaflaub 1997b, 636–37. Some indication of the fluidity of the Greek world is suggested by Starr, who points out that at least one-half of the potters and black- and red-figure vase painters we know of in Athens had foreign names (1982, 430).

10. Raaflaub 1997b, 636. See also Finley 1978, 72–73.

11. The adoption by Achilles of the "rhetoric of slaves and the countryside" also appears when he compares himself to a mother bird who provides food for her young but receives nothing for herself. See A. Edwards 1993, 69.

12. Turner 1974, 39.

13. See Turner 1974, 23–59, 231–71, and 1988, 33–71.

14. On autonomy as a way of life, see Douglas 1978, 42–43; Thompson 1982; Wildavsky 1987, 3–21; and Thompson, Ellis, and Wildavsky 1990.

15. Whitman 1958, 193.

16. See also von Reden 1995, 21, who suggests, "Yet as Achilles has lost the prize of valour, he has lost the faith in human society in which recompense is supposed to be granted for risking one's life before life is lost."

17. See Zanker, who suggests that Achilles narrows the meaning of *moira* from portion to simply death (1996, 81).

18. Arist. *Rhet.* 2.8.2. Helpful in my thinking about the expression of pity is Konstan 1999.

19. Arist. *Rhet.* 2.8.2.

20. Zanker 1996, 23, 92.

21. Arist. *Rhet.* 2.2.3. For statements of Achilles' anger, see 1.192, 1.224, 9.260–61, 9.299, and 9.646.

22. I have translated *chreô* as "want."

23. Benveniste 1973, 288.

24. Donlan 1993, 165.

25. Stanley 1993, 116.

26. Arieti 1986, 16.

27. Whitman 1958, 191. It has always troubled me why Homer would compose a dialogue in which neither side understood the other. It seems far more satisfactory to at least hold open the possibility of there being some understanding, albeit profound disagreement, about the values each party brings to the conversation.

28. See Arieti 1986, 17–18, and Beye 1993, 137.

29. Whitman 1958, 187.

30. Saxonhouse 1988, 36, 34–35.

31. The inadequacy of this claim is consistent with a number of statements throughout the *Iliad*. See 4.32, 13.729, and 22.670.

32. Arist. *Pol.* 1253a3–7, 1253a32–34, 1253a38–40.

33. Arist. *Pol.* 1253a29.

34. For a critique of this Aristotelian approach to interpreting the *Iliad*, see Rose 1992, 46–52.

35. Jaeger 1967, 8; Whitman 1958, 218; Redfield 1994, 218; see Saxonhouse 1988, 40–44.

36. See Havelock 1978, 131–33.

37. Turner 1974, 240.

38. Whitman 1958, 206. Jaeger sees the rhythms of the shield as revealing the "deep sense of the harmony between man and nature" in which life is seen as "governed by universal laws" (1967, 50–51)

39. Schadewaldt 1959, 357, 363, 369. Writes Schadewaldt, "Der Schild des Achilleus ist nicht in einer wirklichen Werkstatt, sondern der Gedankenwerkstatt Homers entstanden" [The shield of Achilles did not come into being in a real workshop, but rather in Homer's mental workshop] (357). Though not discussing the shield of Achilles, Heidegger seems to give philosophic expression to this notion of art. He rejects art as representational (1971b, 37). Instead, he suggests that art "gathers around itself" the relations of being: "birth and death, disaster and blessing, victory and disgrace, endurance and decline acquire the shape of destiny for human being" (1971b, 42).

40. Schadewaldt 1959, 363. Schadewaldt notes: "Mit seinem Entschluß, den toten Freund an Hektor zu rächen, hat Achilleus sich selbst zum Tod entschieden, und der Tod steht ihm von nun an zur Seite. In diesem Augenblick gibt der Gott ihm seinen Schild in die Hand, dessen Wahrzeichen das Leben selber ist" [With his decision, to take vengeance on Hektor for his dead friend, Achilles has submitted himself to death, and from now on death stands at his side. In this moment the god puts the shield, the emblem of which is life itself, in his hand.] (1959, 371). See also Taplin 1980.

41. Reinhardt 1961, 405.
42. Atchity 1978, 175. Atchity writes that the shield is a "prephilosophical conceptual statement" that universalizes the "visionary scope" of the poem (1978, 160, also 173).
43. Schein 1984, 141–42. See also M. Edwards 1987, 284–85.
44. Atchity 1978, 175.
45. Becker 1990, 145.
46. Strife: 4.440, 5.518, 5.740, 11.3, 11.73; Confusion: 5.593; Death: 2.302, 12.326.
47. See, for example, 5.140, 5.161, 11.113–22, 11.173–76, 11.472–84, 15.585–88, 15.630, 16.156–62, and 16.485.
48. Turner 1986, 102.

CHAPTER 5

1. Rose notes that the factors associated with social position, including "'inheritance, remote divine sanction, age, personal wealth and number of followers,'" are "subjected to withering irony" (1997, 185, quoting Donlan 1979, 53). Rose argues that the epic defends the principles of achievement on the battlefield and the leader's "generosity in his direct relationship with his followers" as a basis for legitimacy (1997, 186, 192; see also Rose 1992). My discussion broadens this argument by looking at how principles of achievement take on a particular political meaning.
2. For discussions that emphasize such ascriptive characteristics, see Donlan 1979 (conflict between "position authority" and "leadership authority"); Calhoun 1962, 434–38; Easterling 1989; Lenz 1993; and Mondi 1980.
3. For discussions that emphasize the power of leaders to reward and penalize, see Donlan 1998, Andreyev 1991a, McGlew 1989, Qviller 1981, Rihll 1991, and Carneiro 1981 (on chiefdoms generally)
4. To use a slightly different language, though leadership maintains an ability to coerce and to reward ("condign" and "compensatory" powers in Galbraith's terms), what changes is "conditioned" power, or a change in how people believe power should be exercised (Galbraith 1983). This change in belief is associated not with personal qualities but with the organizational basis of power. For an application of this notion of power to the *Iliad*, see Rihll 1991, though I disagree with her conclusion that we see in epic the conditioning of values

supportive of a move toward monarchy (49–50). For suggestive arguments about the development of conditioned power that place the *basileis* in a larger public context, see Donlan 1997b (who uses Weberian categories); Raaflaub 1997b, 641–45; 1997c; 1997e; and Gschnitzer 1991.

5. For useful contrasts between ancient and modern conceptions of rights, see the collection of essays in Ober and Hedrick 1996.

6. The term is from Lenz 1993.

7. Gschnitzer 1965.

8. Glotz 1930, 7. See also Maine 1888, 35.

9. Bonner and Smith 1930, 9.

10. Benveniste 1973, 382, 323–26.

11. Köstler 1968, 180, 175.

12. Köstler writes, "Die Ordnung ist patriarchalish. Alles kommt auf die Persönlichkeit des Königs an" [The order is patriarchal. Everything depends on the personality of the king.] (1968, 182).

13. Jones 1956, 28.

14. Deger-Jalkotzy 1970, 80–88.

15. Easterling 1989, 114.

16. Lenz 1993, 217, 81–82.

17. Mondi 1980, 203, 205, 208, 205, 206.

18. Lenz, for example, specifically rejects the scepter as a symbol of public authority (1993, 160).

19. See, particularly, Gschnitzer (1965) who argues convincingly against seeing the Homeric *basileus* as a remnant of a Mycenaean monarch.

20. Mondi 1980, 208–209.

21. Mondi 1980, 211.

22. Mondi 1980, 212. The notion of "vulgarization" itself points to an assumption that usage corrupts etymological purity.

23. Mondi suggests that the secularization of *krainein* is "post-Homeric" (1980, 206), though *krainein* shows up in the context of leadership in *Od.* 8.391

24. Deger-Jalkotzy 1991, 62–63.

25. Donlan 1989b, 18–19; 1985, 298.

26. Raaflaub 1993, 51; Ulf 1990, 89; Gagarin 1986, 27; Griffin 1980, 11; Nagy 1979, 180.

27. Lenz 1993, 335.

28. Finley 1979, 82, 110.

29. Posner 1979, 35.

30. Benveniste 1973, 382.

31. Havelock 1978, 135, 30.

32. Havelock 1963, 101.

33. Havelock 1978, 130, 132, 136.

34. Havelock 1978, 124. See also Havelock 1963, 61–86.

35. Havelock 1978, 124, 132, 135.

36. Havelock 1978, 14.

37. Havelock 1983.

38. Havelock 1983, 25. See also Havelock 1978, ch. 13.

39. Havelock 1983, 14, 20, 13.

40. Havelock 1978, 37. See also Gagarin 1986, 47.

41. Gagarin (1973), too, in his discussion of *dikê*, seems to draw a distinction between justice as a process or set of procedures and justice as having a moral sense. He concludes that *dikê* in Homer "extends only to the particular area of peaceful litigation" and, since there is little discussion of peaceful litigation in Homer, the word is "insignificant" (1973, 87).

42. Havelock 1978, 36.

43. Havelock 1978, 136–37, referring to 16.387–88.

44. Adkins 1983, 215, 212, 214.

45. On a similar note, see Gluckman 1965, 201–202; Gearing 1968, 114; and Gagarin 1986, 6–7, for their discussions of the interpenetration of custom, law, and right.

46. Turner 1988, 78.

47. Weber 1978, 30.

48. See Snodgrass 1971, 1980, Coldstream 1977, Osborne 1996, and Rose 1997.

49. See de Polignac 1995, Starr 1986, and Raaflaub 1997e.

50. See Tandy 1997.

51. See Qviller 1981.

52. See Morris 1987, Raaflaub 1997b, 1997c, and Donlan 1989b.

53. Weber 1978, 272.

54. One difficulty with reconstructing early history is that events may, in fact, be later traditions that are read back in time. In the case of Athens, see Raaflaub 1988.

55. See Diod. 7.9; Oost 1972, 10–11; Roebuck 1972, 106; and Salmon 1984, 56–57. The precise nature of the oligarchy is difficult to establish. Some have suggested that the single monarch was replaced by three elected officials: a *prytanis* (who performed royal functions), a *basileus* (who performed religious functions), and a *polemarch* (who

collected fines [Nic. Dam. 90 F 57.5] and likely served as the chief military officer). See Roebuck 1972, 106; Will 1955, 298–306. Others have argued that the *prytanis* and *basileus* refer to the same official. See Oost 1972, 10–11, and Salmon 1984, 56–57.

56. Roebuck 1972, 106.

57. Diod. 7.9; Oost 1972, 11; Roebuck 1972, 106; and Salmon 1984, 56–57.

58. Hignett 1958, 38–46.

59. Legon 1981, 57.

60. Shared decision-making among the *basileis* or *gerontes* has been noted by Lenz 1993, 218–25; Carlier 1984, 182–87; Andreyev 1991a, 344; Donlan 1989b, 25 (as a culmination of the unstable chiefdom system); Drews 1983; and Raaflaub 1996, 151, 1997b, 643 (as "established institution" that was "held responsible for communal decisions"); and Ulf 1990. See also Patzek (1992, 131–32) and Flaig (1994) on the importance of consensus in Homeric society.

61. Lenz 1993, 10, 300. See also Andreyev 1991a.

62. Weber 1978, 272, 281.

63. Mention of shared decision-making among the elite appears at 2.53–86, 2.402–40, 3.146–60, 4.322–23, 4.344, 7.323–44, 9.70–178, 9.422, 12.210–50, 13.726–47, 14.27–134, 15.283–84, 18.243–313, 18.497–508, 18.510–11, 22.99–110

64. See, especially, Donlan 1998 and Qviller 1981. More generally, see Earle 1991.

65. See Yaron 1993, 20, 24.

66. Benveniste's suggestion that "where there is no *génos* and no king there can be no *thémis* or assembly" (1973, 383) conforms to Agamemnon's claim. I do not think, however, that Benveniste's argument sufficiently accounts for how *themis* becomes a claim on the leader, rather than a claim of the leader.

67. Havelock 1978, 123–24. See further citations of this notion of restoration in the following section on the funeral games.

68. Van Wees 1992, 35.

69. References to *themis* as cosmic or divine are numerous. Hera complains to Zeus that Ares, who is killing Achaian warriors "out of due order" (*kosmon*), knows "nothing of *themistas*" (5.759, 761). On several occasions, Agamemnon says that he will swear an oath that he never "lay" with Briseis "as is natural (*themis*) for people" (9.133–34, 9.276, 19.177).

70. That *themis* originates with the gods does not necessarily make the invocation of *themis* either exclusionary (i.e., nonpublic) or static. There is a long history that follows the epic in which the heavens are invoked to support the extension of rights. For example, in Solon's reforms that extended the role of the people, the magistrates, assembly, and law courts swore oaths to the gods (Freeman 1976, 82). The beginning of the Gortyn law code begins with an appeal to the gods. And, for more modern examples, the Declaration of Independence makes an appeal to the Divine, as did Martin Luther King in his demand for the extension of civil rights in the United States.

71. There is an ongoing controversy in Homeric scholarship about whether this final passage, in particular, is a later addition. I am convinced of the evidence suggesting that the ideas are consistent and contemporaneous with other aspects of the poem. The argument here provides further corroboration for inclusion of this passage in that it seems completely consistent with a broader process of regularization in which *themis* is extended into a set of political relationships.

72. Finley 1981, 131–33.

73. Adkins (1960, 56), for example, looks at the chariot races as revealing a "microcosm" of "the tangle of values" in Greek society. Farenga (1998) argues that funerary practices, and the genealogical narratives associated with these practices, were important for instigating a "cognitive revolution" (197) in which new ideas could be introduced while tying these ideas to a past. For the role of rituals as "social dramas" that promote reflection on society, see Turner 1981.

74. Redfield 1994, 210.

75. See Scully 1990, 127, and Seaford 1994, 159–64.

76. Farenga 1998, 199, 198. See also Seaford, who emphasizes the "integrative power of lamentation" (1994, 173).

77. Finley 1979, 80–81, 110, and Edmunds 1989, 28.

78. See Farenga 1998, 201.

79. By contrast, see the description of the death and burial of Sarpedon (16.455–57).

80. See Burkert 1985, 191–92. For discussions of hero-cults and cults of the dead in the context of the emergent polis, see Snodgrass 1980, 38–42; de Polignac 1995, 128–49; Antonaccio 1993, 1994; Whitley 1995, 59, 1988; and Sourvinou-Inwood 1990, 1993.

81. Wickersham and Pozzi 1991, 5. See also Burkert 1985, 193.

82. Nagy 1990, 269.

83. See Nagy 1990, 272, 275; Donlan 1980, 10–11; Kullmann 1985; and M. Edwards 1987, 130–31.

84. Dodds (1957, 32) sees this statement as "a reflex of later conditions which, by an inadvertence common in Homer, has been allowed to slip into a simile." Arguments that this role of Zeus is consistent with the *Iliad* are made by Lloyd-Jones 1971 and Yamagata 1994, ch. 5.

85. Stanley (1993, 230), for example, sees Achilles' role as embodying the internalization of value, neglecting his role in resolving real conflicts that emerge. King (1987, 37–38) sees only the "isolated figure" of Achilles in the funeral games. And Schein (1984, 156) describes Achilles' "mood" as "a controlled, detached sociability."

86. Finley 1979, 80–81, 110.

87. See 18.501–508 and van Wees 1992, 34.

88. See Arendt 1958, 236–43.

89. Stanley (1993, 225–26) suggests that this valedictory reward, the final time we see Nestor, is suggestive of "a Nestor of many words but few deeds, whose contribution to the present remains in doubt." This seems contrary to the tone of the funeral games and to the respect paid to Nestor throughout the *Iliad*. Achilles can move beyond Nestor without necessarily removing him.

90. Similar words are spoken by Poulydamas to Hektor: "Hektor, you are too intractable to listen to reason. / Because the god has granted you the actions of warfare / therefore you wish in counsel also to be wise beyond others. / But you cannot choose to have all gifts given to you together. / To one man the god has granted the actions of warfare, / to one to be a dancer, to another the lyre and the singing, / and in the breast of another Zeus of the wide brow establishes / wisdom, a lordly thing, and many take profit beside him / and he saves many, but the man's own thought surpasses all others" (13.726–34).

91. See 1.259–73, 7.124–60, 11.669–802.

CHAPTER 6

1. Donlan 1985, 293–94.

2. I label this approach an "integrationist model" to distinguish it from "stratification models" that are more Marxian in their orientation.

3. Talmon (1960), for example, draws on the connection of a plebiscite to voting in his discussion of modern forms of totalitarianism.

4. See Strasburger 1982, 495; Glotz 1930, 7; Bonner and Smith 1930, 9; Köstler 1968; Andreyev 1991a, 340; and Mondi 1980.

5. See Finley 1979; Donlan 1979, 1989b, 1993, 1997b, 1998; Donlan and Thomas 1993; Qviller 1981; Raaflaub 1989, 1991, 1993, 1997a; van Wees 1992; Ulf 1990, 223–31; Gschnitzer 1991; and Thalmann 1998, 255–71.

6. See, especially, Donlan 1998; Qviller 1981; and Humphreys 1978, 69. On chiefdoms, more generally, see Earle 1991.

7. See Morris 1986, Rose 1997, Thalmann 1998, Tandy 1997, de Ste. Croix 1981, Wood and Wood 1978, and Bintliff 1982. These approaches adopt, in various forms, stratification models of state development that draw their theoretical impetus from Marx. Important for Homeric scholarship is Fried (1967), who argues that the maintenance by an elite of differential access to resources serves as the impetus for state formation.

8. Morris 1986, 123–25.

9. Tandy 1997, 192, 152.

10. Thalmann 1998, 13, 284.

11. Tandy 1997, 192, 171–72, 175, 180.

12. Thalmann 1998, 284, 269, 281 n. 26.

13. See Rose (1997) for a much more complex and interactive understanding of class relations.

14. See Raaflaub 1991, 1993, 1997a, 1997b, 1997d; Hölkeskamp 1997; Donlan 1989b, 1997b, 1998; Ulf 1990; van Wees 1992, 31–36; Gagarin 1986, 27; Griffin 1980, 11; Gschnitzer 1991; Olson 1995, 188; Ruzé 1997, 19–29; and Carlier 1984, who writes "C'est le roi qui décide, mais il décide *en public*" (186). Mentions of the assembly in the *Iliad* appear at 1.54–305, 2.84–398, 2.788–808, 7.345–79, 7.381–412, 7.414–20, 9.9–79, 18.243–313, 19.34–237. Though *laos* and *demos* are not synonymous, their meanings overlap (e.g., 18.301: "let him give them to the people [*laoisi*], to use them in common [*katadêmoborêsai*]"; *Od.* 16.95–96, 114: "Do the people [*laoi*] / hate you throughout this place [*dêmon*].... It is not that all the people [*dêmos*] hate me"). Both terms refer to the people of a community. *Laos* and *laoi* often refer to the followers of a leader, whereas *demos* refers to both a named territory and the people of the territory (see Snell and Erbse, eds., *Lexikon des frühgriechischen Epos* [*LfgrE*], 275–78, 1633–44; Benveniste 1973, 371–76; Donlan 1989; Casevitz 1992; and Haubold 2000). *Plêthos* seems to refer frequently to an undifferentiated multitude (see *Il.* 2.488, 11.305, 11.360, 11.405, 15.295, 17.31, 17.221, 20.197, 22.458; *Od.* 11.514,

16.105). *Plêthos* is not used as a pejorative term for demos or *laos*, though. *Plêthos*, *demos*, and *laos* are all used to refer to the mass of disorderly people (compare *Il.* 2.143, 2.198, and 2.191). And the *plêthos* are not portrayed only unsympathetically. They express approval when Odysseus silences Thersites (*Il.* 2.278); Ajax appeals to Achilles on behalf of the *plêthos* (*Il.* 9.641); and the *plêthos* march in an orderly way back to the ships (*Il.* 15.305).

15. See Carlier 1984, 186; Ruzé 1984, 248–49; and Raaflaub 1997b, 15.

16. Raaflaub 1997d, 55.

17. Raaflaub 1997a, 636.

18. Raaflaub 1997d, 55. See also Raaflaub 1997b, 11–20.

19. Raaflaub 1997a, 636. See also Raaflaub 1997d.

20. Raaflaub 1997d, 55. See also Raaflaub 1991, 230–38.

21. Raaflaub 1997d, 55.

22. Donlan 1989b, 16, 14, 14–15. See also Luce 1978, 9: "The name of the *polis* is also the name of the entire territory."

23. Donlan 1998, 69.

24. Donlan 1997b, 43–44. See also Gschnitzer, who argues that "der in der Ilias nur 'vorstaatliche' oder 'vorrechtliche' Zustände sieht" [in the *Iliad* one sees only early state or early legal positions] (1991, 196).

25. Donlan 1997b, 39.

26. See Donlan 1997b, 42–43.

27. See Sahlins 1972. For Donlan's application of reciprocity to Homeric economy, see Donlan 1997a and bibliography.

28. Donlan 1998, 56. Using a different language, Lenz, following Qviller, describes the "exploitation inherent in these 'gifts.'" See Qviller 1981, 123, and Lenz 1993, 217.

29. Donlan 1998, 55, 54, 56.

30. Donlan 1997b, 42–43.

31. Others, too, have seen in the epic a notion of politics in transition. Luce comments that the polis appears "under its autocratic ruler, but not without some rudiments of a wider political structure" (1978, 11). This is also suggested in a number of articles by Raaflaub (see 1991, 1993, 1997b, 1997d) and Qviller 1981.

32. Weber 1978, 266–67.

33. Similarly, in Book 9 the heralds "summon calling by name each man into the assembly" (9.11) to take "their seats in assembly" (9.13). The association of a space with an assembly is suggested, as well, when Patroklos is depicted as running to the ships "where the Achaians

had their assembly" (11.806). This formalization of a space suggests not only that such meetings of the people were somewhat common, but that a space became identified and defined by this activity.

34. Suggestive of these charismatic elements, as well, is how one group of Achaians long for their leader, Protesilaos (2.703–10), and how Nireus cannot attract a following because he was "a man of poor strength" (2.675). Athene also advises Odysseus on how to restore order to the fleeing assembly of Achaians (2.172–81).

35. See also 3.181, 3.224, and 7.41.

36. Comparison to noise: 14.393–401. Personal prowess: 5.297–302, 8.321, 16.784–85, 18.160, 18.228–29, 20.285. Communal strength: 13.834–35, 15.312–13, 16.78–79, 17.262–66. Divine terror: 5.784–92, 5.859–63, 11.10–14, 14.147–52, 15.321–27, 20.48–53.

37. See Lendon 2000.

38. Weber 1978, 268.

39. Breiner 1996, 21.

40. Schofield 1986, 14.

41. Martin 1989, 37.

42. See Martin 1989, 17.

43. See Schofield (1986) for his discussion of *euboulia*, or good counsel, as an important attribute of good leadership in the *Iliad*. This public ethic that I am suggesting here, and that Schofield also suggests, stands in contrast to Finley's suggestion that soundness and good sense are not heroic virtues (1979, 115–17).

44. On the theme of the role of the leader in protecting the people, see Haubold 2000, 37–40, 47–100.

45. Finley 1979, 80.

46. Andreyev 1991a, 342.

47. Weber 1978, 267.

48. Oost 1972, 24. See also Drews 1972.

49. Ober 1989, 65.

50. Glotz 1928, 136, and de Ste. Croix 1981, 281 (quoting Glotz).

51. De Ste. Croix 1981, 280–81. Wood and Wood, who characterize the polis as emerging from a class struggle for the "liberation of a producing class," simply skip over any discussion of the appearance of tyranny in the seventh and sixth centuries (1978, 29).

52. See McGlew 1993; Raaflaub 1997c, 39; Manville 1990, 162–73; Kolb 1977; Shapiro 1989; Stahl 1987; and Eder 1992.

53. Arist. *Pol.* 1315b12–34.

54. See Herod. 3.142–43, and Robinson 1997, 118–20.

55. Heraclea Pontica: Arist. *Pol.* 1304b31–34 and Robinson 1997, 111–13. Mesopotamia: Jacobsen 1970a and 1970b. See Robinson 1997, 17–25, for a summary of the literature on early non-Greek democracy.

56. Jacobsen provides some corroboration to this argument in his discussion of early political development in Mesopotamia. He identifies a "primitive democracy" in early Mesopotamia that corresponds, in significant ways, to our discussion of the operation of plebiscitary politics. In particular, "the ruler must lay his proposals before the people, first the elders, then the assembly of the townsmen, and obtain their consent, before he can act" (1970b, 163). Over time, though, Mesopotamia veers in a more autocratic direction due to a natural desire of leaders to maintain their position (1970a, 142–43), the accumulation of powers in one leader through claims of perpetual emergency (particularly war) (1970a, 143–45), and the appearance of a new model of autocratic rule with the kingship of Kish, which successfully established control by force over large territories (1970a, 145–47). Jacobsen describes a process in which the assembly, which is not institutionalized, is particularly vulnerable to the assertions of the more autocratic claims to charismatic authority by the king (1970a, 146–47). This move to autocracy is, in turn, supported by the development of claims of divine election and the institutionalization of the "dynastic principle," in which the king would designate his successor (1970a, 148–51). Critiques of Jacobsen can be addressed largely, I think, by substituting "plebiscitary politics" for "primitive democracy." This provides a way to understand the political role of the people without, in turn, positing a sovereignty of the people. Mesopotamia provides a case in which the autocratic elements of plebiscitary leadership assert themselves and then get institutionalized.

57. Arist. *Pol.* 1310b12–17.

58. See Weber's discussion of demagoguery in 1978, 1449–51.

59. Oost 1972, 20.

60. Herod. 1.64.

61. Arist. *Ath. Pol.* 14.4, 15.4.

62. Sinos 1993, 83–84.

63. Connor 1987, 44.

64. On the elective tyranny of Pittacus of Mytilene, see Arist. *Pol.* 1285a34–1285b4. On the tyranny of Cypselus in Corinth, see Arist. *Pol.* 1310b29–32 and Nic. Dam. 90 F 57. On attempts by Maeandrius to surrender the tyranny in Samos, see Herod. 3.142–43. On the rise of Deioces in Medes, see Herod. 1.96–101. On Theagenes at Megara,

see Arist. *Pol.* 1305a25–26, and on Lygdamis at Naxos, see Arist. *Pol.* 1305a37–1305b1.

65. Salmon 1984, 205–209, 231–39, 235. Thucydides mentions a role of the Corinthian assembly (*xullogos*) in negotiations between Corinth and Argos (5.30.5). For the role of the *probouloi* and its relationship to an assembly in oligarchies, in general, see Arist. *Pol.* 1298b26–35.

66. Herod. 3.142.

67. See Herod. 1.59, Thuc. 6.54.5, Arist. *Ath. Pol.* 14.3, 16.2, 16.8–10, and Plut. *Sol.* 31.

68. Salmon 1984, 205–207, 234–36.

69. McGlew 1993, 215.

70. Ober 1993, 216. See also Ober 1997.

71. Ober 1997, 69, 68–69,

72. Raaflaub 1996, 144; see also Rauflaub 1997c.

73. Raaflaub 1997c, 45–46.

74. This dynamic seems to be suggested in the discussion of Peisistratus's leadership by Gouschin 1999.

75. Raaflaub 1996, 144.

76. I will set aside the problem that there is no historical example of a successful, sustained, and leaderless democratic revolution.

77. Raaflaub 1997e, 89.

78. As examples, see *Il.* 1.73, 1.253, 2.78, 2.283, 4.361, 6.79, 13.135, 13.345 (divided in purpose), 15.50, 22.264 (divided in purpose), *Od.* 2.160, 2.228, 7.158.

79. I agree here with Raaflaub 1997c, 41.

80. I think we can understand *apodidomi* in this context as suggesting that Cleisthenes grants or offers what is due to the *dêmos*. Cleisthenes does not, in any absolute sense, "hand over" government (as translated by Rackham), but promises to increase the share of control by the *dêmos*.

81. Ober sees Herodotus as contradictory at this point. In resolving this seeming contradiction, Ober states that he "[does] not accept the historical agent Herodotus proposes here" and notes that Herodotus "elsewhere views the demos as the main agent of democratic change" (Ober 1997, 83). Certainly, we do not have to believe or disbelieve Herodotus on all things. But I find it less than comfortable to pick and choose when and how we are going to believe Herodotus when he is talking about the same thing.

82. Ober 1989, 66–67.

83. Ober 1993, 216. See also Ober 1989, 68–69, 84–86, for the role of the elite in leading reforms.
84. Ober 1993, 228.

CHAPTER 7

1. Kant 1959, 5.
2. Gagarin, for example, defines morality as a "disinterested concern for others" and ethics as a general cultural orientation in which norms of behavior are grounded in "prudential self-interest" (1987, 287–88).
3. Snell 1930. See also Snell 1982 and Erbse 1986, 1990.
4. Fränkel 1962, 89 (1975, 80). See also Böhme 1929, 76.
5. Live in the moment: Fränkel 1962, 93 (1975, 84); see also Schadewaldt 1959, 266–67, and 1955, 137–38. Act according to forms of society: Fränkel 1962, 89 (1975, 80); see also Auerbach 1953; Bakhtin 1981; and Finley 1979, 25, 113, 115.
6. Dodds 1957.
7. Redfield 1994, 21.
8. Critiques and modifications of these arguments have been offered by Wolff 1929, Whitman 1958, Long 1970, Lloyd-Jones 1971, Sharples 1983, Gaskin 1990, Schmitt 1990, Williams 1993, Cairns 1993, Yamagata 1994, Zanker 1994, and Gill 1996.
9. Redfield 1994, 116.
10. Pitt-Rivers 1974, 21–22.
11. Cairns 1993, 142.
12. Cairns 1993, 16. No Greek term corresponds to the term "self-esteem." Cairns has made a strong argument for showing how *aidôs*, and terms used in conjunction with *aidôs*, involves issues of esteem. Though I begin with this notion of esteem, I seek to justify its usage in my argument.
13. Williams 1985, 12. See also Ricoeur 1992, 172.
14. Crotty 1994, 75, 78–79, 79 n. 6, 6, 8.
15. Zanker 1996, 73, 97, 125.
16. See Burkert 1955; Segal 1971; Atchity 1978, 164; MacLeod 1982; Schein 1984; King 1987; Lynn-George 1988; Griffin 1980; Beye 1993; Crotty 1994; and Muellner 1996. Griffin writes that with the death of Patroklos, Achilles now "accepts his own death" (1980, 96). In fact, what is distinctive about Achilles is that "he is able to contemplate

and accept his own death more fully and more passionately than any other hero" (95). Segal also suggests that "Achilles shows an awareness of death as part of a more comprehensive order" (1971, 73).

17. Nagy 1979, 83.

18. Sinos sees Patroklos's entrance into battle as a ritual substitute for Achilles' unwillingness to recognize his obligations to the *philoi*. "Patroklos recognizes the social obligation of Achilles to the φίλοι; it is he who dies for the φίλοι, but as Achilles. His act is a ritual act uniting the φίλοι with Achilles, in the person of the substitute, Patroklos" (1980, 42).

19. Lord suggests that the death of Patroklos marks a change in the pattern of the story from a "pattern of the wrath" of Achilles, which leads to his withdrawal, to one of a "feud" with Hektor, which leads to his return (1960, 150).

20. Nagy 1979, 113, 97.

21. See Nagy 1979, 97–102. Muellner (1996) does not sustain this distinction in his discussion of Achilles. Rather, he describes Achilles' actions and reactions only at the level of epic convention. This is why Muellner does not see Achilles as an ethical actor, but rather as being "propel[led]" by the "poem's overall teleology and conventions" (1996, 161).

22. "To suffer-with another" appears in classical Greek as *sullupeisthai*, and is associated with a feeling for one who is intimate. The term does not appear in the *Iliad*, but I think this sense is conveyed in Achilles' reaction to the death of Patroklos.

23. Heidegger 1979, 327.

24. See Cairns 1993, 57–58.

25. Vernant 1991, 67. See also Segal 1971.

26. This scene is often interpreted as a prefiguring of Achilles' own death. On the relationship between Patroklos's and Achilles' death, see Schadewaldt 1959, 155–202; Schein 1984, 129–33; and Muellner 1996, 155–69.

27. Crotty 1994, 46, 48. There is considerable ambiguity in Crotty's argument at this point. He does not want to suggest that pity and mourning are the same things. Pity becomes something like a second-order mourning: pity arises from the memory of mourning (1994, 75). This distinction between pity and mourning is blurred, though, when Crotty uses Achilles' mourning for Patroklos as an example of the visceral character of pity in his chapter "*Eleos* and the Warrior Society" (1994, 49–50).

28. Crotty 1994, 49.

29. Konstan (1999) suggests that Andromache, in fact, attempts to create this distance by projecting a future in which Hektor is dead.

30. Arist. *Rhet.* 2.8.12.

31. Muellner describes this alienation of Achilles from himself (1996, 136–43), but does not ascribe any cognitive status to this alienation.

32. I disagree with Sinos on this point when he claims that "Achilles' only recognition of his social obligation to the φίλοι is, as we might expect, linked with the name Patroklos" (1980, 43). The death of Patroklos certainly precipitates the remorse, but it is a remorse (and a sense of responsibility) that is specifically extended to his treatment of his other companions.

33. "Because the actor always moves among and in relation to other acting beings," suggests Arendt, "he is never merely a 'doer' but always and at the same time a sufferer" (1958, 190).

34. See Arist. *NE* 1156a–1157a.

35. See also Ricoeur, who describes this esteem as a love of "the other *as being the man he is*" (1992, 183).

36. Arist. *NE* 1156a, 1157b.

37. Arist. *NE* 1157b.

38. Both intimates and comrades are referred to as *philos*. See Benveniste for a discussion of the "complex network of associations" referred to by *philos* (1973, 288).

39. Lynn-George 1988, 232, quoting Cunliffe 1963.

40. Lynn-George 1988, 232.

41. Heidegger 1971b, 204.

42. Heidegger 1971c, 63. Crotty suggests that the performance of the ceremony of supplication gives rise to a "transient, but profound, 'community'" between Achilles and Priam (1994, 21).

43. See Richardson 1985, 344.

44. Lord 1960, 190.

45. See Seaford 1994, 10, 174, and Crotty 1994, 83.

46. Redfield 1994, 219.

47. Crotty 1994, 75.

48. Rabel characterizes Priam's appeal as "rhetorically inept" and reflective of the "narrator's habitual irony" (1997, 201–202).

49. There is practical reason, as well, why Priam does not establish an identity of himself with Peleus, and that is that Achilles would then be cast as Hektor. That, of course, would be unacceptable to Achilles. And

Priam notes the difference. Peleus may still have hope, "But for me, my destiny was evil [*panapotmos*]. I have had the noblest / of sons in Troy, but I say not one of them is left to me" (24.493–94). The one who was left and "who guarded my city and people, that one / you killed a few days since as he fought in defence of his country" (24.499–500). Priam has now lost everything, having "gone through what no other mortal on earth has gone through" (24.505). He ends with an expression of supplication: "I put my lips to the hands of the man who has killed my children" (24.506).

50. This interpretation runs contrary to the suggestion that the urns are an "artistic" motif used by the poet to "satisfy his audience's desire to find an order and rationality in human experience" (M. Edwards 1987, 136).

51. See Arist. *Rhet.* 2.8.7, 2.8.16.

52. See Richardson 1985, 329, on the appearance of the theme of endurance in later literature.

53. Griffin 1980, 102.

54. Whitman 1958, 219. See also Crotty, who suggests that the "understanding of grief" results in "delight" (1994, 103).

55. Rabel 1997, 205.

56. Crotty 1994, 99, 84.

57. Schein 1984, 159. See also Burkert 1955, 107; MacLeod 1982, 16; and Zanker 1996, 125.

58. Notably, see Burkert 1955, 126–34; Seaford 1994; and Zanker 1996, 135–36. Burkert shows how pity relates to, and is brought into tension with, an aristocratic ethic. Seaford argues that Priam's supplication stops the excessive mourning of Achilles. This allows the *Iliad* to end by emphasizing a "public death ritual" suggestive of a polis society, as opposed to the lavish private rituals of early Dark Age society (Seaford 1994, 182). I would disagree with Seaford that this implies a sixth-century dating of the *Iliad* (1994, 144–54). As we saw in chapter 1, there was in the eighth century an increasing public organization of community life and interaction between communities that points toward a progressive enlargement of aspects of recognition, cooperation, and obligation toward other groups. Along these lines, Zanker suggests that the establishment of a "morality beyond reciprocity" would be important in Dark Age society for binding "the distinct community of *aristoi* in crossing 'tribal' boundaries" (1996, 135).

59. Arendt 1958, 188–92.

60. See Heidegger 1979 for his discussion of "understanding" as a "projecting towards a potentiality-for-Being" (385–89). Though the term

is from Heidegger, my discussion more closely follows Arendt. My notion of projection points to a disagreement with Schadewaldt. Schadewaldt suggests that Achilles' decision is one of "pure presence" (*reine Gegenwart*) that arises from his "*ganzen Sein in einem Zustand der Erhebung*" [whole being in a state of exaltation] (1959, 267). There is an interesting parallel to Heidegger's notion of "*ecstases.*" For Schadewaldt the moment of "Exaltation" (*Erhebung*) does not "know" a "Before" (*Vorher*) or "After" (*Nachher*) but exists at the moment of "what has been and what is to come" (*des Gewesenen und des Kommenden*). So for Heidegger the "*ecstases*" of temporality is the experience of a "pure sequence of 'nows'" that bring together the "phenomena of the future (*Zukunft*), the character of having been (*Gewesenheit*), and the Present (*Gegenwart*)" (1962, 377 [1979, 329]). For Schadewaldt, Achilles' decision is not directed by any burden of the past or anticipation of the future, but exists as a pure moment in time. Heidegger, on the other hand, suggests that the coming together of the past, present, and future makes possible the projecting-forward of the individual into the future. I am arguing that Achilles engages in just such a projecting-forth as he binds himself and his community, through a promise, to Priam.

61. I am drawing on Arendt 1958, 236–47.

62. Arendt 1958, 237. Arendt writes, "Without being forgiven, released from the consequences of what we have done, our capacity to act would, as it were, be confined to one single deed from which we would never recover; we would remain the victims of its consequences forever" (1958, 237).

63. Benveniste 1973, 286.

64. See Arendt 1958, 241.

65. Arendt 1958, 244.

66. See Benveniste 1973, 278–81.

67. Richardson 1985, 346.

68. Foucault 1997, 287.

69. See Zanker 1996, 117–18.

70. See Havelock 1983, 15–20.

71. Havelock 1983, 19, 20.

72. Havelock 1978, 8–9.

73. Arendt 1978, 1.100, 102, 105.

74. Arendt 1978, 1.104, 108.

75. Heidegger 1971c, 42, 35; 1971d, 218.

76. Heidegger 1971a, 157.

References

ANCIENT SOURCES

Alc.   Alcaeus. In *Greek Lyric.* 1982. Translated by David Campbell. 5 vols. Cambridge: Harvard University Press.

Arist.

Ath. Pol.   *The Constitution of Athens.* 1996. In *The Politics, and the Constitution of Athens.* Edited by Stephen Everson. Cambridge: Cambridge University Press.

NE   *Nicomachean Ethics.* 1962. Translated by Martin Ostwald. Indianapolis: Bobbs-Merrill.

Poet.   *The Poetics.* 1951. Translated by S. H. Butcher. New York: Dover

Pol.   *The Politics.* 1996. Edited by Stephen Everson. Cambridge: Cambridge University Press.

Rhet.   *The 'Art' of Rhetoric.* 1982. Translated by John Henry Freese. Cambridge: Harvard University Press.

Diod.   *Diodorus of Sicily.* 1952. Translated by C. H. Oldfather. 12 vols. Cambridge: Harvard University Press.

Herod.   *Herodotus.* 1938. Translated by A. D. Godley. 4 vols. Cambridge: Harvard University Press.

Hesiod Theog.   *Theogony.* 1966. Edited by M. L. West. Oxford: Clarendon.

Homer
 Il. *Iliad.* 1951. Translated by Richmond Lattimore. Chicago: University of Chicago Press.
 Od. *Odyssey.* 1967. Translated by Richmond Lattimore. New York: Harper.
Nic. Dam. Nicolaus of Damascus. 1961. In *Die Fragmente der griechischen Historiker,* edited by Felix Jacoby. Leiden: Brill.
Plato *Rep.* *The Republic.* 1974. Translated by Desmond Lee. New York: Penguin
Plut.
 Mor. *Moralia.* 1927. Translated by Frank Cole Babbitt. London: Heinemann.
 Sol. *Life of Solon.* In *Plutarch's Lives.* 1914–59. Translated by Bernadotte Perrin. London: Heinemann.
Schol. Ap. Rhod. *Scholia in Apollonium Rhodium Vetera.* 1958. Edited by Carolus Wendel. Berlin: Weidmannsche.
Sch. Pi. *Scholia in Pindari Epinicia.* 1884–91. Edited by Eugenius Abel. Berlin: S. Calvary.
Thuc. Thucydides. *The Peloponnesian War.* 1972. Translated by Rex Warner. New York: Penguin.

SOURCES CITED

Adkins, Arthur W. H. 1960. *Merit and Responsibility: A Study in Greek Values.* Oxford: Clarendon.

———. 1982. "Values, Goals, and Emotions in the *Iliad.*" *Classical Philology* 77 (October): 292–326.

———. 1983. "Orality and Philosophy." In *Language and Thought in Early Greek Philosophy,* edited by Kevin Robb. La Salle, Ill.: Hegeler Institute.

———. 1997. "Homeric Ethics." In *A New Companion to Homer.* Leiden: Brill.

Alcock, Susan. 1995. "Pausanias and the *Polis:* Use and Abuse." In *Sources for the Ancient Greek City-State: Acts of the Copenhagen Polis Centre.* Vol. 2. Edited by Mogens Herman Hansen. Copenhagen: Munksgaard, 326–44.

Althusser, Louis. 1971. "Ideology and Ideological State Apparatuses (Notes towards an Investigation)." In *Lenin and Philosophy and Other*

Essays. Translated by Ben Brewster. New York: Monthly Review Press, 127–186.

Amory Parry, Anne. 1971. "Homer as Artist." *Classical Quarterly* 21: 1–15.

Andersen, Øivind. 1976. "Some Thoughts on the Shield of Achilles." *Symbolae Osloenses* 51: 5–18.

———. 1987. "Myth, Paradigm and 'Spatial Form' in the *Iliad.*" In *Homer, Beyond Oral Poetry: Recent Trends in Homeric Interpretation,* edited by J. M. Bremer, I. J. F. de Jong, and J. Kalff. Amsterdam: B. R. Grüner, 1–13.

Anderson, Benedict R. O'G. 1991. *Imagined Communities: Reflections on the Origin and Spread of Nationalism.* 2d ed. New York: Verso.

Andrewes, Antony. 1967. *The Greeks.* New York: Norton.

Andreyev, Yu. 1991a. "Greece of the Eleventh to Ninth Centuries B.C. in the Homeric Epics." In *Early Antiquity,* edited by I. M. Diakanoff. Translated by Alexander Kirjanov. Chicago: University of Chicago Press, 328–48.

———. 1991b. "The World of Crete and Mycenae." In *Early Antiquity,* edited by I. M. Diakanoff. Translated by Alexander Kirjanov. Chicago: University of Chicago Press, 309–27.

Antonaccio, Carla. 1993. "The Archaeology of Ancestors." In *Cultural Poetics in Archaic Greece,* edited by Carol Dougherty and Leslie Kurke. Oxford: Oxford University Press, 46–70.

———. 1994. "Contesting the Past: Hero Cult, Tomb Cult, and Epic in Early Greece." *American Journal of Archaeology* 98: 389–410.

———. 1995. "Lefkandi and Homer." In *Homer's World: Fiction, Tradition, Reality,* edited by Øivind Andersen and Matthew Dickie. Bergen: P. Åström, 5–27.

Arendt, Hannah. 1958. *The Human Condition.* Chicago: University of Chicago Press.

———. 1962. "Action and the 'Pursuit of Happiness.'" In *Politische Ordnung und menschliche Existenz: Festgabe für Eric Voegelin zum 60. Geburtstag,* edited by Alois Dempf, Hannah Arendt, and Friedrich Engel-Janosi. München: Beck.

———. 1968a. "Karl Jaspers: A Laudatio." In *Men in Dark Times.* New York: Harvest.

———. 1968b. "Karl Jaspers: Citizen of the World?" In *Men in Dark Times.* New York: Harvest.

———. 1968c. "What Is Freedom?" In *Between Past and Future.* New York: Penguin.

———. 1972. "On Violence." In *Crises of the Republic.* New York: Harvest.

———. 1978. *The Life of the Mind.* San Diego: Harcourt Brace Jovanovich.

———. 1982. *Lectures on Kant's Political Philosophy.* Edited by Ronald Beiner. Chicago: University of Chicago Press.

———. 1994. "What Is Existential Philosophy?" In *Essays in Understanding: 1930–1954,* edited by Jerome Kohn. New York: Harcourt Brace.

Arieti, James. 1986. "Achilles' Alienation in *Iliad* 9." *Classical Journal* 82 (October–November): 1–27.

Arnhart, Larry. 1993. *Political Questions: Political Philosophy from Plato to Rawls.* 2d ed. Prospect Heights, Ill.: Waveland Press.

Atchity, Kenneth. 1978. *Homer's* Iliad*: The Shield of Memory.* Carbondale: Southern Illinois University Press.

Auerbach, Erich. 1953. *Mimesis: The Representation of Reality in Western Literature.* Translated by Willard Trask. Garden City, N.Y.: Doubleday Anchor.

Austin, M. M., and P. Vidal-Naquet. 1977. *Economic and Social History of Ancient Greece: An Introduction.* Translated by M. M. Austin. Berkeley: University of California Press.

Austin, Norman. 1975. *Archery at the Dark of the Moon: Poetic Problems in the* Odyssey. Berkeley: University of California Press.

Bakhtin, M. M. 1981. *The Dialogic Imagination: Four Essays by M. M. Bakhtin.* Edited by Michael Holquist. Translated by Caryl Emerson and Michael Holquist. Austin: University of Texas Press.

———. 1990. *Art and Answerability: Early Philosophical Essays by M. M. Bakhtin.* Edited by Michael Holquist and Vadim Liapunov. Translated by Vadim Liapunov. Austin: University of Texas Press.

Bakhtin, M. M., and P. N. Medvedev. 1985. *The Formal Method in Literary Scholarship: A Critical Introduction to Sociological Poetics.* Translated by Albert J. Wehrle. Cambridge: Harvard University Press.

Bakker, Egbert. 1995. "Noun-Epithet Formulas, Milman Parry, and the Grammar of Poetry." In *Homeric Questions,* edited by Jan Paul Crielaard. Amsterdam: J. C. Gieben, 97–125.

———. 1997a. *Poetry in Speech: Orality and Homeric Discourse.* Ithaca, N.Y.: Cornell University Press.

———. 1997b. "Storytelling in the Future: Truth, Time, and Tense in Homeric Epic." In *Written Voices, Spoken Signs: Tradition, Performance, and the Epic Text,* edited by Egbert Bakker and Ahuvia Kahane. Cambridge: Harvard University Press, 11–36.

Barnes, H. E. 1974. *The Meddling Gods: Four Essays on Classical Themes.* Lincoln: University of Nebraska Press.

Becker, Andrew Sprague. 1990. "The Shield of Achilles and the Poetics of Homeric Description." *American Journal of Philology* 111: 139–53.

Benhabib, Seyla. 1990a. "Epistemologies of Postmodernism: A Rejoinder to Jean-François Lyotard." In *Feminism/Postmodernism,* edited by Linda J. Nicholson. New York: Routledge, 107–30.

————. 1990b. "Hannah Arendt and the Redemptive Power of Narrative." *Social Research* 57 (spring): 167–96.

Benjamin, Walter. 1968. "The Storyteller: Reflections on the Works of Nikolai Leskov." In *Illuminations,* edited by Hannah Arendt. Translated by Harry Zohn. New York: Schocken Books.

Benveniste, Emile. 1973. *Indo-European Language and Society.* Translated by Elizabeth Palmer. Coral Gables, Fla.: University of Miami Press.

Berry, E. G. 1940. *The History and Development of the Concept of ΘEIA MOIRA and ΘEIA TUXH Down to and Including Plato.* Ph.D. diss., University of Chicago.

Beye, Charles Rowan. 1974. "Male and Female in the Homeric Poems." *Ramus* 3: 87–101.

————. 1993. *Ancient Epic Poetry: Homer, Apollonius, Virgil.* Ithaca, N.Y.: Cornell University Press.

Bintliff, John. 1982. "Settlement Patterns, Land Tenure and Social Structure: A Diachronic Model." In *Ranking, Resource, and Exchange: Aspects of the Archaeology of Early European Society,* edited by Colin Renfrew and Stephen Shennan. Cambridge: Cambridge University Press, 106–11.

Blegan, Carl, Hazel Palmer, and Rodney Young. 1964. *Corinth: The North Cemetery.* Vol. 13. Princeton, N.J.: American School of Classical Studies.

Blome, Peter. 1984. "Lefkandi und Homer." *Würzburger Jahrbücher für die Altertumwissenschaft* 10: 9–21.

Bloom, Harold. 1973. *The Anxiety of Influence: A Theory of Poetry.* New York: Oxford University Press.

————. 1982. *Agon: Towards a Theory of Revisionism.* New York: Oxford University Press, 1982.

Böhme, Joachim. 1929. *Die Seele und das Ich im homerischen Epos.* Leipzig: B. G. Teubner.

Bolter, J. David. 1977. *Achilles' Return to Battle: A Structural Study of Books 19–22 of the* Iliad. Ph.D. diss., University of North Carolina.

Bonner, Robert, and Gertrude Smith. 1930. *The Administration of Justice from Homer to Aristotle.* Chicago: University of Chicago Press.

Bowle, John. 1948. *Western Political Thought: An Historical Introduction from the Origins to Rousseu.* New York: Oxford University Press.

Breiner, Peter. 1996. *Max Weber and Democratic Politics.* Ithaca, N.Y.: Cornell University Press.

Bremer, J. M. 1987. "The So-Called 'Götterapparat' in *Iliad* XX–XXII." In *Homer, Beyond Oral Poetry: Recent Trends in Homeric Interpretation,* edited by J. M. Bremer, I. J. F. de Jong, and J. Kalff. Amsterdam: B. R. Grüner, 31–46.

Broneer, Oscar. 1942. "Hero Cults in the Corinthian Agora." *Hesperia* 11: 128–61.

Brown, Richard Harvey. 1987. *Society as Text: Essays on Rhetoric, Reason, and Reality.* Chicago: University of Chicago Press.

Burkert, Walter. 1955. *Zum altgriechischen Mitleidsbegriff.* Ph.D. diss., Friedrich-Alexander-Universität.

———. 1976. "Das hunderttorige Theben und die Datierung der Ilias." *Wiener Studien* 89: 5–21.

———. 1985. *Greek Religion.* Translated by John Raffan. Cambridge: Harvard University Press. Originally published as *Griechische Religion der archaischen und klassischen Epoche* (Stuttgart: Kohlhammer, 1977).

———. 1995. "Greek *Poleis* and Civic Cults: Some Further Thoughts." In *Studies in the Ancient Greek Polis,* edited by Mogens Herman Hansen and Kurt Raaflaub. Stuttgart: Franz Steiner.

Butler, Judith. 1995. "For a Careful Reading." In *Feminist Contentions: A Philosophical Exchange,* edited by Seyla Benhabib, Judith Butler, Drucilla Cornell, and Nancy Fraser. New York: Routledge.

Cairns, Douglas. 1993. *Aidôs: The Psychology and Ethics of Honour and Shame in Ancient Greek Literature.* Oxford: Oxford University Press.

Calhoun, George. 1927. *The Growth of Criminal Law in Ancient Greece.* Berkeley: University of California Press.

———. 1962. "Polity and Society (i) The Homeric Picture." In *A Companion to Homer,* edited by Alan J. B. Wace and Frank H. Stubbings. New York: Macmillan, 431–52.

Cambitoglou, Alexander, Ann Birchall, J. J. Coulton, and J. R. Green. 1988. *Zagora 2: Excavation of a Geometric Town on the Island of Andros.* 2 vols. Athens: Athens Archaeological Society.

Cambitoglou, Alexander, J. J. Coulton, Judy Birmingham, and J. R. Green. 1971. *Zagora I.* Sidney: Sidney University Press.

Caputo, John. 1987. *Radical Hermeneutics: Repetition, Deconstruction, and the Hermeneutic Project.* Bloomington: Indiana University Press.

Carlier, Pierre. 1984. *La Royauté en Grèce avant Alexandre.* Strasbourg: AECR.

Carneiro, Robert. 1981. "The Chiefdom: Precursor of the State." In *The Transition to Statehood in the New World,* edited by Grant Jones and Robert Kautz. Cambridge: Cambridge University Press, 37–79.

Carroll, Noël. 1990. "Interpretation, History and Narrative." *Monist* 73 (April): 134–66.

Cartledge, Paul. 1983. "'Trade and Politics' Revisited: Archaic Greece." In *Trade in the Ancient Economy,* edited by Peter Garnsey, Keith Hopkins, and C. R. Whittaker. Berkeley: University of California Press, 1–15.

Casevitz, Michel. 1992. "Sur le concept de 'peuple.'" In *La langue et les textes en grec ancien: Actes du colloque Pierre Chantraine,* edited by Françoise Létoublon. Amsterdam: J. C. Gieben, 193–99.

Caskey, Miriam Ervin. 1981. "Ayia Irini, Kea: The Terracotta Statues and the Cult in the Temple." In *Sanctuaries and Cults in the Aegean Bronze Age,* edited by Robin Hägg and Nanno Marinatos. Stockholm: Almqvist and Wiksell, 127–35.

Catlin, George. 1939. *The Story of the Political Philosophers.* New York: Whittlesey House.

Catling, R. W. V., and I. S. Lemos. 1990. *Lefkandi II, The Protogeometric Building at Toumba. Part 1, The Pottery.* Edited by M. R. Popham, P. G. Calligas, and L. H. Sackett. Thames: British School of Archaeology at Athens.

Cawkwell, G. L. 1992. "Early Colonisation." *Classical Quarterly* 42: 289–303.

Claessen, Henri J. M., and Peter Skalník. 1978. "The Early State: Theories and Hypotheses." In *The Early State,* edited by Claessen and Skalník. The Hague: Mouton.

Clark, Matthew. 1997. *Out of Line: Homeric Composition beyond the Hexameter.* Lanham, Md.: Rowman & Littlefield.

Claus, David. 1975. "Aidôs in the Language of Achilles." *TAPA* 105: 13–28.

Clay, J. S. 1983. *The Wrath of Athena: Gods and Men in the* Odyssey. Princeton, N.J.: Princeton University Press.

Clemente, Guido. 1991. "Concluding Reflections." In *City States in Classical Antiquity and Medieval Italy,* edited by Anthony Molho, Kurt Raaflaub, and Julie Emlen. Ann Arbor: University of Michigan Press.

Cohen, Ronald. 1978a. Introduction to *Origins of the State: The Anthropology of Political Evolution*, edited by Ronald Cohen and Elman R. Service. Philadelphia: Institute for the Study of Human Issues.

―――. 1978b. "State Foundations: A Controlled Comparison." In *Origins of the State: The Anthropology of Political Evolution*, edited by Ronald Cohen and Elman R. Service. Philadelphia: Institute for the Study of Human Issues.

―――. 1978c. "State Origins: A Reappraisal." In *The Early State*, edited by Henri J. M. Claessen and Peter Skalník. The Hague: Mouton.

Cohen, Ronald, and Middleton, John. 1967. Introduction to *Comparative Political Systems: Studies in the Politics of Pre-Industrial Societies*, edited by Cohen and Middleton. Garden City, N.Y.: Natural History Press.

―――. 1970. Introduction to *From Tribe to Nation in Africa: Studies in the Incorporation Process*, edited by Ronald Cohen and John Middleton. Scranton, Pa.: Chandler.

Coldstream, J. N. 1968. *Greek Geometric Pottery: A Survey of Ten Local Styles and Their Chronology*. London: Methuen.

―――. 1977. *Geometric Greece*. New York: St. Martin's Press.

―――. 1983. "Gift Exchange in the Eighth Century B.C." In *The Greek Renaissance of the Eighth Century B.C.: Tradition and Innovation*, edited by Robin Hägg. Stockholm: P. Åström, 201–206.

Cole, Susan. 1995. "Civic Cult and Civic Identity." In *Sources for the Ancient Greek City-State: Acts of the Copenhagen Polis Centre*. Vol. 2. Edited by Mogens Herman Hansen. Copenhagen: Munksgaard, 292–325.

Connor, W. R. 1987. "Tribes, Festivals and Processions: Civic Ceremonial and Political Manipulation in Archaic Greece." *Journal of Hellenic Studies* 107: 40–50.

Cook, J. M. 1958–59. "Old Smyrna, 1948–1951." *The Annual of the British School at Athens* 53–54: 1–34.

Cornford, F. M. 1907. *Thucydides Mythistoricus*. London: E. Arnold.

Coulson, William, Donald Haggis, Margaret Mook, and Jennifer Tobin. "Excavations on the Kastro at Kavousi: An Architectural Overview." *Hesperia* 66: 315–90.

Coulton, J. 1993. "The Toumba Building: Description and Analysis of the Architecture." In *Lefkandi II, The Protogeometric Building at Toumba. Part 2, The Excavation, Architecture and Finds*, edited by M. R. Popham, P. G. Calligas, and L. H. Sackett, with J. Coulton and H. W. Catling. Oxford: British School of Archaeology at Athens, 33–70.

Crielaard, Jan Paul. 1995. "Homer, History and Archaeology." In *Homeric Questions*, edited by Crielaard. Amsterdam: J. C. Gieben, 201–88.

Crielaard, Jan Paul, and Jan Driessen. 1994. "The Hero's Home: Some Reflections on the Building at Toumba, Lefkandi." *Topoi* 4: 251–70.

Crotty, Kevin. 1994. *The Poetics of Supplication: Homer's* Iliad *and* Odyssey. Ithaca, N.Y.: Cornell University Press.

Cunliffe, Richard. 1963. *A Lexicon of the Homeric Dialect*. London: Blackie.

Dalby, Andrew. 1995. "The *Iliad*, the *Odyssey* and Their Audience." *Classical Quarterly* 45: 269–79

Davies, John. 1997. "The 'Origins of the Greek *Polis*': Where Should We Be Looking?" In *The Development of the Polis in Archaic Greece*, edited by Lynette Mitchell and P. J. Rhodes. London: Routledge.

Deger-Jalkotzy, Sigrid. 1970. *Herrschaftsformen bei Homer*. Wien: Notring.

———. 1991. "Diskontinuität und Kontinuität: Aspekte politischer und sozialer Organisation in mykenischer Zeit und in der Welt der Homerischen Epen." In *La transizione dal Miceneo all' alto arcaismo. Dal palazzo alla città*, edited by D. Musti, A. Sacconi, L. Rocchetti, M. Rocchi, E. Scarfa, L. Sportiello, and M. E. Giannotta. Rome: Consiglio Nazionale della Ricerche, 53–66.

De Jong, Irene. 1987a. *Narrators and Focalizers: The Presentation of the Story in the* Iliad. Amsterdam: B. R. Grüner.

———. 1987b. "Silent Characters in the *Iliad*." In *Homer, Beyond Oral Poetry: Recent Trends in Homeric Interpretation*, edited by J. M. Bremer, I. J. F. de Jong, and J. Kalff. Amsterdam: B. R. Grüner, 105–21.

———. 1997. "Homer and Narratology." In *A New Companion to Homer*, edited by Ian Morris and Barry Powell. Leiden: Brill, 305–25.

Deleuze, Gilles. 1994. *Difference and Repetition*. Translated by Paul Patton. New York: Columbia University Press.

Demargne, Pierre, and Henri van Effenterre. 1937. "Recherches a Dréros." *Bulletin de correspondance hellénique* 61: 5–32.

De Polignac, François. 1994. "Mediation, Competition, and Sovereignty: The Evolution of Rural Sanctuaries in Geometric Greece." In *Placing the Gods: Sanctuaries and Sacred Space in Ancient Greece*, edited by Susan Alcock and Robin Osborne. Oxford: Clarendon Press, 3–18.

———. 1995. *Cults, Territory, and the Origins of the Greek City-State*. Chicago: University of Chicago Press. Originally published as *Naissance de la cité grecque* (Paris: Découverte, 1984).

Derrida, Jacques. 1981a. *Dissemination*. Translated by Barbara Johnson. Chicago: University of Chicago Press.

————. 1981b. "The Law of Genre." Translated by Avital Ronell. In *On Narrative*, edited by W. J. T. Mitchell. Chicago: University of Chicago Press.

De Ste. Croix, G. E. M. 1981. *The Class Struggle in the Ancient Greek World: From the Archaic Age to the Arab Conquests*. Ithaca, N.Y.: Cornell University Press.

Detienne, Marcel. 1996. *The Masters of Truth in Archaic Greece*. Translated by Janet Lloyd. New York: Zone Books. Originally published as *Les Maîtres de vérité dans la Grèce archaïque* (Paris: F. Maspero, 1967).

Dickie, Matthew. 1995. "The Geography of Homer's World." In *Homer's World: Fiction, Tradition, Reality*, edited by Øivind Andersen and Matthew Dickie. Bergen: P. Åström, 29–56.

Dienstag, Joshua Foa. 1997. *Dancing in Chains: Narrative and Memory in Political Theory*. Stanford, Calif.: Stanford University Press.

Dietrich, B. C. 1973. *The Origins of Greek Religion*. Berlin: de Gruyter.

Disch, Lisa Jane. 1994. *Hannah Arendt and the Limits of Philosophy*. Ithaca, N.Y.: Cornell University Press.

Dobbs, Darrell. 1987. "Reckless Rationalism and Heroic Reverence in Homer's *Odyssey*." *American Political Science Review* 81 (June): 491–508.

Dodds, E. R. 1957. *The Greeks and the Irrational*. Boston: Beacon Press.

————. 1968. "Homer: I. Homer and the Analysts, II. Homer and the Unitarians." In *Fifty Years (and Twelve) of Classical Scholarship*. Rev. ed. Edited by Maurice Platnauer. New York: Barnes & Noble, 1–13.

Donlan, Walter. 1973. "The Tradition of Anti-Aristocratic Thought in Early Greek Poetry." *Historia* 22: 145–54.

————. 1979. "The Structure of Authority in the *Iliad*." *Arethusa* 12: 51–70.

————. 1980. *The Aristocratic Ideal in Ancient Greece*. Lawrence, Kans.: Coronado Press.

————. 1981–82. "Reciprocities in Homer." *Classical World* 75: 137–75.

————. 1985. "The Social Groups of Dark Age Greece." *Classical Philology* 80: 293–308.

————. 1989a. "Homeric τέμενος and the Land Economy of the Dark Age." *Museum Helveticum* 46: 129–45.

————. 1989b. "The Pre-State Community in Greece." *Symbolae Osloenses* 64: 5–29.

————. 1989c. "The Unequal Exchange between Glaucus and Diomedes in Light of the Homeric Gift-Economy." *Phoenix* 43: 1–15.

———. 1993. "Duelling with Gifts in the *Iliad*: As the Audience Saw It." *Colby Quarterly* 24: 155–72.

———. 1997a. "The Homeric Economy." In *A New Companion to Homer*, edited by Ian Morris and Barry Powell. Leiden: Brill, 649–67.

———. 1997b. "The Relations of Power in the Pre-State and Early State Polities." In *The Development of the Polis in Archaic Greece*, edited by Lynette Mitchell and P. J. Rhodes. London: Routledge.

———. 1998. "Political Reciprocity in Dark Age Greece: Odysseus and His *Hetairoi*." In *Reciprocity in Ancient Greece*, edited by Christopher Gill, Norman Postlethwaite, and Richard Seaford. Oxford: Oxford University Press, 151–71.

Donlan, Walter, and Carol G. Thomas. 1993. "The Village Community of Ancient Greece: Neolithic, Bronze, and Dark Ages." *Studi Micenei ed Egeo-Anatolici* 31: 61–71.

Douglas, Mary. 1966. *Purity and Danger: An Analysis of Concepts of Pollution and Taboo.* London: Routledge & Kegan Paul.

———. 1978. *Cultural Bias.* Occasional paper no. 34. London: Royal Anthropological Institute of Great Britain and Ireland.

———. 1982. *Natural Symbols: Exploration in Cosmology.* New York: Pantheon.

Douglas, Mary, and Aaron Wildavsky. 1982. *Risk and Culture.* Berkeley: University of California Press.

Drews, Robert. 1972. "The First Tyrants in Greece." *Historia* 21: 129–44.

———. 1983. *Basileus: The Evidence for Kingship in Geometric Greece.* New Haven, Conn.: Yale University Press.

Drolet, Michael. 1994. "The Wild and the Sublime: Lyotard's Post-Modern Politics." *Political Studies* 42: 259–73.

Dunbabin, T. J. 1948. *The Western Greeks: The History of Sicily and South Italy from the Foundation of the Greek Colonies to 480 B.C.* Oxford: Clarendon Press.

Earle, Timothy. 1991. "Property Rights and the Evolution of Chiefdoms." In *Chiefdoms: Power, Economy, and Ideology*, edited by Earle. Cambridge: Cambridge University Press, 71–99.

Easterling, P. E. 1989. "Agamemnon's *Skêptron* in the *Iliad*." In *Images of Authority*, edited by Mary Margaret Mackenzie and Charlotte Roueché. Cambridge: Cambridge Philological Society, 104–121.

Easton, David. 1959. "Political Anthropology." In *Biennial Review of Anthropology: 1959*, edited by Bernard J. Siegal. Stanford, Calif.: Stanford University Press, 210–62.

Eder, Walter. 1986. "The Political Significance of the Codification of Law in Archaic Societies: An Unconventional Hypothesis." In *Social Struggles in Archaic Rome: New Perspectives on the Conflict of the Orders*, edited by Kurt Raaflaub. Berkeley: University of California Press, 262–300.

———. 1992. "Polis und Politai: Die Auflösung des Adelsstaates und die Entwicklung des Polisbürgers." In *Euphronios und seine Zeit*, edited by W.-D. Heilmeyer and I. Wehgartner. Berlin: Staatliche Museen, 24–38.

Edmunds, Lowell. 1975. *Chance and Intelligence in Thucydides*. Cambridge: Harvard University Press.

———. 1989. "Commentary on Raaflaub." In *Proceedings of the Boston Area Colloquium in Ancient Philosophy*. Vol. 4. Edited by John Cleary and Daniel Shartin. New York: University Press of America.

Edwards, A. T. 1993. "Homer's Ethical Geography: Country and City in the *Odyssey*." *TAPA* 123: 27–78.

Edwards, Carol. 1983. "The Parry-Lord Theory Meets Operational Structuralism." *Journal of American Folklore* 96: 151–69.

Edwards, Mark W. 1987. *Homer: Poet of the Iliad*. Baltimore: Johns Hopkins University Press.

Ehrenberg, Victor. 1943. "An Early Source of Polis-Constitution." *Classical Quarterly* 37: 14–18.

———. 1960. *The Greek State*. New York: Barnes & Noble.

———. 1967. *From Solon to Socrates: Greek History and Civilization during the 6th and 5th centuries B.C.* London: Methuen.

Elliot, William, and Neil McDonald. 1949. *Western Political Heritage*. New York: Prentice-Hall.

Emerson, Caryl. 1993. "Irreverent Bakhtin and the Imperturbable Classics." *Arethusa* 26: 123–39.

Erbse, Hartmut. 1986. *Untersuchungen zur Funktion der Götter im homerischen Epos*. Berlin: de Gruyter.

———. 1990. "Nachlese zur Homerischen Psychologie." *Hermes* 118: 1–17.

Euben, J. Peter. 1990. *The Tragedy of Political Theory: The Road Not Taken*. Princeton, N.J.: Princeton University.

Evans-Pritchard, E. E. 1952. *Social Anthropology*. Glencoe, Ill.: Free Press.

———. 1962. "The Divine Kingship of the Shilluk of the Nilotic Sudan." In *Essays in Social Anthropology*. New York: Free Press.

Fagerström, Kåre. 1988. *Greek Iron Age Architecture: Developments through Changing Times*. Göteborg: P. Åström.

Farenga, Vincent. 1998. "Narrative and Community in Dark Age Greece: A Cognitive and Communicative Approach to Early Greek Citizenship." *Arethusa* 31: 179–206.

Feeney, D. C. 1991. *The Gods in Epic: Poets and Critics of the Classical Tradition.* Oxford: Clarendon Press.

Felsch, Rainer C. S. 1981. "Mykenischer Kult im Heiligtum bei Kalapodi?" In *Sanctuaries and Cults in the Aegean Bronze Age*, edited by Robin Hägg and Nanno Marinatos. Stockholm: Almqvist and Wiksell, 81–89.

Felson-Rubin, Nancy. 1993. "Bakhtinian Alterity, Homeric Rapport." *Arethusa* 26: 159–71.

―――. 1994. *Regarding Penelope: From Character to Poetics.* Princeton, N.J.: Princeton University Press.

Fenik, Bernard. 1968. *Typical Battle Scenes in the* Iliad: *Studies in the Narrative Techniques of Homeric Battle Description.* Wiesbaden: F. Steiner.

Ferguson, Yale. 1991. "Chiefdoms to City-States: The Greek Experience." In *Chiefdoms: Power, Economy, and Ideology*, edited by Timothy Earle. Cambridge: Cambridge University Press, 169–92.

Finkelberg, Margalit. 1998. "*Timê* and *Aretê* in Homer." *Classical Quarterly* 48: 14–28.

Finley, J. H., Jr. 1942. *Thucydides.* Cambridge: Harvard University Press.

Finley, M. I. 1973. *The Ancient Economy.* London: Chatto & Windus.

―――. 1975. "Anthropology and the Classics." In *The Use and Abuse of History.* New York: Viking Press: 102–19.

―――. 1979. *The World of Odysseus.* 2d ed. New York: Penguin.

―――. 1981. *Early Greece: The Bronze and Archaic Ages.* London: Chatto & Windus.

―――. 1982. *Economy and Society in Ancient Greece.* Edited by Brent Shaw and Richard Saller. New York: Viking.

―――. 1983. *Politics in the Ancient World.* Cambridge: Cambridge University Press.

Finnegan, Ruth. 1977. *Oral Poetry: Its Nature, Significance and Social Context.* Cambridge: Cambridge University Press.

Fischer-Hansen, Tobias. 1996. "The Earliest Town-Planning of the Western Greek Colonies. With Special Regard to Sicily." In *Introduction to an Inventory of Poleis*, edited by Mogens Herman Hansen. Copenhagen: Munksgaard, 317–73.

Flaig, Egon. 1994. "Das Konsensprinzip in homerischen Olymp. Überlegungen zum göttlichen Entscheidungsprozess Ilias 4.1–72." *Hermes* 122: 13–31.

Foley, Anne. 1988. *The Argolid 800–600 B.C.: An Archaeological Survey.* Göteborg: P. Åström.

Foley, John. 1997. "Traditional Signs and Homeric Art." In *Written Voices, Spoken Signs: Tradition, Performance, and the Epic Text,* edited by Egbert Bakker and Ahuvia Kahane. Cambridge: Harvard University Press, 56–82.

Fontenrose, Joseph. 1978. *The Delphic Oracle: Its Responses and Operation.* Berkeley: University of California Press.

Ford, Andrew. 1992. *Homer: The Poetry of the Past.* Ithaca, N.Y.: Cornell University Press.

Forrest, W. G. 1966. *The Emergence of Greek Democracy, 800–400 B.C.* New York: McGraw-Hill.

Fortes, M., and E. E. Evans-Pritchard. 1940. Introduction to *African Political Systems,* edited by Forest and Evans-Pritchard. London: Oxford University Press.

Fossey, John. 1988. *Topography and Population of Ancient Boiotia.* Chicago: Ares.

Foucault, Michel. 1972. *The Archaeology of Knowledge and the Discourse on Language.* Translated by A. M. Sheridan Smith. New York: Pantheon.

———. 1980. "Two Lectures." In *Power/Knowledge: Selected Interviews and Other Writings 1972–1977,* edited by Colin Gordon. New York: Pantheon Books.

———. 1983. "On the Genealogy of Ethics: An Overview of Work in Progress." In *Michel Foucault, Beyond Structuralism and Hermeneutics,* by Hubert L. Dreyfus and Paul Rabinow. 2d ed. Chicago: University of Chicago Press.

———. 1984a. "An Interview with Michel Foucault." In *The Foucault Reader,* edited by Paul Rabinow. New York: Pantheon Books.

———. 1984b. "Politics and Ethics: An Interview." In *The Foucault Reader,* edited by Paul Rabinow. New York: Pantheon Books.

———. 1997. "The Ethics of the Concern for Self as a Practice of Freedom." In *Ethics: Subjectivity and Truth.* Vol. 1. Edited by Paul Rabinow. Translated by Robert Hurley and others. New York: New Press.

Fränkel, Hermann. 1962. *Dichtung und Philosophie des frühen Griechentums.* München: Beck. Translated by Moses Hadas and James Willis as *Early Greek Poetry and Philosophy* (Oxford: Blackwell, 1975).

Freeman, Kathleen. 1976. *The Work and Life of Solon: With a Translation of his Poems.* New York: Arno Press.

Fried, Morton H. 1967. *The Evolution of Political Society: An Essay in Political Anthropology.* New York: Random House.

Friedman, J., and M. J. Rowlands. 1977. "Notes Towards an Epigenetic Model of the Evolution of 'Civilisation.'" In *The Evolution of Social Systems,* edited by Friedman and Rowlands. Trowbridge: Duckworth, 201–76.

Friedrich, Paul, and James Redfield. 1978. "Speech as a Personality Symbol: The Case of Achilles." *Language* 54: 263–87.

Gagarin, Michael. 1973. "*Dikê* in the *Works and Days.*" *Classical Philology* 68 (April): 81–94.

———. 1986. *Early Greek Law.* Berkeley: University of California Press.

———. 1987. "Morality in Homer." *Classical Philology* 82: 285–306.

Gagarin, Michael, and Paul Woodruff. 1995. *Early Greek Political Thought from Homer to the Sophists.* Cambridge: Cambridge University Press.

Galbraith, John Kenneth. 1983. *The Anatomy of Power.* Boston: Houghton Mifflin.

Gaskin, Richard. 1990. "Do Homeric Heroes Make Real Decisions?" *Classical Quarterly* 40: 1–15.

Gates, Bill. 1995. "Bill Gates: How the American Spirit Gives Us an Edge in Business." *USAir Magazine* 61 (March): 63.

Gearing, Fred. 1968. "Sovereignties and Jural Communities in Political Evolution." In *Essays on the Problem of Tribe,* edited by June Helm. Seattle: University of Washington Press, 111–19.

Geddes, A. G. 1984. "Who's Who in 'Homeric' Society?" *Classical Quarterly* 34: 17–36.

Geertz, Clifford. 1973a. "Ideology as a Cultural System." In *The Interpretation of Cultures.* New York: Basic Books, 193–233.

———. 1973b. "Thick Description: Toward an Interpretative Theory of Culture." In *The Interpretation of Cultures.* New York: Basic Books, 3–30.

Gill, Christopher. 1990. "The Character–Personality Distinction." In *Characterization and Individuality in Greek Literature,* edited by Christopher Pelling. Oxford: Oxford University Press, 1–31.

———. 1996. *Personality in Greek Epic, Tragedy, and Philosophy: The Self in Dialogue.* Oxford: Clarendon Press.

Glotz, Gustave. 1928. *La cité Grecque.* Paris: La Renaissance du Livre. Translated as *The Greek City and Its Institutions* (New York: Knopf, 1930).

Gluckman, Max. 1965. *Politics, Law and Ritual in Tribal Society.* New York: Aldine.

Gouschin, Valerij. 1999. "Pisistratus' Leadership in A.P. 13.4 and the Establishment of the Tyranny of 561/60 B.C." *Classical Quarterly* 49: 14–23.

Graham, A. J. 1971. "Patterns of Early Greek Colonization." *Journal of Hellenic Studies* 91: 35–47.

Greene, William. 1944. *Moira: Fate, Good, and Evil in Greek Thought.* Cambridge: Harvard University Press.

Greenhalgh, P. A. L. 1972. "Patriotism in the Homeric World." *Historia* 21: 528–37.

Griffin, Jasper. 1980. *Homer on Life and Death.* Oxford: Clarendon.

Gschnitzer, Fritz. 1965. "BASILEUS: Ein terminologischer Beitrag zur Frühgeschichte des Königtums bei den Griechen." *Innsbrucker Beiträge zur Kulturwissenschaft* 11: 99–112.

———. 1981. *Griechische Sozialgeschichte: Von der mykenischen bis zum Ausgang der klassischen Zeit.* Wiesbaden: Franz Steiner.

———. 1991. "Zur homerischen Staats- und Gesellschaftsordnung: Grundcharakter und geschichtliche Stellung." In *Zweihundert Jahre Homer-Forschung: Rückblick und Ausblick,* edited by Joachim Latacz. Stuttgart: B. G. Teubner, 182–204.

Gunnell, John G. 1987. *Political Philosophy and Time: Plato and the Origins of Political Vision.* Chicago: University of Chicago Press.

Haas, Jonathan. 1982. *The Evolution of the Prehistoric State.* New York: Columbia University Press.

Hägg, Robin. 1974. *Die Gräber der Argolis in submykenischer, protogeometrischer und geometrischer Zeit.* Uppsala: Acta Universitatis Upsaliensis.

———. 1983. "Burial Customs and Social Differentiation in 8th-Century Argos." In *The Greek Renaissance of the Eighth Century B.C.: Tradition and Innovation.* Edited by Hägg. Stockholm: P. Åström.

Hainsworth, J. B. 1992. "The Criticism of an Oral Homer." In *Homer: Readings and Images,* edited by C. Emlyn-Jones, L. Hardwick, and J. Purkis. London: Duckworth.

Hall, Jonathan. 1997. *Ethnic Identity in Greek Antiquity.* Cambridge: Cambridge University Press.

Hallowell, John, and Jene Porter. 1997. *Political Philosophy: The Search for Humanity and Order.* Scarborough, Ont.: Prentice-Hall Canada.

Halverson, John. 1985. "Social Order in the 'Odyssey.'" *Hermes* 113: 129–45.

Hansen, Mogens Herman. 1993. "Introduction: The Polis as a Citizen-State." In *The Ancient Greek City-State,* edited by Hansen. Copenhagen: Munksgaard, 7–29.

————. 1995. "The 'Autonomous City-State': Ancient Fact or Modern Fiction." In *Studies in the Ancient Greek Polis*, edited by Hansen and Kurt Raaflaub. Stuttgart: Franz Steiner.

Hansen, Mogens Herman, and Kurt Raaflaub, eds. 1995. *Studies in the Ancient Greek Polis*. Stuttgart: Franz Steiner.

Haubold, Johannes. 2000. *Homer's People: Epic Poetry and Social Formation*. Cambridge: Cambridge University Press.

Havel, Václav. 1991. "Stories and Totalitarianism." In *Open Letters: Selected Writings 1965–1990*, edited by Paul Wilson. New York: Knopf.

————. 1997. "Academy of Performing Arts." In *The Art of the Impossible: Politics as Morality in Practice*. Translated by Paul Wilson. New York: Knopf.

Havelock, Eric. 1963. *Preface to Plato*. Cambridge: Harvard University Press, Belknap Press.

————. 1978. *The Greek Concept of Justice: From Its Shadow in Homer to Its Reality in Plato*. Cambridge: Harvard University Press.

————. 1983. "The Linguistic Task of the Presocratics." In *Language and Thought in Early Greek Philosophy*, edited by Kevin Robb. La Salle, Ill.: Hegeler Institute.

Heidegger, Martin. 1971a. "Building Dwelling Thinking." In *Poetry, Language, Thought*. Translated by Albert Hofstadter. New York: Harper & Row, 145–61.

————. 1971b. "Language." In *Poetry, Language, Thought*. Translated by Albert Hofstadter. New York: Harper & Row, 189–210.

————. 1971c. "The Origin of the Work of Art." In *Poetry, Language, Thought*. Translated by Albert Hofstadter. New York: Harper & Row, 17–87.

————. 1971d. ". . . Poetically Man Dwells. . . ." In *Poetry, Language, Thought*. Translated by Albert Hofstadter. New York: Harper & Row, 213–29.

————. 1979. *Being and Time*. Translated by John Macquarrie and Edward Robinson. New York: Harper & Row. Originally published as *Sein und Zeit* (Tübingen: Max Niemeyer, 1962).

Hignett, Charles. 1958. *A History of the Athenian Constitution to the End of the Fifth Century B.C.* Oxford: Clarendon Press.

Hoffmann, Wilhelm. 1956. "Die Polis bei Homer." In *Festschrift Bruno Snell*, edited by H. Erbse. München: Beck, 153–65.

Hölkeskamp, Karl-Joachim. 1994. "Tempel, Agora und Alphabet: Die Entstehungsbedingungen von Gesetzgebung in der archaischen Polis." In *Rechtskodifizierung und soziale Normen im interkulturellen*

Vergleich, edited by Hans-Joachim Gehrke. Tübingen: Gunter Narr, 135–64.

———. 1997. *"Agorai* bei Homer." In *Volk und Verfassung im vorhellenistischen Griechenland,* edited by Walter Eder and Karl-Joachim Hölkeskamp. Stuttgart: Franz Steiner, 1–19.

Holoka, James. 1991. "Homer, Oral Poetry Theory, and Comparative Literature: Major Trends and Controversies in Twentieth-Century Criticism." In *Zweihundert Jahre Homer-Forschung,* edited by Joachim Latacz. Stuttgart: B. G. Teubner, 456–81.

Holway, Richard. 1989. "Poetry and Political Thought in Archaic Greece: The *Iliad,* the *Theogony,* and the Rise of the *Polis.*" Ph.D. diss., University of California, Berkeley.

Humphreys, S. C. 1978. *Anthropology and the Greeks.* London: Routledge & Kegan Paul.

Huxley, G. L. 1969. *Greek Epic Poetry: From Eumelos to Panyassis.* Cambridge: Harvard University Press.

Jacobsen, Thorkild. 1970a. "Early Political Development in Mesopotamia." In *Toward the Image of Tammuz and Other Essays on Mesopotamian History and Culture,* edited by William Moran. Cambridge: Harvard University Press, 132–56.

———. 1970b. "Primitive Democracy in Ancient Mesopotamia." In *Toward the Image of Tammuz and Other Essays on Mesopotamian History and Culture,* edited by William Moran. Cambridge: Harvard University Press, 157–70.

Jacopin, Pierre-Yves. 1988. "On the Syntactic Structure of Myth, or the Yakuna Invention of Speech." *Cultural Anthropology* 3 (May): 131–59.

Jaeger, Werner. 1967. *Paideia: The Ideals of Greek Culture.* Translated from the second German edition by Gilbert Highet. Vol. 1. New York: Oxford University Press.

Jakobson, Roman. 1960. "Closing Statement: Linguistics and Poetics." In *Style in Language,* edited by Thomas Sebeok. New York: Wiley: 350–77.

Jameson, Fredric. 1984. Foreword to *The Postmodern Condition: A Report on Knowledge,* by Jean-François Lyotard. Translated by Geoff Bennington and Brian Massumi. Minneapolis: University of Minnesota Press, vii–xxi.

———. 1991. *Postmodernism, or, The Cultural Logic of Late Capitalism.* Durham, N.C.: Duke University Press.

Janko, Richard. 1982. *Homer, Hesiod and the Hymns: Diachronic Development in Epic Diction.* Cambridge: Cambridge University Press.

————. 1998. "The Homeric Poems as Oral Dictated Texts." *Classical Quarterly* 48: 135–67.

Janszen, Nick. 1997. "The Divine Comedy of Homer: Defining Political Virtue through Comic Depictions of the Gods." In *Justice v. Law in Greek Political Thought,* edited by Leslie Rubin. Lanham, Md.: Rowman & Littlefield, 69–81.

Jeffery, L. H. 1976. *Archaic Greece: The City-States c. 700–500 B.C.* London: Ernest Benn.

————. 1990. *The Local Scripts of Archaic Greece: A Study of the Origin of the Greek Alphabet and Its Development from the Eighth to the Fifth Centuries B.C.* Rev. ed. Oxford: Clarendon Press.

Jones, J. Walter. 1956. *The Law and Legal Theory of the Greeks: An Introduction.* Oxford: Clarendon Press.

Kant, Immanuel. 1959. *Foundations of the Metaphysics of Morals.* Translated by Lewis White Beck. Indianapolis: Bobbs-Merrill.

Katz, Marylin. 1991. *Penelope's Renown: Meaning and Indeterminacy in the* Odyssey. Princeton, N.J.: Princeton University Press.

Kelly, Thomas. 1976. *A History of Argos to 500 B.C.* Minneapolis: University of Minnesota Press.

King, Katherine Callen. 1987. *Achilles: Paradigms of the War Hero from Homer to the Middle Ages.* Berkeley: University of California Press.

Kirk, G. S. 1962. *The Songs of Homer.* Cambridge: Cambridge University Press.

————. 1976. *Homer and the Oral Tradition.* Cambridge: Cambridge University Press.

————. 1985. *The* Iliad: *A Commentary.* Vol. 1: Books 1–4. Cambridge: Cambridge University Press.

Klosko, George. 1993. *History of Political Theory: An Introduction.* Vol. 1. Fort Worth, Tex.: Harcourt Brace.

Kolb, Frank. 1977. "Die Bau-, Religious- und Kulturpolitik der Peisistratiden." *Jahrbuch des Deutschen Archäologischen Instituts* 92: 99–138.

Konstan, David. 1999. "Ancient Pity." Paper presented at the "For Passions and Perspectives: Representing Emotions in Antiquity" conference, Columbia University, November 13.

Köstler, Rudolf. [1950] 1968. "Die Homerische Rechts- und Staatsordnung." In *Zur Griechischen Rechtsgeschichte,* edited by Erich Berneker. Darmstadt: Wissenschaftliche Buchgesellschaft, 172–95.

Kristiansen, Kristian. 1991. "Chiefdoms, States, and Systems of Social Evolution." In *Chiefdoms: Power, Economy, and Ideology,* edited by Timothy Earle. Cambridge: Cambridge University Press, 16–43.

Kullmann, W. 1985. "Gods and Men in the *Iliad* and the *Odyssey*." *Harvard Studies in Classical Philology* 89: 1–23.

———. 1995. "Homers Zeit und das Bild des Dichters von den Menschen der mykenischen Kultur." In *Homer's World: Fiction, Tradition, Reality*, edited by Øivind Andersen and Matthew Dickie. Bergen: P. Åström, 57–75.

Lambrinudakis, V. 1981. "Remains of the Mycenaean Period in the Sanctuary of Apollon Maleatas." In *Sanctuaries and Cults in the Aegean Bronze Age*, edited by Robin Hägg and Nanno Marinatos. Stockholm: Almqvist and Wiksell, 59–65.

Latacz, Joachim. 1996. *Homer: His Art and His World*. Translated by James Holoka. Ann Arbor: University of Michigan Press.

Legon, Ronald. 1981. *Megara: The Political History of a Greek City-State to 336 B.C.* Ithaca, N.Y.: Cornell University Press.

Lendon, J. E. Forthcoming. "Voting by Shouting in Sparta."

Lenz, John. 1993. "Kings and the Ideology of Kingship in Early Greece (c. 1200–700 B.C): Epic, Archaeology and History." Ph.D. diss., Columbia University.

Lesky, Albin. 1961. *Göttliche und menschliche Motivation im homerischen Epos*. Heidelberg: Carl Winter.

Lessing, Gotthold Ephraim. 1984. *Laocoön: An Essay on the Limits of Painting and Poetry*. Baltimore: Johns Hopkins University Press.

Lloyd-Jones, Hugh. 1971. *The Justice of Zeus*. Berkeley: University of California Press.

Long, A. A. 1970. "Morals and Values in Homer." *Journal of Hellenic Studies* 90: 121–39.

———. 1992. "Stoic Readings of Homer." In *Homer's Ancient Readers: The Hermeneutics of Greek Epic's Earliest Exegetes*, edited by Robert Lamberton and John Keaney. Princeton, N.J.: Princeton University Press.

Lord, Albert Bates. 1951. "Composition by Theme in Homer and Southslavic Epos." *TAPA* 82: 71–80.

———. 1960. *The Singer of Tales*. Cambridge: Harvard University Press.

Losco, Joseph, and Leonard Williams. 1992. *Political Theory: Classic Writings, Contemporary Views*. New York: St. Martin's Press.

Louden, Robert B., and Paul Schollmeier, eds. 1996. *The Greeks and Us: Essays in Honor of Arthur W. H. Adkins*. Chicago: University of Chicago Press.

Lowenstam, Steven. 1993. *The Scepter and the Spear: Studies on Forms of Repetition in the Homeric Poems*. Lanham, Md.: Rowman & Littlefield.

Luban, David. 1983. "Explaining Dark Times: Hannah Arendt's Theory of Theory." *Social Research* 50: 215–48.

Luce, J. V. 1975. *Homer and the Heroic Age.* New York: Harper & Row.

———. 1978. "The Polis in Homer and Hesiod." *Proceedings of the Royal Irish Academy* 78: 1–15.

Lynn-George, Michael. 1988. *Epos: Word, Narrative and the Iliad.* Atlantic Highlands, N.J.: Humanities Press.

Lyotard, Jean-François. 1984. *The Postmodern Condition: A Report on Knowledge.* Translated by Geoff Bennington and Brian Massumi. Minneapolis: University of Minnesota Press.

———. 1988. *The Differend: Phrases in Dispute.* Translated by Georges Van Den Abbeele. Minneapolis: University of Minnesota Press.

———. 1989. "Universal History and Cultural Differences." In *The Lyotard Reader,* edited by Andrew Benjamin. Oxford: Blackwell: 314–23.

———. 1991. *The Inhuman: Reflections on Time.* Stanford, Calif.: Stanford University Press.

MacCary, W. Thomas. 1982. *Childlike Achilles: Ontogeny and Phylogeny in the* Iliad. New York: Columbia University Press.

MacIntyre, Alasdair. 1984. *After Virtue.* 2d ed. Notre Dame, Ind.: University of Notre Dame Press.

———. *Whose Justice? Which Rationality?* Notre Dame, Ind.: University of Notre Dame Press.

Mackie, Hilary. 1996. *Talking Trojan: Speech and Community in the* Iliad. Lanham, Md.: Rowman & Littlefield.

MacLeod, C. W. 1982. *Homer, Iliad, Book XXIV.* Cambridge: Cambridge University Press.

Maine, Henry. 1888. *Lectures on the Early History of Institutions.* New York: Holt.

Mair, Lucy. 1962. *Primitive Government.* Baltimore: Penguin.

Malinowski, Bronislaw. 1926. *Crime and Custom in Savage Society.* London: Kegan Paul.

Malkin, Irad. 1998. *The Returns of Odysseus: Colonization and Ethnicity.* Berkeley: University of California Press.

Manville, Philip Brook. 1990. *The Origins of Citizenship in Ancient Athens.* Princeton, N.J.: Princeton University Press.

Margolis, Joseph. 1993. "Redeeming Foucault." In *Foucault and the Critique of Institutions,* edited by John Caputo and Mark Yount. University Park: Pennsylvania State University Press, 41–59.

Martin, R. P. 1989. *The Language of Heroes: Speech and Performance in the* Iliad. Ithaca, N.Y.: Cornell University Press.

Mauss, Marcel. [1954] 1967. *The Gift: Forms and Functions of Exchange in Archaic Societies.* New York: Norton.

Mazarakis Ainian, Alexander. 1997. *From Rulers' Dwellings to Temples: Architecture, Religion and Society in Early Iron Age Greece (1100–700 B.C.).* Jonsered: Paul Åströms Förlag.

McDonald, Lee. 1968. *Western Political Theory.* 3 vols. New York: Harcourt Brace Jovanovich.

McDonald, William. 1943. *The Political Meeting Places of the Greeks.* Baltimore: Johns Hopkins University Press.

McGlew, James. 1989. "Royal Power and the Achaean Assembly at *Iliad* 2.84–393." *Classical Antiquity* 8 (October): 283–95.

———. 1993. *Tyranny and Political Culture in Ancient Greece.* Ithaca, N.Y.: Cornell University Press.

McGowan, John. 1991. *Postmodernism and Its Critics.* Ithaca, N.Y.: Cornell University Press.

McIlwain, Charles. 1968. *The Growth of Political Thought in the West: From the Greeks to the End of the Middle Ages.* New York: Cooper Square.

Meier, Christian. 1990. *The Greek Discovery of Politics.* Translated by David McLintock. Cambridge: Harvard University Press.

Meiggs, Russell, and David Lewis, eds. 1969. *A Selection of Greek Historical Inscriptions to the End of the Fifth Century B.C.* Oxford: Clarendon Press.

Miller, Paul Allen, and Charles Platter. 1993. "Introduction." *Arethusa* 26: 117–21.

Miller, Stephen. 1978. *The Prytaneion: Its Function and Architectural Form.* Berkeley: University of California Press.

Mireaux, Emile. 1959. *Daily Life in the Time of Homer.* New York: Macmillan.

Mondi, Robert. 1980. "ΣΚΗΡΤΟΥΧΟΙ ΒΑΣΙΛΕΙΣ: An Argument for Divine Kingship in Early Greece." *Arethusa* 13: 203–16.

Morgan, Catherine. 1988. "Corinth, the Corinthian Gulf and Western Greece during the Eighth Century BC." *Annual of the British School at Athens* 83: 313–38.

———. 1993. "The Origins of Pan-Hellenism." In *Greek Sanctuaries: New Approaches,* edited by Nanno Marinatos and Robin Hägg. London: Routledge, 18–44.

———. 1994. "The Evolution of a Sacral 'Landscape': Isthmia, Perachora, and the Early Corinthian State." In *Placing the Gods: Sanctuaries and Sacred Space in Ancient Greece,* edited by Susan E. Alcock and Robin Osborne. Oxford: Clarendon Press, 105–42.

Morgan, Catherine, and Todd Whitelaw. 1991. "Pots and Politics: Ceramic Evidence for the Rise of the Argive State." *American Journal of Archaeology* 95: 79–108.

Moore, Sally, and Barbara Myerhoff. 1977. "Introduction: Secular Ritual: Forms and Meanings." In *Secular Ritual*, edited by Moore and Myerhoff. Amsterdam: Van Gorcum.

Morris, Ian. 1986. "The Use and Abuse of Homer." *Classical Antiquity* 5 (April): 81–138.

———. 1987. *Burial and Ancient Society: The Rise of the Greek City-State.* Cambridge: Cambridge University Press.

———. 1991. "The Early Polis as City and State." In *City and Country in the Ancient World*, edited by John Rich and Andrew Wallace-Hadrill. New York: Routledge, 25–57.

———. 1997. "The Art of Citizenship." In *New Light on a Dark Age: Exploring the Culture of Geometric Greece*, edited by Susan Langdon. Columbia: University of Missouri Press, 9–43.

Muellner, Leonard. 1976. *The Meaning of Homeric εὔχομαι through Its Formulas.* Innsbruck: Innsbrucker Beiträge zur Sprachwissenschaft.

———. 1996. *The Anger of Achilles: Mênis in Greek Epic.* Ithaca, N.Y.: Cornell University Press.

Murray, Oswyn. 1980. *Early Greece.* Stanford, Calif.: Stanford University Press.

———. 1990. "Cities of Reason." In *The Greek City: From Homer to Alexander*, edited by Oswyn Murray and Simon Price. Oxford: Clarendon Press.

Myrsiades, Kostas, ed. 1987. *Approaches to Teaching Homer's* Iliad *and* Odyssey. New York: Modern Language Association of America.

Naas, Michael. 1995. *Turning: From Persuasion to Philosophy: A Reading of Homer's* Iliad. Atlantic Highlands, N.J.: Humanities Press.

Nagler, Michael. 1974. *Spontaneity and Tradition: A Study in the Oral Art of Homer.* Berkeley: University of California Press.

Nagy, Gregory. 1979. *The Best of the Achaeans: Concepts of the Hero in Archaic Greek Poetry.* Baltimore: Johns Hopkins University Press.

———. 1990. *Greek Mythology and Poetics.* Ithaca, N.Y.: Cornell University Press.

———. 1992. "Homeric Questions." *TAPA* 122: 17–60.

———. 1996. *Poetry as Performance: Homer and Beyond.* Cambridge: Cambridge University Press.

———. 1997. "The Shield of Achilles: Ends of the *Iliad* and the Beginnings of the *Polis*." In *New Light on a Dark Age: Exploring the Culture of Geometric Greece,* edited by Susan Langdon. Columbia: University of Missouri Press, 194–207.

Newton, Adam Zachary. 1995. *Narrative Ethics.* Cambridge: Harvard University Press.

Nicholls, R. V. 1958–59. "Old Smyrna: The Iron Age Fortifications and Associated Remains on the City Perimeter." *The Annual of the British School at Athens* 53–54: 35–137.

Nietzsche, Friedrich. 1974. *The Gay Science.* Translated by Walter Kaufmann. New York: Vintage.

——. 1994a. *On the Genealogy of Morality.* Edited by Keith Ansell-Pearson. Translated by Carol Diethe. Cambridge: Cambridge University Press.

——. 1994b. "Homer on Competition." In *On the Genealogy of Morality,* edited by Keith Ansell-Pearson. Translated by Carol Diethe. Cambridge: Cambridge University Press.

Nilsson, Martin P. 1968. *Homer and Mycenae.* New York: Cooper Square.

Nimis, Steve. 1986. "The Language of Achilles: Construction vs. Representation." *Classical World* 79: 217–25.

Nussbaum, Martha. 1986. *The Fragility of Goodness: Luck and Ethics in Greek Tragedy and Philosophy.* Cambridge: Cambridge University Press.

——. 1990. *Love's Knowledge: Essays on Philosophy and Literature.* Oxford: Oxford University Press.

——. 1995. *Poetic Justice: The Literary Imagination and Public Life.* Boston: Beacon Press.

Ober, Josiah. 1989. *Mass and Elite in Democratic Athens: Rhetoric, Ideology, and the Power of the People.* Princeton, N.J.: Princeton University Press.

——. 1993. "The Athenian Revolution of 508/7 B.C.E.: Violence, Authority, and the Origins of Democracy." In *Cultural Poetics in Archaic Greece,* edited by Carol Dougherty and Leslie Kurke. Oxford: Oxford University Press, 215–32.

——. 1997. "Revolution Matters: Democracy as Demotic Action (A Response to Kurt A. Raaflaub)." In *Democracy 2500? Questions and Challenges,* edited by Ian Morris and Kurt Raaflaub. Dubuque, Iowa: Kendall/Hunt, 67–85.

Ober, Josiah, and Charles Hedrick, eds. 1996. *Dêmokratia: A Conversation on Democracies, Ancient and Modern.* Princeton, N.J.: Princeton University Press.

O'Brien, Joan. 1993. *The Transformation of Hera: A Study of Ritual, Hero, and the Goddess in the* Iliad. Lanham, Md.: Rowman & Littlefield.

Olson, S. Douglas. 1995. *Blood and Iron: Stories and Storytelling in Homer's Odyssey*. Leiden: Brill.

Ong, Walter. 1982. *Orality and Literacy: The Technologizing of the Word*. London: Methuen.

Oost, Stewart. 1972. "Cypselus the Bacchiad." *Classical Philology* 67 (January): 10–30.

Osborne, Robin. 1991. "Pride and Prejudice, Sense and Subsistence: Exchange and Society in the Greek City." In *City and Country in the Ancient World*, edited by John Rich and Andrew Wallace-Hadrill. London: Routledge.

————. 1996a. *Greece in the Making, 1200–479 BC*. London: Routledge.

————. 1996b. "Pots, Trade and the Archaic Greek Economy." *Antiquity* 70: 31–44.

Ostwald, Martin. 1996. "Shares and Rights: 'Citizenship' Greek Style and American Style." In *Dēmokratia: A Conversation on Democracies, Ancient and Modern*, edited by Josiah Ober and Charles Hedrick. Princeton, N.J.: Princeton University Press, 49–61.

Page, D. 1959. *History and the Homeric Iliad*. Berkeley: University of California Press.

Papadopoulos, John. 1996. Review of *Homer's World: Fiction, Tradition, Poetry*, edited by Øivind Andersen and Matthew Dickie. Bryn Mawr Classical Review 5.

Parke, H. W. 1967. *The Oracles of Zeus*. Oxford: Blackwell.

Parry, Adam. 1956. "The Language of Achilles." *TAPA* 87: 1–7.

————. 1987. *Introduction to The Making of Homeric Verse: The Collected Papers of Milman Parry*, edited by Adam Parry. Oxford: Clarendon.

Parry, Anne Amory. 1971. "Homer as Artist." *Classical Quarterly* 21: 1–15.

Parry, Milman. [1928] 1987a. "Homeric Formulae and Homeric Metre." *The Making of Homeric Verse: The Collected Papers of Milman Parry*, edited by Adam Parry. New York: Oxford University Press, 191–239.

————. [1928] 1987b. "The Traditional Epithet in Homer." In *The Making of Homeric Verse: The Collected Papers of Milman Parry*, edited by Adam Parry. New York: Oxford University Press, 1–190.

————. [1930] 1987c. "Studies in the Epic Technique of Oral Verse-Making. I. Homer and Homeric Style." In *The Making of Homeric Verse: The Collected Papers of Milman Parry*, edited by Adam Parry. New York: Oxford University Press, 266–324.

————. [1933] 1987d. "The Traditional Metaphor in Homer." In *The Making of Homeric Verse: The Collected Papers of Milman Parry*, edited by Adam Parry. New York: Oxford University Press, 365–75.

Patzek, Barbara. 1992. *Homer und Mykene: Mündliche Dichtung und Geschichtsschreibung.* München: R. Oldenbourg.

Pausanias. 1898. *Pausanias's Description of Greece.* 6 vols. Translated by J. G. Frazer. London: Macmillan.

Payne, Humfry, and others. 1940. *Perachora: The Sanctuaries of Hera Akraia and Limenia.* Oxford: Clarendon Press.

Peradotto, John. 1990. *Man in the Middle Voice: Name and Narration in the* Odyssey. Princeton, N.J.: Princeton University Press.

————. 1992. "Disauthorizing Prophecy: The Ideological Mapping of *Oedipus Tyrannus.*" *Transactions of the American Philological Association* 122: 9–15.

Pitkin, Hanna. 1972. *Wittgenstein and Justice.* Berkeley: University of California Press.

Pitt-Rivers, Julian. 1974. "Honour and Social Status." In *Honour and Shame: The Values of Mediterranean Society,* edited by J. G. Peristiany. Chicago: University of Chicago Press, 19–77.

Pohlenz, Max. 1956. "Furcht und Mitleid? Ein Nachwort." *Hermes* 84: 49–74.

Polanyi, Karl. 1944. *The Great Transformation: The Political and Economic Origins of Our Time.* Boston: Beacon Press.

Popham, M. R. 1993a. "The Main Excavation of the Building (1981–3)." In *Lefkandi II, The Protogeometric Building at Toumba. Part 2, The Excavation, Architecture and Finds,* edited by M. R. Popham, P. G. Calligas, and L. H. Sackett, with J. Coulton and H. W. Catling. Oxford: British School of Archaeology at Athens, 7–31.

————. 1993b. "The Sequence of Events, Interpretation and Date." In *Lefkandi II, The Protogeometric Building at Toumba. Part 2, The Excavation, Architecture and Finds,* edited by M. R. Popham, P. G. Calligas, and L. H. Sackett, with J. Coulton and H. W. Catling. Oxford: British School of Archaeology at Athens, 97–101.

Popham, M. R., P. G. Calligas, and L. H. Sackett, eds., with J. Coulton and H. W. Catling. 1993. *Lefkandi II, The Protogeometric Building at Toumba. Part 2, The Excavation, Architecture and Finds.* Oxford: British School of Archaeology at Athens.

Popham, M. R., L. H. Sackett, with P. G. Themelis, eds. 1980. *Lefkandi I: The Iron Age, Text.* Thames: British School of Archaeology at Athens.

Posner, R. A. 1979. "The Homeric Version of the Minimal State." *Ethics* 90: 27–46.

Powell, Barry. 1991. *Homer and the Origins of the Greek Alphabet.* Cambridge: Cambridge University Press.

Price, Theodora Hadzistelious. 1973. "Hero-Cult and Homer." *Historia* 22: 129–44.

Pucci, Pietro. 1987. *Odysseus Polutropos: Intertextual Readings in the Odyssey and in the* Iliad. Ithaca, N.Y.: Cornell University Press.

———. 1998a. "Honor and Glory in the *Iliad.*" In *The Song of the Sirens: Essays on Homer,* by Pietro Pucci. Lanham, Md.: Rowman & Littlefield, 179–230.

———. 1998b. Preface to *The Song of the Sirens: Essays on Homer.* Lanham, Md.: Rowman & Littlefield, ix–xiii.

———. 1998c. "The Proem of the *Odyssey.*" In *The Song of the Sirens: Essays on Homer,* by Pietro Pucci. Lanham, Md.: Rowman & Littlefield, 11–29.

Qviller, Bjørn. 1981. "The Dynamics of the Homeric Society." *Symbolae Osloenses* 56: 109–55.

Raaflaub, Kurt. 1988. "Athenische Geschichte und mündliche Über-lieferung." In *Vergangenheit in mündlicher Überlieferung,* edited by Jürgen von Ungern-Sternberg and Hansjörg Reinau. Stuttgart: B. G. Teubner, 197–225.

———. 1989. "Homer and the Beginning of Political Thought in Greece." *Proceedings of the Boston Area Colloquium Series in Ancient Philosophy* 4: 1–25.

———. 1991. "Homer and die Geschichte des 8.Jh.s v. Chr." In *Zweihundert Jahre Homer-Forschung,* edited by Joachim Latacz. Stuttgart: B. G. Teubner, 205–56.

———. 1993. "Homer to Solon: The Rise of the Polis, The Written Sources." In *The Ancient Greek City-State,* edited by Mogens Herman Hansen. Copenhagen: Munksgaard, 41–105.

———. 1996. "Equalities and Inequalities in Athenian Democracy." In *Dêmokratia: A Conversation on Democracies, Ancient and Modern,* edited by Josiah Ober and Charles Hedrick. Princeton, N.J.: Princeton University Press, 139–74.

———. 1997a. "Greece." In *Ancient History: Recent Work and New Directions,* edited by Carol Thomas. Claremont, Calif.: Regina Books, 1–35.

———. 1997b. "Homeric Society." In *A New Companion to Homer,* edited by Ian Morris and Barry Powell. Leiden: Brill.

———. 1997c. "Politics and Interstate Relations in the World of Early Greek *Poleis:* Homer and Beyond." *Antichthon* 31: 1–27.

———. 1997d. "Power in the Hands of the People: Foundations of Athenian Democracy." In *Democracy 2500? Questions and Challenges,* edited by Ian Morris and Kurt Raaflaub. Dubuque, Iowa: Kendall/ Hunt.

———. 1997e. "Soldiers, Citizens and the Evolution of the Early Greek *Polis.*" In *The Development of the Polis in Archaic Greece,* edited by Lynette G. Mitchell and P. J. Rhodes. New York: Routledge, 49–59.

———. 1998a. "A Historian's Headache: How to Read 'Homeric Society'?" In *Archaic Greece: New Approaches and New Evidence,* edited by Nick Fisher and Hans van Wees. London: Duckworth, 169–93.

———. 1998b. "Homer, the Trojan War, and History." *Classical World* 91: 387–403.

———. 2000. "Poets, Lawgivers, and the Beginnings of Political Reflection in Archaic Greece." In *The Cambridge History of Greek and Roman Political Thought,* edited by Christopher Rowe and Malcolm Schofield. Cambridge: Cambridge University Press, 23–59.

Rabel, Robert. 1997. *Plot and Point of View in the* Iliad. Ann Arbor: University of Michigan Press.

Radcliffe-Brown, A. R. 1940. Preface to *African Political Systems,* edited by M. Fortes and E. E. Evans-Pritchard. London: Oxford University Press.

———. 1952. *Structure and Function in Primitive Society.* London: Cohen & West.

Rawls, John. 1971. *A Theory of Justice.* Cambridge: Harvard University Press.

Rayner, Steve. 1988. "The Rules That Keep Us Equal: Complexity and Costs of Egalitarian Organization." In *Rules, Decisions, and Inequality in Egalitarian Societies,* edited by James Flanagan and Steve Rayner. Aldershot: Avebury.

Redfield, James. 1994. *Nature and Culture in the* Iliad: *The Tragedy of Hektor.* Durham, N.C.: Duke University Press.

Reece, Steve. 1993. *The Stranger's Welcome: Oral Theory and the Aesthetics of the Homeric Hospitality Scene.* Ann Arbor: University of Michigan Press.

Reinhardt, Karl. 1961. *Die Ilias und Ihr Dichter.* Edited by Uvo Hölscher. Göttingen: Vandenhoeck & Ruprecht.

Richardson, Nicholas. 1985. *The* Iliad: *A Commentary.* Vol. 6: Books 21–24. Cambridge: Cambridge University Press.

Richardson, Scott. 1990. *The Homeric Narrator.* Nashville, Tenn.: Vanderbilt University Press.

Ricoeur, Paul. 1981. "Narrative Time." In *On Narrative,* edited by W. J. T. Mitchell. Chicago: University of Chicago Press.

————. 1983a. "Action, Story and History: On Re-reading *The Human Condition*." *Salmagundi* 60: 60–72.

————. 1983b. "The Narrative Function." In *Hermeneutics and the Human Sciences*, edited and translated by John B. Thompson. Cambridge: Cambridge University Press, 274–96.

————. 1984, 1985, 1988. *Time and Narrative.* 3 vols. Translated by Kathleen Blamey and David Pellauer. Chicago: University of Chicago Press.

————. 1992. *Oneself as Another.* Translated by Kathleen Blamey. Chicago: University of Chicago Press.

Rihll, T. E. 1991. "The Power of the Homeric βασιλεῖς." In *Homer 1987*, edited by J. Pinsent and H. V. Hurt. Liverpool: Liverpool Classical Monthly, 39–50.

Rihll, T. E., and A. G. Wilson. 1991. "Modelling Settlement Structures in Ancient Greece: New Approaches to the Polis." In *City and Country in the Ancient World*, edited by John Rich and Andrew Wallace-Hadrill. London: Routledge, 58–95.

Robb, Kevin. 1994. *Literacy and Paideia in Ancient Greece.* New York: Oxford University Press.

Robinson, Eric. 1997. *The First Democracies: Early Popular Government Outside Athens.* Stuttgart: Franz Steiner.

Roebuck, Carl. 1972. "Some Aspects of Urbanization in Corinth." *Hesperia* 41: 96–127.

Rogin, Michael. 1983. *Subversive Genealogy: The Politics and Art of Herman Melville.* Berkeley: University of California Press.

Rose, Peter. 1988. "Thersites and the Plural Voices of Homer." *Arethusa* 21: 4–25.

————. 1992. *Sons of the Gods, Children of Earth: Ideology and Literary Form in Ancient Greece.* Ithaca, N.Y.: Cornell University Press.

————. 1997. "Ideology in the *Iliad*: Polis, *Basileus, Theoi.*" *Arethusa* 30: 151–99.

Roussel, Denis. 1976. *Tribu et Cité.* Paris: Annales Littéraires de L'Université de Besançon.

Rowe, John Carlos. 1993. "The Writing Class." In *Politics, Theory, and Contemporary Culture*, edited by Mark Poster. New York: Columbia University Press, 41–82.

Rubino, Carl A. 1993. "Opening Up the Classical Past: Bakhtin, Aristotle, Literature, Life." *Arethusa* 26: 141–57.

Ruijgh, C. J. 1995. "D'Homère aux origines proto-Mycéniennes de la tradition épique." In *Homeric Questions*, edited by Jan Paul Crielaard. Amsterdam: J. C. Gieben, 1–96.

Runciman, W. G. 1982. "Origins of States: The Case of Archaic Greece." *Comparative Studies in Society and History* 24: 351–77.

———. 1990. "Doomed to Extinction: The *Polis* as an Evolutionary Dead-End." In *The Greek City: From Homer to Alexander*, edited by Oswyn Murray and Simon Price. Oxford: Clarendon Press, 347–67.

Runnels, Curtis, and Tjeerd Van Andel. 1987. "The Evolution of Settlement in the Southern Argolid, Greece." *Hesperia* 56: 303–34.

Russo, Joseph. 1968. "Homer against His Tradition." *Arion* 7 (summer): 275–95.

———. 1978. "How, and What, Does Homer Communicate? The Medium and Message of Homeric Verse." In *Communication Arts in the Ancient World*, edited by Eric A. Havelock and Jackson P. Hershbell. New York: Hastings House, 39–52.

Ruzé, François. 1984. "Plethos, Aux origines de la majorité politique." In *Aux origines de l'Hellénisme: La Crète et la Grèce*. Paris: Publications de la Sorbonne, 247–63.

———. 1997. *Délibération et pouvoir dans la cité grecque: De Nestor à Socrate.* Paris: Sorbonne.

Sabine, George. 1950. *A History of Political Theory.* Rev. ed. New York: Holt.

Sahlins, Marshall. 1967. "The Segmentary Lineage: An Organization of Predatory Expansion." In *Comparative Political Systems: Studies in the Politics of Pre-Industrial Societies*, edited by Ronald Cohen and John Middleton. Garden City, N.Y.: Natural History Press.

———. 1968. *Tribesmen.* Englewood Cliffs, N.J.: Prentice-Hall.

———. 1972. *Stone Age Economics.* Chicago: Aldine-Atherton.

Sahlins, Marshall, and Elman Service, eds. 1960. *Evolution and Culture.* Ann Arbor: University of Michigan Press.

Sakellarious, M. B. 1989. *The Polis-State, Definition and Origin.* Athens: Research Centre for Greek and Roman Antiquity.

Sale, W. M. 1994. "The Government of Troy: Politics in the *Iliad*." *GRBS* 35: 5–102.

Salmon, J. B. 1984. *Wealthy Corinth: A History of the City to 338 BC.* Oxford: Clarendon Press.

Saussure, Ferdinand de. 1959. *Course in General Linguistics.* Edited by Charles Bally and Albert Sechehaye, in collaboration with Albert Riedlinger. Translated by Wade Baskin. New York: McGraw-Hill.

Saxonhouse, A. W. 1988. "*Thymos*, Justice, and Moderation of Anger in the Story of Achilles." In *Understanding the Political Spirit: Philo-*

sophical Investigations from Socrates to Nietzsche, edited by C. H. Zuckert. New Haven, Conn.: Yale University Press.

Schadewaldt, Wolfgang. 1955. "Furcht und Mitleid? Zur Deutung des Aristotelischen Tragödiensatzes." *Hermes* 83: 129–71.

———. 1959. *Von Homers Welt und Werk: Aufsätze und Auslegungen zur Homerischen Frage.* 3d ed. Stuttgart: K. F. Koehler.

Schein, Seth. 1984. *The Mortal Hero.* Berkeley: University of California Press.

Schmitt, Arbogast. 1990. *Selbständigkeit und Abhängigkeit menschlichen Handelns bei Homer.* Stuttgart: Franz Steiner.

Schmitt-Pantel, Pauline. 1990. "Collective Activities and the Political in the Greek City." In *The Greek City: From Homer to Alexander,* edited by Oswyn Murray and Simon Price. Oxford: Clarendon Press, 199–213.

Schofield, Malcolm. 1986. "*Euboulia* in the *Iliad.*" *Classical Quarterly* 36: 6–31.

Scholes, Robert, and Robert Kellogg. 1966. *The Nature of Narrative.* New York: Oxford University Press.

Scully, Stephen. 1981. "The Polis in Homer: A Definition and Interpretation." *Ramus* 10: 1–34.

———. 1990. *Homer and the Sacred City.* Ithaca, N.Y.: Cornell University Press.

Seaford, Richard. 1994. *Reciprocity and Ritual: Homer and Tragedy in the Developing City-State.* Oxford: Clarendon Press.

Sealey, Raphael. 1976. *A History of the Greek City States ca. 700–338 B.C.* Berkeley: University of California Press.

Segal, Charles. 1971. *The Theme of the Mutilation of the Corpse in the* Iliad. Leiden: Brill.

———. 1986. *Interpreting Greek Tragedy: Myth, Poetry, Text.* Ithaca, N.Y.: Cornell University Press.

———. 1992. "Bard and Audience in Homer." In *Homer's Ancient Readers: The Hermeneutics of Greek Epic's Earliest Exegetes,* edited by Robert Lamberton and John Keaney. Princeton, N.J.: Princeton University Press.

Service, Elman. 1962. *Primitive Social Organization: An Evolutionary Perspective.* New York: Random House.

———. 1975. *Origins of the State and Civilization: The Process of Cultural Evolution.* New York: Norton.

Shannon, Richard Stoll. 1975. *The Arms of Achilles and Homeric Compositional Technique.* Leiden: Brill.

Shapiro, H. A. 1989. *Art and Cult under the Tyrants in Athens.* Mainz am Rhein: Philipp von Zabern.

Shapiro, Michael J. 1992. *Reading the Postmodern Polity: Political Theory as Textual Practice.* Minneapolis: University of Minnesota Press.

Sharples, R. W. 1983. "'But Why Has My Spirit Spoken With Me Thus?': Homeric Decision-Making." *Greece and Rome* 30 (April): 1–7.

Shipley, Graham. 1987. *A History of Samos, 900–188 B.C.* Oxford: Clarendon Press.

Sinn, Ulrich. 1996. "The Influence of Greek Sanctuaries on the Consolidation of Economic Power." In *Religion and Power in the Ancient Greek World,* edited by Pontus Hellström and Brita Alroth. Uppsala: Motala Grafiska, 67–74.

Sinos, Dale. 1980. *Achilles, Patroklos and the Meaning of* Philos. Innsbruck: Innsbrucker Beiträge zur Sprachwissenschaft.

Sinos, Rebecca. 1993. "Divine Selection: Epiphany and Politics in Archaic Greece. In *Cultural Poetics in Archaic Greece: Cult, Performance, Politics,* edited by Carol Dougherty and Leslie Kurke. Oxford: Oxford University Press, 73–91.

Snell, Bruno. 1930. "Das Bewußtsein von eigenen Entscheidungen im frühen Griechentum." *Philologus* 85: 141–58.

———. [1953] 1982. *The Discovery of the Mind in Greek Philosophy and Literature.* New York: Dover.

Snell, Bruno, and Hartmut Erbse, eds. 1982. *Lexikon des frühgriechischen Epos.* Göttingen: Vandenhoek & Ruprecht.

Snodgrass, A. M. 1964. *Early Greek Armour and Weapons.* Edinburgh: University Press.

———. 1965. "The Hoplite Reform and History." *Journal of Hellenic Studies* 85: 110–22.

———. 1971. *The Dark Ages of Greece.* Edinburgh: University Press.

———. 1974. "An Historical Homeric Society?" *JHS* 94: 114–25.

———. 1980. *Archaic Greece.* Berkeley: University of California Press.

———. 1982. "Central Greece and Thessaly." In *The Cambridge Ancient History.* 2d ed. Vol. 3, part 1. Cambridge: Cambridge University Press.

———. 1991. "Archaeology and the Study of the Greek City." In *City and Country in the Ancient World,* edited by John Rich and Andrew Wallace-Hadrill. New York: Routledge, 1–23.

Sourvinou-Inwood, Christiane. 1990. "What Is *Polis* Religion?" In *The Greek City: From Homer to Alexander,* edited by Oswyn Murray and Simon Price. Oxford: Clarendon Press.

————. 1993. "Early Sanctuaries, the Eighth Century and Ritual Space: Fragments of a Discourse." In *Greek Sanctuaries: New Approaches*, edited by Nanno Marinatos and Robin Hägg. London: Routledge, 1–17.

Stahl, Michael. 1987. *Aristokraten und Tyrannen im archaischen Athen.* Stuttgart: Franz Steiner.

Stanley, K. 1993. *The Shield of Homer: Narrative Structure in the* Iliad. Princeton, N.J.: Princeton University Press.

Starr, Chester G. 1961. *The Origins of Greek Civilization: 1100–650 B.C.* New York: Knopf.

————. 1977. *The Economic and Social Growth of Early Greece 800–500 B.C.* New York: Oxford University Press.

————. 1982. "Economic and Social Conditions in the Greek World." In *The Cambridge Ancient History*, edited by John Boardman and N. G. L. Hammond. 2d ed. Vol. 3, part 3. Cambridge: Cambridge University Press.

————. 1986. *Individual and Community: The Rise of the Polis, 800–500 B.C.* New York: Oxford University Press.

Steiner, Ann. 1992. "Pottery and Cult in Corinth: Oil and Water at the Sacred Spring." *Hesperia* 61: 385–408.

Steuerman, Emilia. 1992. "Habermas vs. Lyotard: Modernity vs. Postmodernity?" In *Judging Lyotard*, edited by Andrew Benjamin. New York: Routledge: 99–118.

Stewart, Susan. 1986. "Shouts on the Street: Bakhtin's Anti-Linguistics." In *Bakhtin: Essays and Dialogues on His Work*, edited by Gary Saul Morson. Chicago: University of Chicago Press.

Stillwell, Agnes Newhall. 1948. *Corinth: The Potters' Quarter.* Vol. 15, part 1. Princeton, N.J.: American School of Classical Studies at Athens.

Strasburger, Hermann. [1952] 1982. "Der soziologische Aspekt der homerischen Epen." In *Studien zur Alten Geschichte*. Vol. 1 of 3, edited by Walter Schmitthenner and Renate Zoepffel. Hildescheim: Georg Olms.

Swartz, Mark, Victor Turner, and Arthur Tuden. 1966. Introduction to *Political Anthropology*, edited by Swartz, Turner, and Tuden. Chicago: Aldine.

Talman, J. L. 1960. *The Origins of Totalitarian Democracy.* New York: Praeger.

Tandy, David. 1997. *Warriors into Traders: The Power of the Market in Early Greece.* Berkeley: University of California Press.

Taplin, Oliver. 1980. "The Shield of Achilles within the *Iliad*." *Greece and Rome*, 2d ser., 27 (April): 1–21.

————. 1990. "Agamemnon's Role in the *Iliad*." In *Characterization and Individuality in Greek Literature*, edited by Christopher Pelling. Oxford: Clarendon Press, 60–82.

————. 1992. *Homeric Soundings: The Shaping of the Iliad*. New York: Oxford University Press.

Thalmann, William. 1988. "Thersites: Comedy, Scapegoats, and Heroic Ideology in the *Iliad*." *TAPA* 118: 1–28.

————. 1998. *The Swineherd and the Bow: Representations of Class in the* Odyssey. Ithaca, N.Y.: Cornell University Press.

Thiele, Leslie Paul. 1997. *Thinking Politics: Perspectives in Ancient, Modern, and Postmodern Political Theory*. Chatham, N.J.: Chatham House.

Thomas, Carol. 1966. "Homer and the Polis." *La Parola del passato* 21: 5–14.

Thomas, Carol, and Craig Conant. *1999. Citadel to City-State: The Transformation of Greece, 1200–700 B.C.E.* Bloomington: Indiana University Press.

Thompson, Michael. 1982. "The Problem of the Centre: An Autonomous Cosmology." In *Essays in the Sociology of Perception*, edited by Mary Douglas. London: Routledge & Kegan Paul.

Thompson, Michael, Richard Ellis, and Aaron Wildavsky. 1990. *Cultural Theory*. Boulder, Colo.: Westview Press.

Turner, Frank. 1997. "The Homeric Question." In *A New Companion to Homer*, edited by Ian Morris and Barry Powell. Leiden: Brill, 123–45.

Turner, Victor. 1974. *Dramas, Fields and Metaphors: Symbolic Action in Human Society*. Ithaca, N.Y.: Cornell University Press.

————. 1981. "Social Dramas and Stories about Them." In *On Narrative*, edited by W. J. T. Mitchell. Chicago: University of Chicago Press, 137–64.

————. 1986. *The Anthropology of Performance*. New York: PAJ Publications.

Ulf, Christoph. 1990. *Die homerische Gesellschaft: Materialien zur analytischen Beschreibung und historischen Lokalisierung*. München: Beck.

Van Wees, Hans. 1988. "Kings in Combat: Battles and Heroes in the *Iliad*." *Classical Quarterly* 38: 1–24.

————. 1992. *Status Warriors: War, Violence and Society in Homer and History*. Amsterdam: J. C. Gieben.

————. 1994. "The Homeric Way of War: The *Iliad* and the Hoplite Phalanx." *Greece and Rome* 41: 1–18, 131–55.

Vattimo, Gianni. 1986. "The End of (Hi)story." *Chicago Review* 35: 20–30.

Verdelis, Nicholas. 1962. "A Sanctuary at Solygeia." *Archaeology* 15 (March): 184–92.

Vernant, Jean-Pierre. 1990a. "The Historical Moment of Tragedy in Greece: Some of the Social and Psychological Conditions." In *Myth and Tragedy in Ancient Greece,* by Vernant and Pierre Vidal-Naquet. Translated by Janet Lloyd. New York: Zone Books.

———. 1990b. "Intimations of the Will in Greek Tragedy." In *Myth and Tragedy in Ancient Greece,* by Vernant and Pierre Vidal-Naquet. Translated by Janet Lloyd. New York: Zone Books.

———. 1990c. "Tensions and Ambiguities in Greek Tragedy." In *Myth and Tragedy in Ancient Greece,* by Vernant and Pierre Vidal-Naquet. Translated by Janet Lloyd. New York: Zone Books.

———. 1991. *Mortals and Immortals.* Edited by Froma Zeitlin. Princeton, N.J.: Princeton University Press.

Vickers, Brian. 1993. *Appropriating Shakespeare: Contemporary Critical Quarrels.* New Haven, Conn.: Yale University Press.

Vivante, Paolo. 1970. *The Homeric Imagination: A Study of Homer's Poetic Perception of Reality.* Bloomington: Indiana University Press.

———. 1982. *The Epithets in Homer: A Study in Poetic Values.* New Haven, Conn.: Yale University Press.

———. 1985. *Homer.* New Haven, Conn.: Yale University Press.

Vlasaki, Maria. 1991. "The Khania Area, ca 1200–700 B.C." In *La transizione dal Miceneo all' alto arcaismo. Dal palazzo alla città.* Edited by D. Musti, A. Sacconi, L. Rocchetti, M. Rocchi, E. Scarfa, L. Sportiello, and M. E. Giannotta. Roma: Consiglio Nazionale della Ricerche.

Von Reden, Sitta. 1995. *Exchange in Ancient Greece.* London: Duckworth.

Wathelet, Paul. 1981. "La langue homérique et le rayonnement littéraire de l' Eubée." *L'Antiquité classique* 50: 819–33.

Weber, Max. 1978. *Economy and Society.* 2 vols. Edited by Guenther Roth and Claus Wittich. Berkeley: University of California Press.

Weil, Simone. 1965. *The* Iliad, *or the Poem of Force.* Wallingford, Pa.: Pendle Hill.

West, M. L. 1966. *Hesiod. Theogony.* Oxford: Clarendon.

———. 1971. *Early Greek Philosophy and the Orient.* Oxford: Clarendon.

———. 1988. "The Rise of the Greek Epic." *Journal of Hellenic Studies* 108: 151–72.

———. 1995. "The Date of the *Iliad.*" *Museum Helveticum* 52: 203–19.

Westbrook, Raymond. 1992. "The Trial Scene in the *Iliad.*" *Harvard Studies in Classical Philology* 94: 53–76.

White, Hayden. 1981. "The Value of Narrativity in the Representation of Reality." In *On Narrative,* edited by W. J. T. Mitchell. Chicago: University of Chicago Press, 1–23.

White, James Boyd. 1984. *When Words Lose Their Meaning: Constitutions and Reconstitutions of Language, Character, and Community.* Chicago: University of Chicago Press.

———. 1994. *Acts of Hope: Creating Authority in Literature, Law, and Politics.* Chicago: University of Chicago Press.

White, Stephen K. 1991. *Political Theory and Postmodernism.* Cambridge: Cambridge University Press.

Whitley, James. 1988. "Early States and Hero Cults: A Re-Appraisal." *Journal of Hellenic Studies* 108: 173–82.

———. 1991. *Style and Society in Dark Age Greece: The Changing Face of a Pre-literate Society 1100–700 BC.* Cambridge: Cambridge University Press.

———. 1995. "Tomb Cult and Hero Cult: The Uses of the Past in Archaic Greece." In *Time, Tradition and Society in Greek Archaeology: Bridging the "Great Divide,"* edited by Nigel Spencer. London: Routledge, 43–63.

Whitman, Cedric. 1958. *Homer and the Heroic Tradition.* Cambridge: Harvard University Press.

Wickersham, John M., and Dora C. Pozzi. 1991. Introduction to *Myth and the Polis.* Ithaca, N.Y.: Cornell University Press.

Wildavsky, Aaron. 1987. "Choosing Preferences by Constructing Institutions: A Cultural Theory of Preference Formation." *American Political Science Review* 81: 3–21.

Will, Édouard. 1955. *Korinthiaka: Recherches sur l'histoire et la civilisation de Corinthe des origines aux guerres médiques.* Paris: E. de Boccard.

Willcock, M. M. 1970. "Some Aspects of the Gods in the *Iliad*." *Bulletin of the Institute of Classical Studies* 17: 1–10.

Willetts, R. F. 1965. *Ancient Crete: A Social History.* London: Routledge & Kegan Paul.

———. 1977. *The Civilization of Ancient Crete.* London: Batsford.

Williams, Bernard. 1981. "Moral Luck." In *Moral Luck: Philosophical Papers 1973–1980.* Cambridge: Cambridge University Press.

———. 1985. *Ethics and the Limits of Philosophy.* Cambridge: Cambridge University Press.

———. 1993. *Shame and Necessity.* Berkeley: University of California Press.

Williams, Charles. 1984. "The Early Urbanization of Corinth." *Annuario della Scuola Archeologica di Atene* 60: 9–20.

Williams, Charles, and Joan Fisher. 1971. "Corinth, 1970: Forum Area." *Hesperia* 40: 1–51.

————. 1973. "Corinth, 1972: The Forum Area." *Hesperia* 42: 1–44.

Wittgenstein, Ludwig. 1953. *Philosophical Investigations.* Translated by G. E. M. Anscombe. New York: Macmillan.

Wolf, F. A. [1795] 1985. *Prolegomena to Homer.* Translated by Anthony Grafton, Glenn Most, and James Zetzel. Princeton, N.J.: Princeton University Press.

Wolff, Erwin. 1929. "Review of Bruno Snell: *Aischylos und das Handeln im Drama.*" *Gnomon* 5: 386–400.

Wolff, Hans Julius. 1946. "The Origin of Judicial Litigation among the Greeks." *Traditio* 4: 31–87.

Wolin, Sheldon. 1960. *Politics and Vision: Continuity and Innovation in Western Political Thought.* Boston: Little, Brown.

————. 1972. "Political Theory as a Vocation." In *Machiavelli and the Nature of Political Thought,* edited by Martin Fleischer. New York: Atheneum.

Wood, Ellen, and Neal Wood. 1978. *Class Ideology and Ancient Political Theory: Socrates, Plato, and Aristotle in Social Context.* Oxford: Blackwell.

Yamagata, Naoko. 1994. *Homeric Morality.* Leiden: Brill.

Yaron, Reuven. 1993. "Social Problems and Policies in the Ancient Near East." In *Law, Politics and Society in the Ancient Mediterranean World,* edited by Baruch Halpern and Deborah Hobson. Sheffield: Sheffield Academic Press, 19–41.

Young-Bruehl, Elisabeth. 1977. "Hannah Arendt's Storytelling." *Social Research* 44: 183–90.

Zaidman, Louise Bruit, and Pauline Schmitt Pantel. 1992. *Religion in the Ancient Greek City.* Translated by Paul Cartledge. Cambridge: Cambridge University Press. Originally published as La Religion grecque (Paris: Armand Colin Editeur, 1989).

Zanker, Graham. 1994. *The Heart of Achilles: Characterization and Personal Ethics in the* Iliad. Ann Arbor: University of Michigan Press.

Zeitlin, Froma. 1996. *Playing the Other: Gender and Society in Classical Greek Literature.* Chicago: University of Chicago Press.

Index of Passages Cited

General Index

Achaians, as political community, 43–46, 218nn.125–27

Achilles, and Agamemnon, 16, 18, 44–45, 77, 81–87, 93–96, 107, 113, 119, 123, 129, 154, 174, 183–84, 192; and anger, 100–101, 174, 176; and assembly, 44–45, 82, 86, 154, 157–58; challenge to Agamemnon's authority, 16–17, 82–86, 103, 129–32; challenge to social system, 59; and charisma, 154–55; dishonored, 94; and embassy, 96–105; and esteem, 16–18, 59, 97–101, 172–82; ethical reflection by, 17–18, 171–75; ethical transformation of, 172–94; and Eumelos, 66–69, 70–71; and fate, 98–99; and forgiveness, 141; and funeral games, 17, 66–71, 76–77, 134–43, 181–82; and Hektor, 65–66, 107, 112, 176–77, 179, 181, 183, 189–94; and honor, 59, 97–101; as leader, 137–43; as *metanastês*, 94–96; and Patroklos, 17–18, 101, 106–107, 109, 174–83, 185–87; perspective, 110, 113; and Phoenix, 98; and pity, 99–100, 174–75, 182–94; and Priam, 18, 107, 173–74, 182–94, 197; relationship to the Achaians, 93–96, 112–13; relationship to Briseis, 104–105; self-sufficiency rejected, 16, 106–107, 182; as self-sufficient (autonomous), 16, 96–105; shield, 105–113; and sorrow, 97; and suffering, 17–18, 100–101, 141, 172–89; and vengeance, 101, 106, 109, 189–91; and view of death, 98–99, 173–74, 178–80, 238–39n.16; vulnerability to another, 18, 175–80; withdrawal from battle, 16, 18, 86–87, 93, 95–96, 192. *See also* Achilles, and esteem; Achilles, and suffering; Achilles, as *metanastês*; Achilles, as self-sufficient; Liminality

Adkins, Arthur, 53–54, 69, 76, 78–79, 125–26

Agamemnon, and Achilles: assembly, 155–56; basis of authority, 82–88, 119; deceived by Zeus, 77, 87–88, 119; delusion, 64; and exercise of authority, 16, 82–92, 129–31, 139; and the funeral games, 137; and Odysseus, 88–89, 156; offer of gifts, 102–104, 112, 123; as venal, 129–30. *See also* Achilles, and Agamemnon

Agathos: and competitive values, 78–79; defined, 59–60; relationship to *aretê*, 69–74

Agency: and autonomy, 49–58, 78; and chance, 15–16, 49–51, 58, 74–79; and Descartes, 50; and ethics, 50–51, 171; and the gods, 15–16, 49–79; in the *Iliad*, 74–79; Kant, 50–51; and politics, 15–16, 49–51; scholarly views, 51–57, 170–71, 218–19n.6